The CEO's Talent MANIFESTO

ALIGN TALENT INVESTMENTS TO
ACHIEVE TARGETED RESULTS

Dr. Chip Cleary and Tom Hilgart

Copyright © 2013 Chip Cleary and Tom Hilgart
All rights reserved.

ISBN-10: 0615765858
ISBN-13: 9780615765853

Library of Congress Control Number: 2013902784
CreateSpace Independent Publishing Platform
North Charleston, South Carolina

Dedication

From Chip:

To my parents, who showed me what it means to have a lifelong commitment to helping people learn.

From Tom:

To my wife and best friend, Shirley Kitzmann, for all of her encouragement and wise counsel.

Contents

Dedication v
Contents vii
Figures ix
Foreword 1
Why We Wrote This Book 5
Tools You Can Use 7
Section 1: Overview of the A2B Methodology 9
Chapter 1: The CEO's Talent Manifesto 11
Chapter 2: Generating Demonstrated Business Value 33
Chapter 3: The Heart of A2B: the Learning Investment
Portfolio 45
Chapter 4: Targeting Business Needs and Aligning
Investments. 69
Chapter 5: The Role of the Business Engagement
Manager 91
Section 2: Defining and Managing a Portfolio of
Learning Investments 111
Chapter 6: How the Pieces Fit Together: Information
Flow under A2B 115
Chapter 7: Governance under A2B 127
Section 3: Managing Your Relationship with a Business
Group 161

Chapter 8: Building Your Relationship 163
Chapter 9: Sustaining Your Relationship 179
Section 4: Managing the Lifecycle of a Learning
Investment 193
Chapter 10: Chartering an Investment. 197
Chapter 11: Chaperoning Execution 237
Chapter 12: Closing the Loop. 247
Section 5: Implementing and Sustaining the A2B
Methodology 259
Chapter 13: Implementing A2B 261
Chapter 14: Sustaining A2B 285
Appendix A: A Step-by-Step Example of the
Ability-to-Execute Alignment Framework 305
Appendix B: Ensuring Robust Core L&D Capabilities 325
Bibliography. 329
About the Authors 335
Notes. 339

Figures

Figure 1: The Aligned-to-Business Methodology 15
Figure 2: An Excerpt from a Learning Investment Portfolio 19
Figure 3: The Value-Added Matrix 21
Figure 4: The Ability-to-Execute-Alignment Framework 22
Figure 5: An Increase in the Strategic Alignment Ratio 24
Figure 6: Business Engagement Manager Responsibilities . . 25
Figure 7: Closing the Loop through the Results Contract and the Results Report 27
Figure 8: Agendas for Quarterly Reviews 29
Figure 9: The Flow of Quarterly and Annual Governance . . 31
Figure 10: The Strategic Alignment Assessment 37
Figure 11: A Hypothetical Program Docket—A Typical Starting Point for Selecting Learning Investments 53
Figure 12: The Hypothetical Docket Extended to Clarify Alignment and Define Success 56
Figure 13: The Value-Added Matrix 60
Figure 14: The Ability-to-Execute Alignment Framework . . . 71
Figure 15: An Example Ability-to-Execute Analysis 76
Figure 16: Business Processes are the Pivot Point in the Alignment Chain 77
Figure 17: An Example Value Chain 83

ix

Figure 18: Scanning the Results for a Single Process 84
Figure 19: The Talent Performance SWOT for a Single Process 85
Figure 20: Example of a Completed Ability-to-Execute Scan..86
Figure 21: Prioritizing Business Processes for Learning Investments...87
Figure 22: The Business Engagement Manager's Key Tasks..94
Figure 23: The Four Key Deliverables under A2B........116
Figure 24: The Ability-to-Execute Scan................119
Figure 25: An Ability-to-Execute Drilldown Analysis......120
Figure 26: The Learning Investment Portfolio..........121
Figure 27: The Value-Added Matrix...................124
Figure 28: Joint Responsibility for Results..............133
Figure 29: Timing of the Annual Process...............137
Figure 30: Agendas for Quarterly Reviews.............150
Figure 31: The Ability-to-Execute Alignment Framework...166
Figure 32: Planning Where to Spend Time "Walking the Beat"...182
Figure 33: The Lifecycle of a Learning Investment.......194
Figure 34: The Ability to Execute Alignment Framework...203
Figure 35: Example Business Process Measures and Targets 207
Figure 36: Example Dialog to Define a Commitment......212
Figure 37: Example Performance Outcomes............215
Figure 38: The Updated Behavior Engineering Model....219
Figure 39: Alternative Sources of Funding..............232
Figure 40: Example Results from Business Leader Interviews 266

Figure 41: Rating Criteria for the BEM Scorecard 294
Figure 42: The Ability-to-Execute Alignment
Framework 306
Figure 43: Desired Business Outcomes 309
Figure 44: The Start of a Drill-Down Analysis 312
Figure 45: Metrics Added for Quality Reviews...........313
Figure 46: Moving a Goal from the Drill Down to the
Top Level 314
Figure 47: Adding Performances for One
Business Process....................................318
Figure 48: Example Performance Analysis...............320
Figure 49: The Solution to Achieve One
Business Outcome 322

Foreword

In 1999, we wrote in *Running Training Like A Business* that "many business leaders say that T&D remains 'out of the loop' strategically, that it too often operates like 'something separate from the business,' and that they don't see enough tangible returns on their T&D investment." We also wrote that executives see a widening gap between the skills and knowledge that businesses require and those that the workforce can offer. In 2012, the fifteenth annual Price-Waterhouse Coopers Global CEO Survey stated that:

- 25 percent of CEOs have cancelled an initiative because they did not have the talent they required;

- 33 percent were unable to pursue a market opportunity; and

- 70 percent were less than "very confident" that they had the talent they required.

It seems like the more things change, the more they stay the same. Has there ever been a clearer mandate for Learning & Development (L&D) than now? I think not! And so, Chip

The CEO's Talent Manifesto

Cleary and Tom Hilgart define the CEO's Talent Manifesto as the new "marching orders" for L&D.

The authors are hot on the trail of the "holy grail" of L&D in this new and exciting book. Alignment to Business, or A2B, as it is referred to in the book, has been and continues to be the most elusive and most critical element of L&D. It is the beginning of the beginning, and without it, everything else is pretty much irrelevant. The authors say, "The most pressing issue that is faced by most L&D organizations is not whether they have the right guns to fire but rather whether they know just where to point them." We can design and develop the best training ever created, and we can deliver it with the best instructors and/or the best technology in the best format. But…if it is not on something important to the business, business executives are not happy—and they shouldn't be. Making investments in learning and development has to deliver the same level of business value that investments in R&D, marketing, sales, manufacturing and service deliver; otherwise, business executives place their investment bets in areas other than L&D and the problems defined in the PWC survey will continue on.

In this book, Chip and Tom have put forth the "Aligned-to-Business Methodology," which provides a set of models and introduces some key new concepts, processes, and tools for L&D, including:

- Portfolio of Investments

- Value-Added Matrix

- Ability-to-Execute Alignment Framework including

Foreword

- o Ability-to-Execute Scan
- o Ability-to-Execute Analysis
- o Ability-to-Execute Map

- "Walking the beat" to keep abreast of the business

- Key Players

- Following learning investments through a full lifecycle, including chartering, chaperoning execution, and closing the loop.

All of these make up the "how-to" of ensuring that the work of L&D is aligned to the business and is delivering measurable value when and where the business requires it.

The authors have also defined a role they call business engagement manager (BEM) to enable the A2B process. The primary job of the BEM is to help business leaders make the right investments to create and manage learning portfolios that generate demonstrated results. I really like that they define BEMs as investment managers whose goal is to enable the business to generate results through investments in learning. And therefore, this role serves as the key interface between the business and L&D. BEMs are business people in learning, and as such, they must think business first and then define ways in which learning can enable business goals. The key measure of success for BEMs is how much business value their learning portfolios produce for the business they serve. This is a great impact-producing role for L&D!

The CEO's Talent Manifesto

Back in 1999, we discussed the critical importance of A2B as the first step in what we called the Value Creation Process, and we asserted that many, if not most, organizations had not figured out how to do it in a way that ensures delivery of measurable value to the business. In 2013, as an industry, we are still trying to figure it out, and that is why this book is so important to the industry and to the people of L&D.

L&D organizations will be wise to make this book required reading for all of their staff. If they do and if they establish the BEM role and execute as described in this book, we will certainly move L&D "from the backroom to the boardroom."

Thanks, Chip and Tom. Well done!

Edward Trolley
Co-author, *Running Training Like a Business*

Why We Wrote This Book

Chip leads the advisory services practice in NIIT, a company that provides managed training services. In 2010, several of my clients asked how they could improve what they called "relationship management" between learning and development (L&D) and the business. They sought ways to better align L&D activities with business priorities.

In response, I began a brief project to research and consolidate best practices—at least, that was the plan.

My search soon ended with the realization that there have been few concrete best practices published that show just how L&D can generate strategic alignment with the business.

Of the best practices I did uncover, the most compelling was a method to ensure alignment, improve prioritization, and clarify results called the "Strategic Learning Portfolio Approach," which Tom had developed when he served as vice president of CNA's Knowledge & Learning Group. CNA was widely acknowledged as generating demonstrated business value from its investments in learning. The Strategic Learning Portfolio Approach went on to become recognized as a best practice by both the Learning & Development Roundtable of the

The CEO's Talent Manifesto

Corporate Executive Board (2004)[1] and Bersin & Associates (2005)[2].

Tom and I decided to collaborate on a book to help close the gap in published best practices. This is the result. It provides a "how-to" guide for targeting the business results that matter most and aligning investments in talent to achieve them. It details an enhanced version of the original Strategic Learning Portfolio Approach, which we have named the *A2B Methodology* (for "Aligned to Business").

Tools You Can Use

To help you implement the A2B Methodology, we provide an A2B "toolbox". In addition to information about A2B, we provide templates, formats, guides, and documents for all of the A2B elements described in this book. Throughout the book, you will find these listed in "Tools You Can Use" boxes.

> You can visit the toolbox at:
> www.aligned-to-business.com

The tools include:

1. The Ability-to-Execute Map template

2. The Business Engagement Manager job description

3. The Annual Learning Investment Planning Meeting guide

4. The Quarterly Learning Investment Plan Review guide

5. The L&D Business Engagement Model presentation

6. The Strategic Account Management Plan template

The CEO's Talent Manifesto

7. The Results Contract template

8. The Learning Design Architecture template

9. The Learning Design Costing Standards template

10. The Learning Solutions Evaluation Standards template

11. The Results Report template

12. The Accountability Principle presentation

13. The Business Engagement Manager Performance Scorecard

14. The L&D Capability Self-Assessment

Section 1: Overview of the A2B Methodology

In this section, we explain the challenge we tackle and the core practices we recommend. Throughout the remaining sections, we dive deep into the practices, illustrating just how to put them to use.

The first two chapters define the problem we tackle. Chapter 1 takes the perspective of the CEO and sets out how the need for companies to develop their talent has grown to become one of the top priorities for many CEOs. In it, we propose that L&D organizations conceive of their role as enabling the company to define and manage a strategically aligned portfolio of investments in learning that improves its ability to execute. You can use the first chapter as a stand-alone piece to socialize these ideas with the leadership and others in your company.

Chapter 2 then assumes the perspective of the learning leader. We summarize the evidence that many L&D organizations can materially improve how they support their companies and, in particular, how they align to the business. We summarize the key challenges that prevent L&D organizations from achieving strategic alignment and describe how the methodology we offer in this book, the "Aligned-to-Business Methodology" (A2B) overcomes each.

The remaining three chapters in this section delve into the three core elements of A2B. If you already know you want to improve alignment and want to cut to the chase on how you can do so, you may wish to jump directly here. Chapter 3 explains the *core deliverable*, the Learning Investment Portfolio. The Learning Investment Portfolio summarizes the investments a company (or business group) makes in learning. We provide a tool for analyzing the portfolio, called the Value Added Matrix, which makes explicit key decisions about how a company allocates its investment; these decisions often remain hidden when companies take only a line-item perspective.

Chapter 4 provides the *core framework* for ensuring alignment: the Ability-to-Execute Alignment Framework. This framework makes clear the chain of causality through which an investment in learning affects a company's ability to execute. The central link in this chain is a focus on identifying a specific business process to be improved on a specific metric. This link enables L&D and the business to "meet in the middle" when defining how learning investments will support the business.

Finally, Chapter 5 explains the *core role*: the *business engagement manager* (BEM). Each BEM serves a set of business groups to enable them to define and manage their portfolios. The BEM supplies the organizational focus required for A2B to succeed.

Chapter 1: The CEO's Talent Manifesto

We rely on our people to run our day-to-day operations, continually improve how we operate, and execute our strategic initiatives.

Too often, we lack the depth of talent we require to win.

We require a talent system that lets us manage our investments in talent as methodically as we manage our other investments. Our talent system must pinpoint specifically what our business requires, align our investments to our priorities, identify concrete business outcomes each investment will generate, make visible whether those outcomes are achieved, and continually improve.

<u>In short, we must align our talent investments to achieve targeted business results.</u>

HR and, in particular, Learning and Development, must provide this talent system.

Companies Thrive on Their "Ability to Execute"

In a world of accelerating change, how do companies excel? Of course, having a compelling strategy matters. Being able to rapidly refine strategy as lessons are learned matters even more. But what many are coming to believe is that what matters the most is the ability to convert strategic intention to reality.[3] In short, organizations thrive based on their *ability to execute.*

Throughout the eighties and nineties, Toyota exhibited an unmatched ability to reduce waste and shrink cycle time, providing it with lower costs and higher quality than its competitors. As a result, by 2010, it had grown to be the world's largest car manufacturer. In the decade leading up to 2010, Apple exhibited an unmatched ability to create leapfrog products using top-notch design. As a result, it captured 35 percent of the total profits made in the computer industry that year.[4] Toyota and Apple both converted their strategic intent to reality. In our words, they developed an unequaled *ability to execute* the business processes that mattered the most to their strategies.

Talent Increasingly Constrains the Ability to Execute

CEOs have long struggled to convert strategic intentions into differentiated capabilities. In today's world, what enables a company to do something better than its competitors? Many previously important competitive barriers have now shrunk. Today, few companies enjoy distinctive access to raw materials, capital, or even technology. In these ways, the world is becoming flat.[5] However, one critical item that remains differentiated is talent—that is, the level at which the people in the company perform the tasks that are most important to it—and whether they do them better, faster, and with fewer errors than competitors' people.

Chapter 1: The CEO's Talent Manifesto

Many business leaders say, "Our people are our most important asset." Talent has always made it onto the CEO's list of priorities. In the past, however, it may not have gotten very high on that list and so did not receive much focus. As one ex-CEO told us, "Sure, training was always on my list of priorities. It was something like number 35. I never really paid as much attention to it as perhaps it warranted." As the importance of many sources of differentiation decreases, the importance of those that remain, like talent, grows. Today, beyond simply making it onto the CEO's list, talent is moving near to the top.

> For many CEOs, talent has moved beyond being one priority among many to making the short list of critical priorities. Why? Because talent gaps are preventing CEOs from executing their strategies.

Consider the results of the Fifteenth Price-Waterhouse Coopers Global CEO Survey (also cited by Ed Trolley in the Forward):

- 25 percent of CEOs have *cancelled an initiative* because they did not have the talent they required;

- 33 percent were *unable to pursue a market opportunity*; and

- 70 percent were *less than "very confident"* that they had the talent they required.

McKinsey & Company surveyed 1,440 executives and reported similar findings. When asked how they ranked the priority of building organizational capabilities:

- Over 90 percent ranked it a top-ten priority.

- Over 50 percent ranked it a top-three priority.

Learning & Development Is Becoming Increasingly Important within the Talent System

For years, we have been warned about the "War for Talent."[6] The thrust has been on how a company can compete for employees. CEOs have been advised they must make their organizations attractive if they are to succeed in hiring and retaining the talent they require. While the war may rage on, hiring is no longer a viable primary approach to address talent gaps. In the PWC survey, CEOs across industries reported that it has become more difficult to hire needed talent. Furthermore, the talent required is becoming increasingly unique as companies stress differentiated skills that set them apart. This focus on differentiation is particularly acute on just those positions for which CEOs are most likely to require investments in talent: the few "pivotal positions" that are most important to the company's success.[7] By definition, one cannot hire such talent.

Since companies increasingly find it challenging to "buy" the talent they need, they must instead "make" it. Said differently, in place of *hunting* for talent, they must turn to *farming* it. Naturally, business leaders from the CEO down look to Learning & Development (L&D) with new urgency. They increasingly ask L&D to provide the kind of mature capability that they have long required from their core operations. They seek a reliable and efficient system to *identify* the capabilities their people require, to systematically *develop* them, to *make results visible*, and to *drive continual improvement*.

Chapter 1: The CEO's Talent Manifesto

We believe few companies enjoy such a mature and reliable system today. This book shows how we can do better. While we focus in particular on Learning & Development, we believe much of what we describe also applies more broadly to strategic HR.

The Aligned-to-Business Methodology

This book presents the *A2B Methodology* ("Aligned to Business"), a system for managing investments in learning and talent.

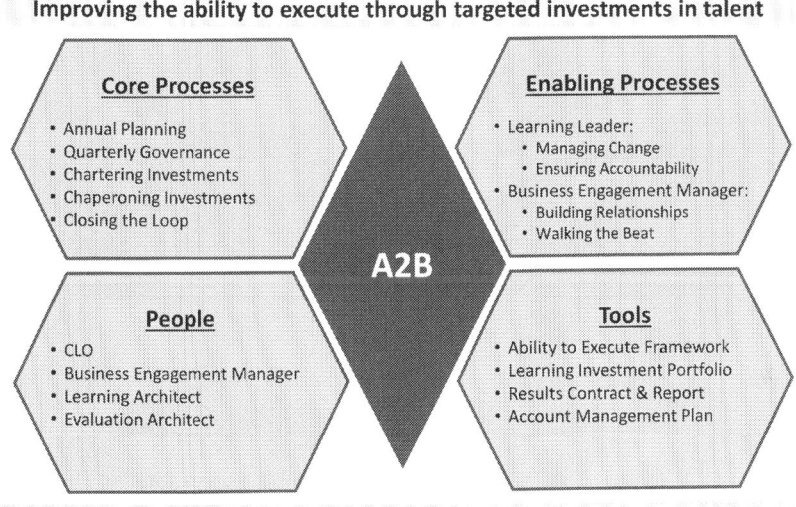

Figure 1: The Aligned-to-Business Methodology

The notion that L&D should become aligned is not new. For many years, in many venues, learning leaders have been exhorted to "get closer to the business," "align with the business," or "address business needs." In the midst of all the exhortations, what has been missing has been concrete guidance on how to proceed. Just *how* can an L&D organization achieve strategic alignment? *This book serves as a "how-to" guide, explaining how an L&D organization can engage with the business to systematically generate strategic alignment.*

As Figure 1 shows, we provide:

- A series of *core processes* for identifying, prioritizing, and managing investments—A2B.

- A series of *enabling processes* that L&D must implement to ensure that A2B works effectively. This includes ensuring the right accountabilities, managing change, and what we call "walking the beat," which is a systematic approach to continually connecting with the business and identifying emerging needs.

- A set of *roles and responsibilities* that L&D must implement. These revolve around the role of the *business engagement managers* (BEMs), a set of individuals who help business groups manage their learning investments and who are judged by the results they achieve.

- A set of *tools and templates* to support the processes. (These are available for download from http://www.aligned-to-business.com).

Below, we summarize the cornerstone ideas upon which A2B is founded. Then, in subsequent chapters, each of these cornerstone ideas is fully developed.

Chapter 1: The CEO's Talent Manifesto

Cornerstone 1: Organize around a Portfolio of Investments in Learning

Some L&D organizations view their role as "providing a service" to the business, so they focus on satisfying their customers' demands. Such L&D organizations often think in technical terms about the service they offer. What content do they provide? How often should they run programs? How much do things cost? Naturally, they come to be viewed by the business as "order-takers."

Assuming this "demand-driven" perspective leads to investments being chosen based on timing rather than value. This approach also expends resources—people and dollars—on a first-come-first-served basis. It places business leaders in the uncomfortable position of being the "order-makers," who need to decide whether launching a new program is a good idea. It also puts pressure on L&D itself to be flexible enough to respond to an unpredictable stream of responses, many of which come with short lead times.

Business leaders want something different. They want a *trusted advisor* who can help them manage investments to achieve specific, important business results. Most business leaders know that they have neither the time nor the expertise to identify on their own the where, when, how, and why behind the many potential investments in learning that they might choose to make. They seek a trusted advisor to clarify and simplify the decisions they face.

A2B asks L&D organizations to view their role as enabling *the business to define and manage a portfolio of investments in learning that improve its ability to execute.* Under this view, the business

17

retains control. The business is the investor, so it must always make the final call on which investments to make. At the same time, L&D facilitates. It is the investment manager, so it must clarify the choices, do the homework, and provide the business with the learning equivalent of compelling investment prospectuses.

When L&D and the business adopt this "investment-driven" perspective, it permeates how they engage, starting even with how they state the L&D workload for the year. During the annual budgeting cycle, most L&D organizations create some form of demand plan. Typically, demand plans list the activities L&D will conduct (e.g., "We'll run ten sessions of this program and twenty sessions of that one.") and the deliverables it will produce (e.g., "We'll create these twenty-seven new programs."). This typical approach positions L&D as a cost center, since it only gives visibility into costs and activities, not results.

Under A2B, we replace the demand plan with a *Learning Investment Portfolio*, which gives business leaders additional visibility. The Learning Investment Portfolio summarizes the value side of the equation. It provides for each program:

1. *Alignment*—How it aligns to business goals. (This answers the question "Why are we considering this program?")

2. *Intended Results*—"What results do we expect to see?" (This answers the question "What counts as success?")

By adding these elements, the A2B approach invites business leaders to adopt an investment perspective. We no longer talk

Chapter 1: The CEO's Talent Manifesto

about "programs" but rather about "investments" and ask "Is this a worthy return?"

The following table shows an excerpt from a Learning Investment Portfolio.

Program Background			Business Alignment			
Business Unit	Program Name	Initiative Supported	Process Improved	Measure	Target	Cost ($K)
Major Accounts	Conducting Service Reviews	Customer Care	Cust. Relationship Mgmt.	Cust. Perceived Quality	95% @ 8 - 10 on Cust. Qual. Survey	$115
Finance	Managing Collections	--	Collections	On Time Payment	90% On Time / 98% < 30 Days PD	$50
Enterprise	Engaging Employees	Best Place to Work	Performance Management	Pivotal Position Engagement & Retention	Engagement 90% / Retention 90%	$72
Customer Service	Building the Brand	Best Place to Work	Onboarding	New Employee Engagement & Retention	Engagement 90% @ 12 weeks / Retention 99% @ 12 weeks	$35
Enterprise	Desktop PC Skills	--	Microsoft Outlook Utilization	Personal Efficiency	100% Certified as "Proficient"	$17
Small Business	Sales Technology	Doubling Small Business Sales	Prospecting/ Qualifying Custs.	New Business - Small Business	2 X in 2 Years	$90
...						
Total						...

Figure 2: An Excerpt from a Learning Investment Portfolio

Since we view the goal of talent investments to be improving a company's ability to execute, creating alignment requires the business and L&D to first identify *the critical business processes that create growth and profitability* and then how a talent investment can impact the performance of those processes. Accordingly, we capture "alignment" by specifying the strategic initiative an investment supports along with the *business process* improved. We then specify the intended results by stating the *business process measure* to be improved and the *target* to be achieved.

Cornerstone 2: Make the Allocation of the Portfolio Visible

The Learning Investment Portfolio enables business leaders to treat each line item as an individual investment. Portfolios typically contain dozens or even hundreds of line items. Business leaders can find it difficult to make wise trade-off decisions without some way to step back from the detail to make broader decisions about how they are placing their learning investment bets. *Business leaders require some way to evaluate the portfolio as a whole instead of as a series of individual investments.*

In response, A2B provides a portfolio analysis to highlight key investment decisions: How much am I investing in advancing the strategy versus running day-to-day operations? How much am I investing in differentiated skills versus generic skills?

In particular, A2B provides a *Value-Added Matrix* that shows the allocation of the overall portfolio (see Figure 3). When companies adopt this perspective, they are often surprised by the results. Most find that they have been investing much less than they would want in what we call "Drivers," that is, programs that advance the strategy through developing differentiated skills. Conversely, they invest more than they want in "Fundamentals," programs based on generic knowledge that support day-to-day operations.

The Value-Added Matrix makes crystal clear the net result of the many individual investment decisions that business leaders must consider and, therefore, improves their control over how they invest in learning.

Cornerstone 3: Align Each Investment with Specific Business-Relevant Targets

An investment is "aligned" when it directly addresses a known business priority to produce a known target result. Alignment is not a binary characteristic; rather, it is a continuum: we speak of "well-aligned, tightly targeted" and "poorly aligned, loosely targeted" investments.

Chapter 1: The CEO's Talent Manifesto

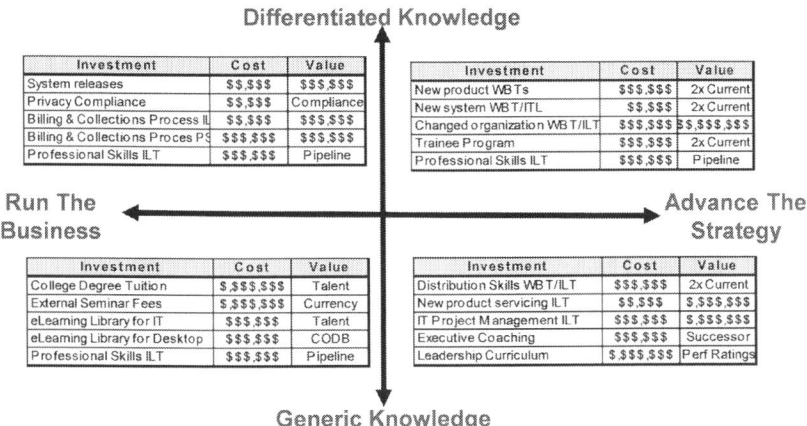

Investment Allocation

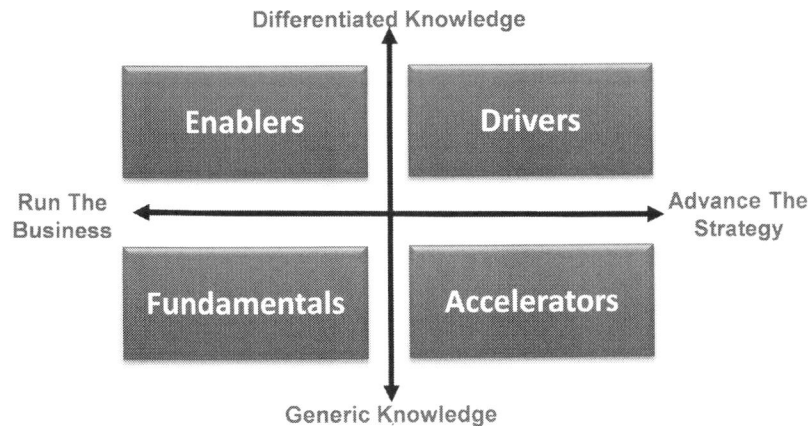

Investment Summary

Figure 3: The Value-Added Matrix

The CEO's Talent Manifesto

How often do business leaders come to your L&D organization saying something like "I want a two-hour course to communicate the following points!" *Most mistakes in aligning talent investments come from being imprecise in what we consider a "business need" and correspondingly focusing too early on too detailed a level of conversation.*

A2B provides a systematic approach business leaders and L&D can use to articulate business "needs" so as to clarify and validate alignment. Our approach is based on the foundational idea that L&D helps business through *improving its ability to execute.* To ensure alignment, we must trace the chain of causality between end business goals and learning solutions.

To trace the chain, we have found it useful to call out four separate levels, resulting in what we call the *Ability-to-Execute Alignment Framework* (see Figure 4).

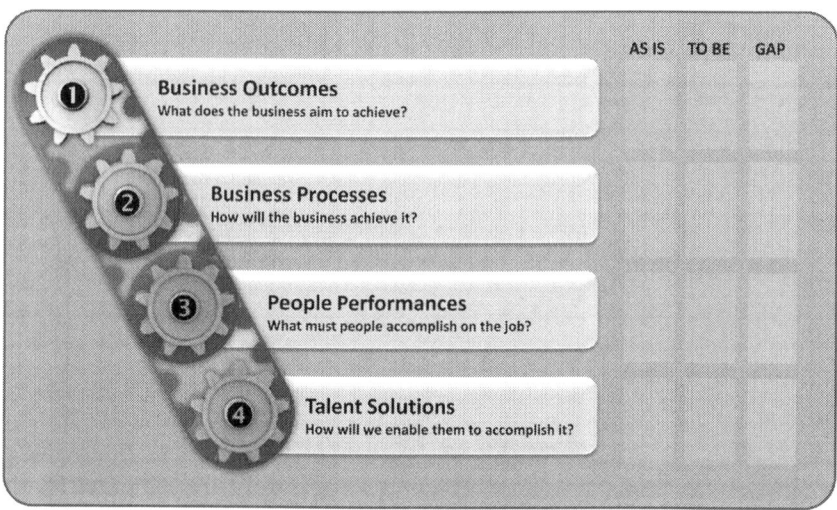

Figure 4: The Ability-to-Execute-Alignment Framework

Chapter 1: The CEO's Talent Manifesto

This framework states that the way L&D:

1. Improves *business outcomes* is by

2. Improving *business processes*, which it does by

3. Improving *people performances*, which it does by

4. Providing targeted, effective, and efficient *talent solutions.*

So, when a business stakeholder comes to "order a solution," the framework shows that it's important to back up and begin asking "Why?" Similarly, when a business stakeholder says, "I have a performance problem and need a solution," it's again important to back up and ask about what business process will be impacted. The framework gives L&D and the business a simple map for tracing alignment and targeting performance.

Under A2B, we talk about the "strategic alignment ratio"; this is the percentage of spending on learning solutions which are aligned to specific business objectives and have specific targets set for business process outcomes. Figure 5 shows what happened in one company over the four years after it began to make the strategic alignment ratio visible for each business unit.

As part of ensuring that investments were aligned, the company also found itself shifting its mix. It reduced investment in "Fundamentals" and dramatically increased its investment in "Drivers." By doing so, it substantially increased value without increasing its total investment.

23

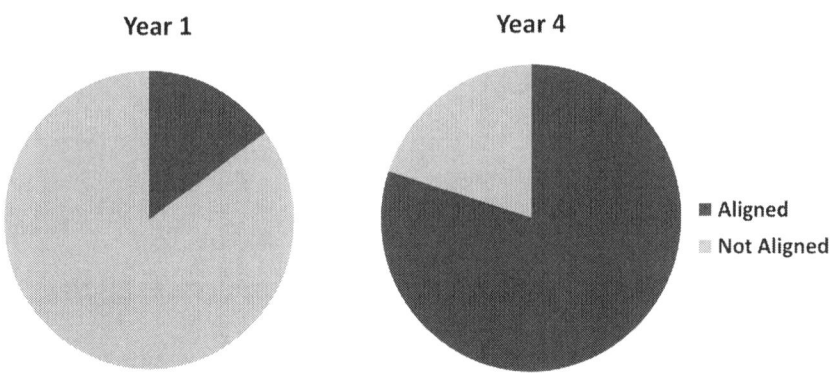

Figure 5: An Increase in the Strategic Alignment Ratio

Cornerstone 4: Implement a Specific Role Accountable for Driving Success

Most L&D organizations are busy places; they execute a remarkable volume of work using a lean set of resources. Most often, the job of generating strategic alignment falls to people who have other pressing responsibilities (e.g., curriculum managers who also manage build plans). The natural result is that when things get busy, the urgent chases out the important. Spending time creating alignment falls to the side in favor of getting today's deliverables out. The problem is that in most L&D organizations, things are *always* busy.

As part of A2B, we stress the need for a dedicated role, the *business engagement manager*, whose primary job is to help business leaders create and manage portfolios that generate demonstrated results. BEMs are investment managers. Their goal is to enable the business to generate results through investments in learning. The BEM leads the effort to determine how investments in talent can achieve targeted business results. Each BEM serves a set of business groups. When BEMs are effective,

Chapter 1: The CEO's Talent Manifesto

they earn the role of trusted advisors to the business leaders they support. Figure 6 identifies their key responsibilities.

The role of the BEM goes beyond a typical "relationship manager" job. This is reflected in how BEMs are evaluated. Relationship managers tend to be evaluated by the volume of work that they generate. That is emphatically not what it is about for the BEM. Instead, as investment managers, *BEMs are judged on how much business value their portfolios produce.*

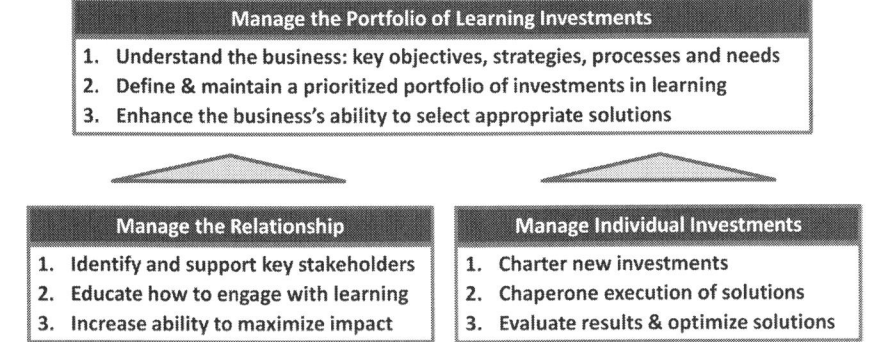

Manage the Portfolio of Learning Investments
1. Understand the business: key objectives, strategies, processes and needs
2. Define & maintain a prioritized portfolio of investments in learning
3. Enhance the business's ability to select appropriate solutions

Manage the Relationship
1. Identify and support key stakeholders
2. Educate how to engage with learning
3. Increase ability to maximize impact

Manage Individual Investments
1. Charter new investments
2. Chaperone execution of solutions
3. Evaluate results & optimize solutions

Figure 6: Business Engagement Manager Responsibilities

The BEM role is central to both implementing A2B and making it an ongoing success. Change needs a champion, and the BEMs provide a focal point. Once in place, BEMs spend their time generating strategic alignment, chaperoning investments to ensure maximum results, and closing the loop to validate that the business got what it paid for when it commissioned an investment.

Generating alignment must be the BEM's goal-above-all-others to prevent them from being distracted. As a rule of thumb, they must spend at least 70 percent of their time on it. In some organizations, the role is full-time; in others, BEMs may have other tasks, e.g., manage a team of content development project managers.

Cornerstone 5: Implement a Governance Process to Ensure the Portfolio Remains on Track

Adopting A2B is not an L&D initiative. Rather, it is a *business* initiative that changes how L&D engages with the business. Under A2B, the focus of L&D moves from providing a service to defining and managing a portfolio of investments that increases the business's ability to execute critical processes. Clearly, L&D cannot effect such a transformation by itself. You need two to dance. Just as clearly, L&D cannot achieve such a transformation only by engaging with the business once a year during budgeting and then afterward hunkering down to execute on the plan. Instead, the business and L&D require a clear method to ensure that:

- The business has visibility into how the portfolio performs.

- L&D has visibility into how the business evolves.

- The business and L&D mutually adjust the portfolio to maximize its performance over time.

In short, L&D and the business require a way to govern the portfolio. A2B provides for this through four tiers of activity.

Tier 1: "Walking the Beat"

As part of A2B, BEMs regularly "walk the beat" to stay current with the business. Walking the beat takes many forms ranging from striking up watercooler conversations to inserting focused questions into meetings dedicated to other topics and arranging touch-base sessions to test out new ideas. Walking the beat may consume 20 to 25 percent of a BEM's time. To

Chapter 1: The CEO's Talent Manifesto

provide BEMs with a structure for investing this time to achieve maximum impact, A2B offers an analysis and planning tool: the Strategic Account Management Plan.

By walking the beat, the BEM comes to understand what is happening in the business while also developing a go-to network of resources to explore needs and understand priorities quickly. When new needs arise, in-flight programs run into challenges, or business plans change, the BEM is there to understand and help L&D respond.

Tier 2: Closing the Loop on Individual Investments

All too often, the last business sponsors hear about a learning investment is when they approve the expense. When business leaders do not get explicit reports back about results, they are likely to suspect that those results are not good. A2B clears away the fog. Under A2B, the BEM is responsible for "closing the loop" by reporting back results, as illustrated in Figure 7.

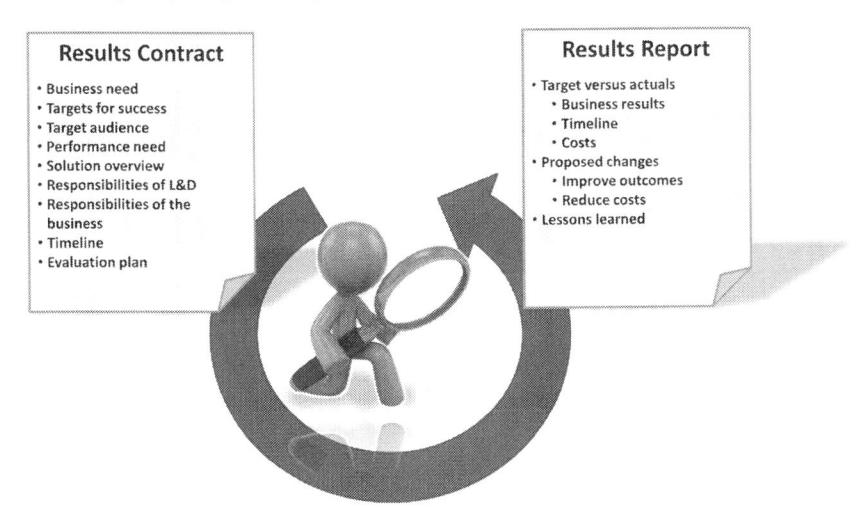

Results Contract
- Business need
- Targets for success
- Target audience
- Performance need
- Solution overview
- Responsibilities of L&D
- Responsibilities of the business
- Timeline
- Evaluation plan

Results Report
- Target versus actuals
  - Business results
  - Timeline
  - Costs
- Proposed changes
  - Improve outcomes
  - Reduce costs
- Lessons learned

Figure 7: Closing the Loop through the Results Contract and the Results Report

The process begins early. At the start of the project, the BEM facilitates agreement to a *Results Contract*. The Results Contract states the target results in business relevant terms. It also makes clear what both L&D and the business will do to ensure success. After the program has been implemented, the BEM provides a *Results Report*. The Results Report guarantees discipline and transparency about whether the business and L&D achieved what they set out to. Where there are gaps, it provides for corrective actions to address them and preventative actions to make the L&D system itself stronger and reduce the chances that a similar gap will recur on other investments.

Tier 3: Quarterly Reviews

Walking the beat and closing the loop work at the level of individual investments. Business leaders and L&D also require the opportunity to step back and consider progress at the level of the overall learning investment portfolio. A2B provides for a structured, quarterly governance process. This process operates at two levels: business group and company-wide (shown in Figure 8).

First, BEMs review progress on the Learning Investment Portfolio with each of their business groups. What is progress against schedule? What is working, and what is not? What add/modify/drop decisions are called for? Then, the learning leader shares the results with a learning council composed of senior executives. A2B defines what should be prepared for each session, what should be accomplished, and how the time should be used.

Chapter 1: The CEO's Talent Manifesto

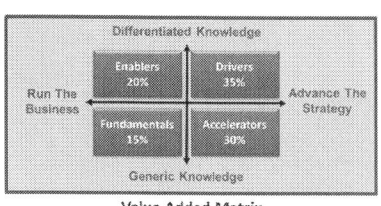

Value Added Matrix

Investment	Cost	Value
New product WBTs	$$$,$$$	2x Current
New system WBT/ITL	$$,$$$	2x Current
GM Development Program	$$$,$$$	$,$$$,$$$
CEO Leadership Forum	$$$,$$$	Successor
Leadership Curriculum	$,$$$,$$$	Perf Ratings

Learning Investment Portfolio

Business Group Update

Update:
- Changes in the business?
- Results from new deployments?
- Progress against schedule?
- Preparation for new development?
- Potential new investments?

Decisions To Be Made
- Changes to the plan?
- Actions to accelerate progress?

Learning Council Update

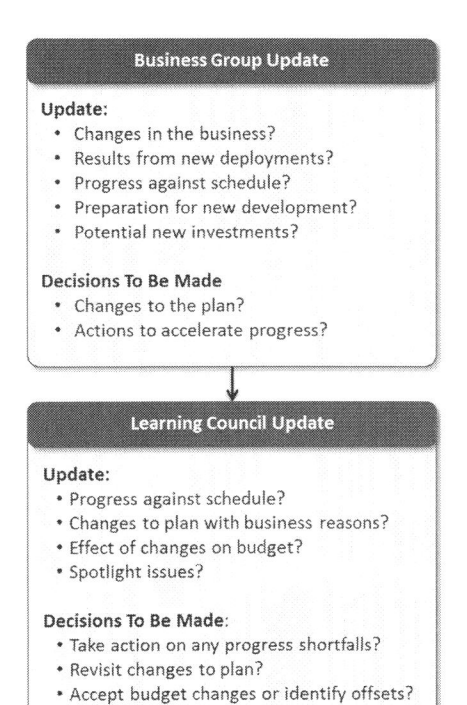

Update:
- Progress against schedule?
- Changes to plan with business reasons?
- Effect of changes on budget?
- Spotlight issues?

Decisions To Be Made:
- Take action on any progress shortfalls?
- Revisit changes to plan?
- Accept budget changes or identify offsets?

Figure 8: Agendas for Quarterly Reviews

Tier 4: Annual Planning

Finally, business leaders and L&D require the opportunity to do periodic deep dives on the Learning Investment Portfolio. This naturally dovetails with a company's annual budgeting process. *We have found the annual planning process to be one of the most distinctive elements of A2B.* Our research indicates that most companies are unclear about how to implement a crisp, data-driven approach to determining the L&D budget. As a result, many resort to coarse approaches, such as baselining against last year's spending ("Seems we need some more learning. Let's give L&D a 10 percent increase.") or against industry averages ("Other banks spend less per employee than we do. Let's give L&D 10 percent less.").

29

The CEO's Talent Manifesto

In contrast, A2B seeks a level of investment that is tuned to each company's specific situation. This level is determined by business executives who make choices based on the concrete opportunities they currently have to invest in learning and improve their ability to execute. This annual process represents a ground-up reset of the annual plan, not just an incremental adjustment to the prior year's spending. Like quarterly governance, annual planning works at two levels. First, BEMs work with their business groups to identify and prioritize opportunities for investment. The output is a business-group-level "Learning Investment Proposal." The learning leader consolidates the results and facilitates a workshop with the learning council to decide upon the Learning Investment Portfolio for the year.

Figure 9 shows the relationship between the quarterly reviews and the annual reset.

The immediate outcome from this governance process is that the business and L&D are mutually clear on the key decisions that define the learning portfolio and the results it achieves. The extra bonus is that the process helps business leaders become wiser investors in L&D over time. Business leaders see how others make investment decisions in their units over time. They discuss these decisions under the facilitation of the learning leader. They receive what amounts to a continuing education in what works and what does not when investing in learning.

Chapter 1: The CEO's Talent Manifesto

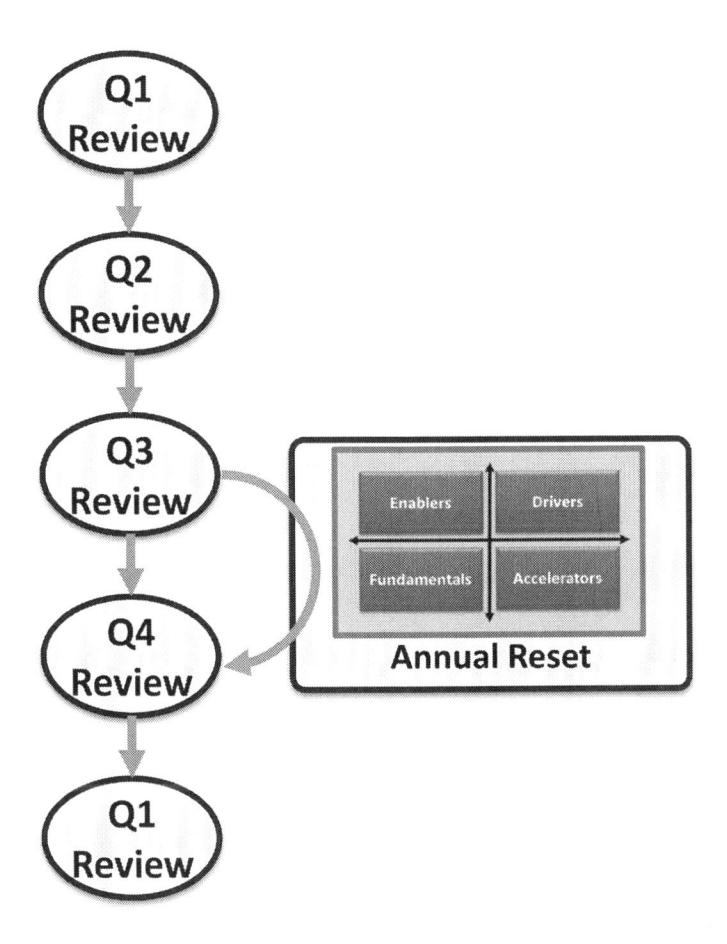

Figure 9: The Flow of Quarterly and Annual Governance

Chapter 2: Generating Demonstrated Business Value
A Long Time Coming…

Those who work in Learning & Development (L&D) have long sought to create compelling value for their companies. Back in 1999, Adelsberg and Trolley formulated the phrase "Running Training Like a Business" to capture their vision for how L&D can contribute to a company.

> What does Running Training like a Business mean?… Being *effective* means delivering training services that tangibly help businesses to achieve their goals. Being *efficient* means making the true costs of training clearly evident and highly acceptable to its customers…Training's mission becomes unashamedly *economic*. Education is still what training does. But business education is a means to business results, not an end in itself.[8]

More than a decade after Trolley released *Running Training Like a Business*, he collaborated with the Corporate University Xchange to evaluate progress. What they found is summarized in the following quote:

> We had thought that given all of the research, writings and discussion around transformation of the training function to a strategic driver in a knowledge economy would have resulted in widespread adoption of practices. However, the data tell us that there are still many areas where learning organizations struggle to run training like a business.[9]

According to the Corporate University Xchange, less than 15 percent of the 150 L&D organizations surveyed provide quantified metrics to demonstrate the value they generate.[10] Our own research indicates that most L&D organizations feel limited in their ability to help business leaders make effective decisions about the learning budget. When we surveyed over fifty L&D organizations, most reported that they were unable to provide business leaders with either a clear decision framework or meaningful benchmarks to consider.[11]

In chapter 1, we showed that many CEOs now see the need to develop talent as a top priority. Given the increasing urgency of talent, you might think that business leaders from the CEO down would see their L&D organizations as heroes within their companies, central to helping them execute their strategies. Unfortunately, when we speak with learning leaders, we find that few believe their L&D organizations are creating the level of impact they desire.

The Challenge: Strategic Alignment

What is stopping L&D organizations from doing better? Why are so few able to generate demonstrably high business value for their companies despite growing business urgency?

Chapter 2: Generating Demonstrated Business Value

We can rule some possibilities out. For instance, learning leaders do not lack motivation. Learning leaders see themselves as businesspeople who drive business results through learning solutions. The 2011 update to *Running Training Like a Business* showed that this vision resonates today even more strongly than it did back in 1999.[12]

Nor is the root cause a dearth of core capability. Most L&D organizations are able to generate commanding value…at least sometimes. They can bring to bear an increasingly powerful set of capabilities to support learning better, faster, and cheaper. They can deploy an increasingly broad and nuanced toolkit of interventions (e.g., eLearning, virtual classrooms, and social networks). They are growing increasingly mature in their core processes for designing, developing, and delivering training. And they are supported by an ecosystem of service providers who themselves are rapidly growing more mature year-by-year.

Instead, we propose the critical root cause lies not in core capabilities but rather in connective tissue. Too often, L&D fails to achieve *strategic alignment*. To use a military metaphor, the problem is not so much that L&D organizations don't have the right guns to fire but rather that they are not clear enough about where to point them and whether they actually hit their target.

What Would It Mean to Be Strategically Aligned?

L&D and business are aligned when they have implemented a portfolio of talent investments that target the company's highest-priority gaps in its ability to execute.

The CEO's Talent Manifesto

L&D achieves strategic alignment by collaborating with business leaders to generate concrete answers to five questions:

1. Where and how can talent investments help us meet our key goals, implement our strategies, and achieve our operational objectives?

2. What defines "success" for each investment we have considered?

3. What priorities have we set among the learning investments we have considered? Does our overall portfolio of investments support our strategic and operating plans?

4. Have our investments achieved the results we sought? If not, what corrective repairs did we make to the solutions? What preventative repairs did we make to avoid shortfalls in future investments?

5. How have we learned from our experience so that we continually get better at using learning investments to grow the business and achieve our goals?

The *sine qua non* of L&D is to improve business performance. Therefore, the best people to judge whether L&D is aligned are the business leaders responsible for it. A quick way to evaluate whether an L&D organization is aligned is to ask senior business leaders to rate the statements shown in Figure 10.

Chapter 2: Generating Demonstrated Business Value

> **Strategic Alignment Assessment**
>
> **To what extent do you believe:**
>
> 1. L&D understands my business goals, strategies, and operational objectives.
> 2. L&D understands the gaps in my "ability to execute" (gaps between my actual results and desired ability to achieve my business goals, implement my strategies, and achieve my operational objectives).
> 3. L&D understands – and helps me understand – where, how, and to what extent people performance gaps create gaps in my ability to execute.
> 4. We have learning investments that target my most important performance gaps.
> 5. Each learning investment has clearly defined target outcomes in business performance.
> 6. We select solutions that reflect my priorities (e.g., cost versus rollout time versus effectiveness).
> 7. My team knows what our responsibilities are to achieve the target outcomes.
> 8. I know how previous investments have performed.
> 9. I know how to use L&D better going forward.
> 10. L&D helps me achieve my most important business goals.

Figure 10: The Strategic Alignment Assessment

To what extent would *your* business leaders view your L&D organization as aligned?

L&D's Role as Steward

Many business leaders are all too ready to "order up" training that they feel may be of benefit. After all, most business leaders have spent sixteen years or more as students. Don't they understand education? Why, then, all the fuss about strategic alignment? Why not have L&D adopt a flexible "fast-follower" strategy—wait until business leaders request support and then be prepared to respond quickly? Why not simply let L&D serve as an order-taker?

The problem is that business leaders are generally not very skilled at ordering up the right solutions. Most of them are aware of this. As an analogy, imagine that you have come down with a stomachache. When might you ask for help from a pharmacist versus a doctor? If your problem is not so bad and you just want help choosing between a couple of off-the-shelf options, you would seek help from a pharmacist. On the other hand, if your problem was more serious and unclear, you would go to the doctor. We believe most talent requirements are complex and so call for the skills of a doctor (albeit one with a particularly good bedside manner).

When L&D takes the order-taker approach, we behave like a doctor who asks his patients to self-diagnose. Maintaining health is complex: issues may have multiple root causes, there are multiple options for treatment, and new treatments arise all the time. Expertise matters. Improving people performance is just the same. No surprise that according to Bersin & Associates, a leading industry research and analyst group, "most L&D staffs are getting out of the mode of 'order-taking' and need to build consulting skills to help business managers solve their performance problems."[13]

Chapter 2: Generating Demonstrated Business Value

Business leaders have limited time to choose which investments they will make. It is simply unrealistic to expect them to become deeply aware of the possibilities provided by L&D or other domains. They will reach out to "order up" a solution when it is central to some challenge they face. But more generally, they look to L&D (or IT or marketing or other support functions) to understand the challenges they face, help identify how the service function can help, and size up the costs and benefits of various options. While business leaders want to (and should) retain the prerogative to decide which investments to make, they look to their functional experts to clarify opportunities and make recommendations. After having signed off on an investment, they then expect their functional experts to provide some evidence of the value of what they "bought" and how to do even better in the future. In short, business leaders expect the people who represent specialty functions to serve as trusted advisors to help them leverage the expertise that function represents and improve the business.

It's L&D's responsibility to bridge the gap and serve as a good business partner. A function that does this well develops a track record over time and becomes a trusted advisor. It's a bit like taking your car to the mechanic. A trustworthy mechanic keeps you in charge of decisions about just what work to do on your car while fixing what ails it without confusion or repeat visits. To do this, when you bring your car in, a trustworthy mechanic makes it easy for you to work through the process of diagnosis. He gives you options for how to proceed and how much to do but leaves the decision to you. And when you put money in, the problem demonstrably goes away. Over the course of a few rounds with such a mechanic, you develop trust.

L&D organizations have plenty of opportunity to work with business leaders to build trust. However, today few do this job well. Not many have a strong ability to collaborate with business leaders, use their time effectively to help them develop a portfolio of L&D investments that are in tight alignment with their business needs, and, finally, close the loop to understand the success of those investments and what lessons were learned so they are able to do even better next time.

When L&D falls short in this job, business leaders are left without a clear vision for how L&D can help them. They can be skeptical of results, feeling about learning like John Wanamaker famously felt about advertising, "I know that half of my investments are wasted. I just don't know which half!" Their companies get substantially less value from L&D than they could were the job to be done well.

The benefits of doing better are compelling. Bersin & Associates use the label "performance consulting" to cover the tasks involved in achieving alignment. They found that few organizations were strong, with only 14 percent of L&D organizations rating themselves as having a strong capability in performance consulting. However, they then found that *those organizations that were strong had 30 percent higher effectiveness ratings, 28 percent higher efficiency ratings, and 26 percent higher alignment ratings. They were seven times more likely to have an excellent measurement program.*[14]

Barriers to Success and How to Overcome Them

We have said that many L&D organizations are weak at creating strategic alignment. The A2B methodology will allow them to build their strength. A2B provides a systematic way

Chapter 2: Generating Demonstrated Business Value

to overcome the barriers that block most organizations from achieving alignment. So just what are these barriers and how does A2B overcome them?

How do we define what counts as a "business need" in a way that clearly defines success?

A2B provides the Ability-to-Execute Alignment Framework, which ensures a clear line of sight and articulates the gaps at each level of the causal chain: business results, business processes, and people performance. Once the causal chain has been made clear, we urge L&D to ask business leaders, "Can you achieve this change without an investment in learning?" If so, no investment is warranted. If not, then the conversation continues.

How do we identify the full set of opportunities where learning investments may be required to support business needs?

To ensure priorities are systematically identified, A2B provides an *Ability-to-Execute Scan*. The scan gives business leaders and L&D a simple and efficient method to get the right opportunities on the table for consideration. To conduct the scan, business leaders and L&D take a top-down look across the set of business processes to identify how they are currently performing, how they must change, and whether and where learning support may be required. Once potential gaps are identified, the Ability-to-Execute Alignment Framework is used to explore them.

The Ability-to-Execute Scan is like an annual checkup with your doctor. It's a brief diagnostic that helps business leaders and

L&D avoid realizing key investment needs belatedly, leading to helter-skelter solutions, or overlooking them altogether.

How do we enable business leaders to confidently prioritize among needs?

As described in chapter 1, A2B provides a Learning Investment Portfolio that helps business leaders decide the shape of the portfolio. It also gives them a set of predefined options through the use of "step-down plans" for selecting the level of investment. Under this approach, business groups and L&D collaborate to identify their desired spending and then how they would cut back if spending were reduced to 85 percent and then again to 70 percent of the desired total. Senior business leaders can then choose between overall levels to get a near fit and, possibly, choose to fine-tune the portfolio from there. Since the A2B governance process makes decisions clear at the group level as well as the business level, business leaders can see how others make investment decisions, leading to wiser decisions over time.

How do we ensure that the L&D organization does not get distracted by the urgency of the day-to-day project work?

As described in chapter 1, the best way we have found to do that is to dedicate a role to it, the role of business engagement manager. BEMs dedicate the majority of their time to generating alignment and are judged on how much business value their portfolios produce. Accordingly, they stand aside from the urgency of L&D operations to ensure alignment and results.

How do we give business leaders confidence that when they make an investment in learning, they can expect it to pay off?

It might seem that evaluation is "issue of the year" in L&D… and has been for many years. In point of fact, the field is growing increasingly sophisticated about impact measurements.[15] However, most organizations lack credible evidence of the results achieved from their learning investments.

Under A2B, we suggest a specific approach to measurement that simplifies the conversation. We focus targets (and therefore evaluation) on the *business process measures* identified as part of the Ability-to-Execute conversation. We build evaluation into the process from the start. When a new learning investment is chartered, A2B calls for a *Results Contract* that clearly stipulates the results sought from an investment, the dependencies on the business that will be required to achieve those results, and how the results will be evaluated. The business engagement manager is then specifically responsible for closing the loop, producing a *Results Review* that shares results, diagnosing any shortfalls, and suggesting appropriate actions.

The first question in the review is: "Did we achieve the desired business process results?" If so, from the business leader's perspective, that's the end of the conversation. Even though several investments might have contributed (a process change, a staffing change, a training program), if they cumulatively achieved the result, the business has "won." Only if the answer is "no" is further diagnosis required.

How do we help the business take ownership of the actions they must take to ensure results?

Learning solutions work best when participants do not consider themselves "done" until they have successfully applied skills learned on the job. Application, feedback, and coaching should typically be part of the overall learning design and are not just an optional add-on. Most of the work of these application components will necessarily fall on the business.

Helping businesses see the value of such actions is a typical change management issue that can be addressed through evidence from pilots. However, to help businesses routinely execute them in the midst of the day-to-day can be a larger challenge. A2B supports such efforts by not sweeping this work under the rug but rather highlighting it from the start as a key risk point. The Results Contract mentioned above contains a clear statement of the responsibilities of both L&D and of the business. Here, L&D has the opportunity to guide the business toward effective approaches…and offer counsel on what is possible if the business chooses not to adopt them.

A Path Forward

Are you seeking to increase the demonstrated results your company achieves from its investments in learning? We argue that the single most important step you can take is to implement a systematic approach to strategic alignment.

Many L&D organizations have struggled to achieve alignment, but we are quite optimistic about the potential to do better. *It is actually not overwhelmingly difficult to create tight strategic alignment. It simply calls for a different approach.*

Chapter 3: The Heart of A2B: the Learning Investment Portfolio
Introduction

It's a tricky business for a company to define and manage an effective portfolio of learning investments. Business leaders are the ones who best understand what their company requires to achieve its goals, drive its strategic initiatives, and fulfill its operational objectives. In some cases, doing so will require people to perform differently. The members of the L&D team are the ones best equipped to determine the kind of learning solutions needed to provide the required skills. So collaboration is a requisite. But the potential complexity of this collaboration is formidable. Even a midsized firm can generate dozens of ideas about how learning could support the business. How can companies ensure that they prioritize the most critical business needs and support the most valuable investments in learning?

A McKinsey & Company survey of 1,440 business leaders found that when senior executives are involved in setting the capabilities agenda, companies are more successful at aligning those agendas with the capability most important to performance and more effective at building the needed skills.[16]

Under A2B, L&D *facilitates* the process while business leaders *decide* which investments to make. The "heavy lifting" to articulate investment options is done by the BEMs, who work hand in hand with business leaders within the business groups they support. In a decentralized L&D structure, investment decisions are then made within business groups. In a centralized structure, investment decisions are made by an executive steering committee or learning council, which is facilitated by the learning leader.

In a world in which there seems to be a never-ending stream of demands on limited L&D resources, having the BEM facilitate the development of a clear Learning Investment Portfolio is the best way we've seen to ensure that a business prioritizes the most useful investments in learning while giving business leaders ownership over the portfolio, clarity on their options and what counts as success, and transparency on whether investments chosen actually produce the results sought.

Illustrating the Problem: An Example

To see why it is so difficult to settle on an effective portfolio, let's consider an example.

Frank is the chief learning officer (CLO) of First National Trust, a hypothetical midsized bank. Year-end is coming up. As usual, his boss, Sarah, the SVP of HR, asks him to pull together a request for next year's L&D budget along with the docket of learning solutions he wants to support. The CFO has indicated that next year is expected to be financially difficult. So, Sarah asks Frank to submit a budget 12 percent lower than this year's.

Chapter 3: The Heart of A2B: the Learning Investment Portfolio

To get started, Frank shares the target with his curriculum managers and polls them to learn what business needs they face. He learns:

- Sam, the head of the retail banking unit, is upgrading the role of the call center. Sam believes it's critical that the existing service reps get extensive new training and that the new-hire program be reworked from the ground up.

- Jake, the CIO, plans to continue the shift to a Java-Oracle technology base. He needs several hundred programmers who currently use Microsoft technologies to learn a whole new set of technologies. He believes it's vital that L&D provide a solution to help him.

- Sarah, the SVP of HR (and Frank's boss), believes that the bank needs to redouble its efforts to develop frontline and midlevel leadership. In the past year, the bank has found it more difficult to recruit frontline leaders. Historically, the bank has been seen as a great place to start a career. However, over the past several years, it has cut back on leadership development. She believes these cuts have caused the difficulties in recruiting new leaders.

Thinking about the results, Frank realizes that the only business leader who has volunteered to step back from a current or planned investment is Jake. He has offered to wind up the extensive project management training IT ran last year. However, that program was due to expire in any case.

In short, Frank has been asked to cut L&D but none of the business or functional leaders has raised *his or her* hand to receive less support. In fact, the opposite is true—in his efforts to stay close to the business, Frank has only uncovered a slew of new requests.

Frank is challenged. How can he respect Sarah's request to cut spending while ensuring that the bank receives the best value from whatever level of investment it does make in L&D? Should he be the one to make the call between whether to fund developing Java programmers or new leaders? In fact, he wonders, as he mulls over what would be best for the bank, whether it is productive for Sarah to set next year's budget level based on a simple adjustment to this year's.

Frank suspects that the answer to both questions is "no." He would rather *facilitate* a process that enables the bank's business leaders to confidently choose both the right level of investment for the bank's situation as well as make trade-off decisions between alternative investments based on how they view their needs. But how can he pull that off?

Why Is It So Hard to Establish the Annual L&D Plan?

Frank wants a better way for his organization to choose "where to point the gun," that is, to choose which investments to make in L&D. Our research shows he is far from alone. Most L&D organizations lack confidence in how they establish their portfolio of L&D investments. To do so effectively, they must overcome several barriers:

- *Multiple business sponsors*—Frank must work with multiple business leaders, each with her and his own

Chapter 3: The Heart of A2B: the Learning Investment Portfolio

priorities. How can he bring them together to make choices about spending?

- *Ad hoc identification of opportunities*—Some business leaders are strong believers in training…perhaps even to the extent that they see training as a solution to needs that training cannot effectively address ("Gee, let's tell 'em to get more engaged!"). Other business leaders may not feel training is useful to close skill gaps beyond what happens naturally on the job ("We'll just have our supervisors keep an eye out and coach when they need to."). Yet others may simply not look far down the path to consider what new skills need to be developed to achieve their goals ("Well, the new application is rolling out next month. I wonder if there should be some training?"). L&D organizations, all else equal, will tend to spend time where leaders like what they do. Without some structured way to make sure that opportunities are identified even-handedly, some critical ones can fail to make it to the table so they are not even considered for prioritization.

- *Incommensurate options*—In theory, it's clear how to prioritize investments. One identifies the ROI of each program and then selects all programs that exceed a target rate. If only it was so crisp in practice. While it's not hard to calculate costs, how does one judge value? How much is a more proficient service rep worth to First National Trust compared to a more proficient Java programmer or a more proficient frontline leader? Determining a hard ROI for training is often quite speculative…as speculative as it is for many other investments. How can First National Trust compare such apples and oranges?

- *Business judgment is required to establish priorities*—It's clear that investment priorities should be in sync with business priorities. That means that the business leadership must set them.

- *Technical expertise is required to define and evaluate solutions*—At the same time, most business leaders do not know how to best leverage L&D (or, for that matter, IT, legal, or any of the other specialized service functions in the company). They can ask for training to achieve goals that training cannot accomplish. They can jump to solutions that are overly costly. L&D must contribute the technical expertise that business leaders require to identify options for solutions and evaluate the trade-offs among them.

- *Collaboration requires business acumen*—While L&D must drive the process, the goal is to improve the business. It's appropriate that business leaders rapidly become impatient with technical specialists who do not speak "the language of business" and who seem unclear on what the business is trying to achieve. For L&D to gain the trust and participation of business leaders, it must use their time wisely and "start at the start" with what the business wants to achieve. This means that L&D must find some way to understand the goals, strategies, and operational objectives of each business group efficiently enough that business leaders do not feel that they have to take baby steps to work through each conversation.

Frank requires a process that integrates many voices, including those of business leaders from across the company as well

Chapter 3: The Heart of A2B: the Learning Investment Portfolio

as those of L&D team members who help those business leaders think through how investments in learning can best enable them to achieve their goals. To put it mildly, putting such a process in place can be a challenge.

No wonder many companies use simpler methods to set L&D budgets and priorities. Some companies set budget levels "top down," based on last year's budget, like Sarah suggested, perhaps adding a delta to consider inflation, how much the business can "afford," or how much others in the industry tend to spend per employee. Others look to L&D to determine for itself how to allocate the budget, which then leads L&D to make choices based on whatever factors it chooses, e.g., which business leader is the loudest of the squeaky wheels or which curriculum manager is the most articulate. Such methods have the advantage of being simple to execute. However, they neither ensure that a business gets the most value from L&D nor do they build confidence in business leaders that L&D is a wise and effective steward of the company's resources.

What's needed is a different approach, a bottom-up, data-driven process in which a company efficiently uncovers the specific opportunities it has to improve business outcomes via learning investments and, based on the actual opportunities found, decides which way to move forward, and, therefore, how much to invest.

The Genesis of the Aligned-to-Business Methodology

Starting in 2000, CNA's CEO launched a company-wide re-evaluation of its business strategies along with a review of the performance and talent management practices that supported those strategies. It was a critical time for the business, and it became clear to the senior leadership that a major issue was the lack of deep enough business acumen across departments to turn the company around so it could compete successfully. Therefore, a prominent element in the turnaround strategy was to develop the expertise that customers and the company could depend on.

The CEO was enthusiastic about and committed to the direction but was also concerned. He knew the current training budget was substantial. If CNA were to adopt the new talent strategy, would it become a bottomless pit? The CEO and the HR leader wanted to know how much implementing the new strategy would cost and what the business would get in return. However, under the company's existing structure, learning was decentralized. There was uneven available detail on where the money went and little accounting for outcomes.

In response, CNA centralized L&D budgeting in a newly formed "Knowledge and Learning Group" (while still leaving L&D decentralized). Tom Hilgart led the initiative to answer the CEO and HR leader's questions: how much would the talent strategy cost, and what results would it produce? To do so, he defined a new approach to establishing the L&D budget based on a data-driven, bottom-up analysis of what the business required.

It's not unusual for stressful situations to lead to new approaches. The approach Tom developed back then has now matured into the A2B Methodology.

A Typical Starting Point

Tom started where most L&D shops start. With the support of the CEO and the HR leader, he asked each learning group to report on the learning solutions they provided the prior year.

Chapter 3: The Heart of A2B: the Learning Investment Portfolio

Figure 11 illustrates a typical format for such a request. (As you will see below, this information forms *part* of what Tom requested, but Tom also made two extensions to it).

Program Background		
Business Unit	**Program Name**	**Cost ($K)**
Major Accounts	Conducting Service Reviews	$115
Finance	Managing Collections	$50
Enterprise	Engaging Employees	$72
Customer Service	Building the Brand	$35
Enterprise	Desktop PC Skills	$17
Small Business	Sales Technology	$90
...	...	...
Total		...

Figure 11: A Hypothetical Program Docket—A Typical Starting Point for Selecting Learning Investments

53

In some shops, a docket like this serves as the key management tool for handling the learning budget. Such shops are behaving as if they manage a collection of training programs, not a portfolio of investments. Where on this docket is the information one seeks when one chooses or reviews an investment?

Extension 1: Ensuring Alignment and Capturing the Definition of Success

CNA was keen to ensure that its investments were tightly aligned with its emerging strategy. But a docket like that in Figure 11 does not capture alignment. The first extension Tom made to his request was to identify how investments were aligned to business goals, strategies, and operational objectives. To do so, he simply requested each learning group to identify for each investment which business need it addresses and which business outcome defines success.

All too often, business leaders are unclear on just what they expect to see from an investment in learning. Sure, training may be helpful, but how will its success actually be judged? Often, it is not…and in such cases, training is, and should be, at serious risk of being seen as a "nice-to-have" cut when budgets are tight. Even though business leaders may sign off on learning investments without thinking through how they will judge them, L&D organizations fail to make "success" clear at their own peril.

Definitions of success are central to A2B. A business need is *not* a desire to improve skills, communicate a message, or build morale. Rather, a business need is a gap in the performance of

Chapter 3: The Heart of A2B: the Learning Investment Portfolio

a *business process*. Under A2B, a definition of success contains three elements:

1. Which specific *business process* is to be improved?

2. What *process measure* characterizes the aspect of the process to be improved?

3. What *target level* of performance on that measure counts as success?

While the next chapter outlines the reason for this approach, one benefit is immediately clear: it puts the business and L&D on the "same side of the table" in seeking to drive the stated improvements, and it greatly simplifies that job of determining whether, in fact, the L&D system actually generates the results it promises.

Figure 12 shows what the hypothetical docket described here might look like after being extended to include such definitions of success.

When Tom asked for this detail as part of his request at CNA, he *hoped* to see clear definitions of success like these for most of the learning investments that CNA was making. He *expected* a mixed bag with a few organizations having clear definitions of success and most not. What he *found* was even less. In the first year the data was gathered, CNA found that the learning groups could provide clear definitions of success for only a small percentage of their learning programs.

The CEO's Talent Manifesto

Program Background			Business Alignment			
Business Unit	Program Name	Initiative Supported	Process Improved	Measure	Target	Cost ($K)
Major Accounts	Conducting Service Reviews	Customer Care	Cust. Relationship Mgmt.	Cust. Perceived Quality	95% @ 8 - 10 on Cust. Qual. Survey	$115
Finance	Managing Collections	--	Collections	On Time Payment	90% On Time 98% < 30 Days PD	$50
Enterprise	Engaging Employees	Best Place to Work	Performance Management	Pivotal Position Engagement & Retention	Engagement 90% Retention 90%	$72
Customer Service	Building the Brand	Best Place to Work	Onboarding	New Employee Engagement & Retention	Engagement 90% @ 12 weeks Retention 99% @ 12 weeks	$35
Enterprise	Desktop PC Skills	--	Microsoft Outlook Utilization	Personal Efficiency	100% Certified as "Proficient"	$17
Small Business	Sales Technology	Doubling Small Business Sales	Prospecting/ Qualifying Custs.	New Business - Small Business	2 X in 2 Years	$90
...	...	...	...	...	...	...
Total						

Figure 12: The Hypothetical Docket Extended to Clarify Alignment and Define Success

Chapter 3: The Heart of A2B: the Learning Investment Portfolio

Our experience is that this method of defining success in terms of business process measures provides an enormous advantage in helping business leaders develop confidence in L&D. As business leaders get used to A2B, they become increasingly concrete and confident in their thinking about how to leverage investments in learning. When they consider their goals, strategies, and operational objectives, they grow accustomed to identifying what changes to business processes are required.[17] With the support of BEMs, business leaders become comfortable considering the question "Can I achieve my goals without this investment?" If they can, then they (and the company) avoid unnecessary L&D investments. However, if they cannot, then they choose between either changing their goals or proceeding with an investment. And after having made the investment, they look for the results. The clarity of the process along with the feedback cycle enables trust to develop and lets business leaders become increasingly confident in their ability to use learning investments to support their goals.

Extension 2: Ensuring Balance in the Portfolio

As CNA was considering how to adjust its learning portfolio, it was concerned that even if individual investments made sense considered individually, the portfolio as a whole might underperform if it includes:

- *Too much investment in "run the business" solutions and too little in "advancing the strategy."* This happens when companies do not eliminate or optimize outdated "run the business" programs over time while also not engaging closely enough with the business to determine how learning investments can advance the strategy.

- *Too much investment in solutions based on generic content and too little in solutions based on differentiated content.* The logic here is similar: programs employing generic content should generally be optimized over time with programs based on differentiated content being where a company is most likely to drive strategic advantage.

These are common concerns that companies have with learning portfolios since "old" programs, left unoptimized, can consume too much budget, making it difficult to appropriately fund new priorities.

To avoid these issues, Tom also asked each learning group to capture whether each investment targets:

- *Strategic or Operational*: Did the solution help CNA advance a critical strategic initiative or, instead, to run the day-to-day operations?

- *Differentiated or Generic*: Was the solution based on differentiated content ("company knowledge") or, instead, on off-the-shelf content ("generic knowledge")?

The Result: The Value-Added Matrix

To summarize, in examining CNA's learning investments, Tom gathered three categories of information:

- A *typical docket* of programs and their costs;

- Additional information specifying *business alignment* in terms of business process, measure, and targeted performance; and

Chapter 3: The Heart of A2B: the Learning Investment Portfolio

- Additional information specifying the *allocation* of the spend (strategic versus operational and differentiated versus generic).

Using this information, Tom developed and his team implemented what we have come to call a *Value-Added Matrix* view of the Learning Investment Portfolio. The matrix organizes the investment portfolio into four quadrants and summarizes the investments in each.

The two quadrants *to the right* of the vertical axis contain investments to advance the company's strategies. We call these investments *Drivers* when they employ differentiated content and *Accelerators* when they employ generic knowledge.

The two quadrants to the left of the vertical axis contain learning programs needed to run the ongoing operations. We call these *Enablers* when they employ differentiated knowledge and *Fundamentals* when they employ generic knowledge.

The two quadrants *above* the horizontal axis, *Drivers* and *Enablers*, contain learning programs that employ content that is unique to the business and unavailable in the marketplace. These are programs that need to be built using subject matter experts from inside the company. The two quadrants below, *Accelerators* and *Fundamentals*, contain learning programs whose content is readily available in the marketplace. These are programs that should be bought and perhaps customized.

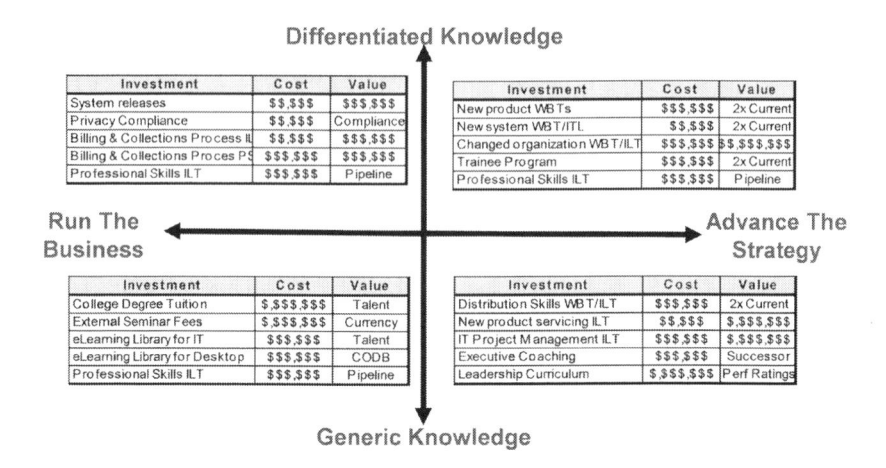

The CEO's Talent Manifesto

Investment Allocation

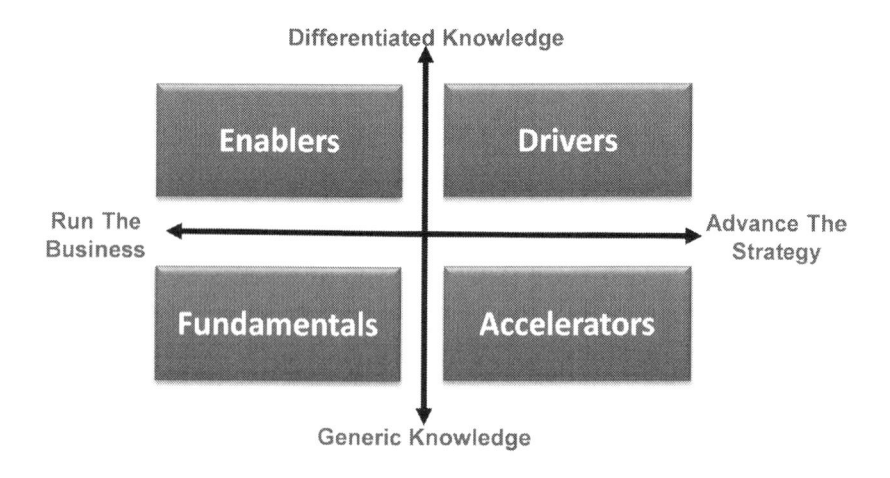

Differentiated Knowledge (upper)

Upper-left quadrant (Run The Business / Differentiated Knowledge):

Investment	Cost	Value
System releases	$$,$$$	$$$,$$$
Privacy Compliance	$$,$$$	Compliance
Billing & Collections Process IL	$$,$$$	$$$,$$$
Billing & Collections Process PS	$$$,$$$	$$$,$$$
Professional Skills ILT	$$$,$$$	Pipeline

Upper-right quadrant (Advance The Strategy / Differentiated Knowledge):

Investment	Cost	Value
New product WBTs	$$$,$$$	2x Current
New system WBT/ITL	$$,$$$	2x Current
Changed organization WBT/ILT	$$$,$$$	$$,$$$,$$$
Trainee Program	$$$,$$$	2x Current
Professional Skills ILT	$$$,$$$	Pipeline

Lower-left quadrant (Run The Business / Generic Knowledge):

Investment	Cost	Value
College Degree Tuition	$,$$$,$$$	Talent
External Seminar Fees	$,$$$,$$$	Currency
eLearning Library for IT	$$$,$$$	Talent
eLearning Library for Desktop	$$$,$$$	CODB
Professional Skills ILT	$$$,$$$	Pipeline

Lower-right quadrant (Advance The Strategy / Generic Knowledge):

Investment	Cost	Value
Distribution Skills WBT/ILT	$$$,$$$	2x Current
New product servicing ILT	$$,$$$	$,$$$,$$$
IT Project Management ILT	$$$,$$$	$,$$$,$$$
Executive Coaching	$$$,$$$	Successor
Leadership Curriculum	$,$$$,$$$	Perf Ratings

Investment Summary

Differentiated Knowledge:
- Enablers (Run The Business)
- Drivers (Advance The Strategy)

Generic Knowledge:
- Fundamentals (Run The Business)
- Accelerators (Advance The Strategy)

Figure 13: The Value-Added Matrix

Chapter 3: The Heart of A2B: the Learning Investment Portfolio

The Value-Added Matrix gives business leaders a welcome tool to understand the allocation of the overall investment they are making and to see whether they are placing the appropriate emphasis on how that investment is distributed in terms of the business value the investment is expected to create. As a simple example, a business that is being run as a cash cow perhaps should allocate most of its investment in running its business whereas a business that is targeting new markets should invest heavily in advancing its strategy.

In the hypothetical example shown in Figure 13, the company has formed a learning investment strategy that allocates 70 percent of its investment to programs that advance strategic capabilities and 30 percent to programs that maintain business operations but are not strategic. Splitting the total using the other dimension, the company is investing 60 percent of its budget in building programs unique to the company and 40 percent in programs purchased from outside. *In short, in the hypothetical example, the company shown is primarily investing in advancing its strategy using differentiated content. Our experience is that many companies would benefit from such an allocation but few companies are likely to achieve it without consciously working at it!*

The Learning Investment Portfolio and the Value-Added Matrix crisply express the strategic alignment of the portfolio of investments and forms the heart of A2B. L&D and the business collaborate to identify what should go into the Learning Investment Portfolio (and what gets left by the wayside). They use the Value-Added Matrix view to refine their choices. Then they collaborate to implement learning solutions that achieve the specific results targeted. And in cases when things don't quite work out, they collaborate again to identify why not and fix both the immediate problem and also the root cause to make the L&D system more reliable each year. As we describe in the next chapter, BEMs provide the motivating force to make it all work, ensuring that opportunities get considered, investments get chartered, and the feedback loop is closed.

The CNA Story: The Impact of Implementing A2B

The impact of implementing A2B can be both immediate and substantial.

CNA L&D began by creating a Value-Added Matrix analysis of their current state. They found that the investment allocation was far from what they wanted:

- Few investments had clear definitions of success. For most, it was unclear what results the investment would produce.

- Only a small percentage of the total was invested in advancing key strategies.

- Several business units ran duplicative programs.

- There was little follow-up with participants after training events. The system lacked focus on transfer to the job and assessing results achieved.

Next, with this homework complete, CNA L&D considered the CEO's question, "How much would the overall learning investment need to be increased for CNA to no longer simply hire experienced talent but instead grow its own, producing the

Chapter 3: The Heart of A2B: the Learning Investment Portfolio

desired level of business acumen?" To generate an answer, the team used the same approach. Tom asked each learning group to use the same portfolio and matrix method to identify its desired investments for the next year. Each learning group collaborated with their business leaders to identify business needs, learning solutions, and an estimated level of investment. For each investment, they identified concrete and measurable targets for success.

The results of the process were surprising. Whereas the CEO's question had been, "How much will we need to increase our investment?" what they actually found was that by insisting on this clear line of sight, *CNA was able to dramatically reduce its budget for the next year…by approximately 50 percent*. Savings mostly came from eliminating low-value training and programs that lacked performance accountabilities. Even after making this dramatic reduction, CNA still had plenty of budget to make the substantial new investments required to implement its new talent strategy.

Benefits from A2B

The chapter began with the tale of Frank from First National Bank, as he wondered how he could set the annual L&D budget. In this chapter, we have described how using A2B to identify a portfolio of targeted investments and analyzing the allocation of those investments using the Value-Added Matrix enables L&D to generate a "custom fit" budget bottom-up based on the specific opportunities the company faces instead of taking a swag based on industry averages. We have hinted at how L&D can use A2B to collaborate with the business, facilitating a process that lets the business decide which investments to make and enables L&D and business leaders to "get on the same side of the table" to define what to expect from them. We have shown how the use of the Value-Added Matrix drives and displays these benefits by adding a value analysis to the type of program docket some L&D organizations use to manage their budgets.

CNA found that by using A2B appropriately, they consistently realized these benefits and more. Companies that implement A2B find they obtain the following benefits.

Increased engagement between business and L&D

The process used to generate the Value-Added Matrix leads to a higher level of engagement between the business and L&D. For instance, as CNA's business leaders worked through year 1, they came to realize that they had been making an unexpectedly high investment in L&D without really actively managing it. They saw how contributing their energy to better manage this investment led to dramatic improvements in cost and value. They also understood how the matrix and the investment detail supporting it gave them the concrete information they required to do so.

Increased confidence of business leaders that L&D acts as a wise steward of company resources

In *Running Training Like a Business*, Adelsberg and Trolley say "business leaders are often sold on learning but not sold on training." Much of that has to do with a lack of confidence that many business leaders have in their company's ability to target investments and determine whether money invested actually produces results. Many business leaders are simply unclear about "Is what you are doing relevant?" The Value-Added Matrix provides clarity on alignment with business priorities…

Chapter 3: The Heart of A2B: the Learning Investment Portfolio

and then goes further to close the loop on whether the company actually gets what it paid for when business leaders make investments.

Increased rationalization of the L&D organizational structure

Many decentralized or federated L&D organizations suffer from duplicative programs. The portfolio roll-up makes such duplication clear. Similarly, many suffer from a lack of the scale required to perform at a level of technical excellence that enables investments to generate results. In the CNA example, the data generated in the first year enabled CNA business leadership to see the cost of decentralization of L&D in terms of duplication, lack of active management of investment, and some places where poor solutions hampered results. As a result, after a couple of years of using the A2B, CNA's business leaders took the decision to centralize not only the budgeting process but also the L&D function itself, forming a centralized Knowledge and Learning Group.

Increased focus on investments that "move the needle"

One issue that vexes many organizations is that it is difficult to invest in learning support to advance key strategic priorities because the budget is consumed by a myriad of moderate-value programs that support day-to-day operations. Such programs gradually accumulate. New ones are added more often than old ones are retired. Changes extend programs more often than they shrink them. As a result, moderate-value training starves out space for strategic investments in L&D.

The Value-Added Matrix clearly focuses business leaders' attention on just that issue. The upper right quadrant focuses squarely on just those investments that tend to generate the highest business impact, namely, strategic programs based on differentiated capabilities. The investment summary view lists what percentage of investment goes to such investments. In the four years after CNA started using the matrix, it steadily increased the percentage invested in this quadrant each year. In part, these increases came because L&D could see more opportunities to support strategic initiatives, given its higher level of engagement. In part, they came because business leaders became increasingly aware of the impact that formal and informal learning could have on the success of their initiative and in part because CNA actively managed down spending in other quadrants.

From the Value-Added Matrix to the A2B Methodology

The Learning Investment Portfolio and Value-Added Matrix provide the heart of the A2B Methodology. At the same time, a company that wishes to deploy it will soon find itself tackling a host of additional questions like:

- What kind of annual planning and governance system is required to keep the matrix current in the face of evolving business needs?

- How does a company deploy this approach across business units?

- Whom should learning leaders select for BEMs and how should they develop them?

- How should individual investments be chartered so that they are set up to succeed?

Chapter 3: The Heart of A2B: the Learning Investment Portfolio

The A2B Methodology provides a practical system to drive strategic alignment by giving structure and process around selecting a portfolio of targeted investments that deliver a value mix fitted to a business's strategy and operating priorities.

Chapter 4: Targeting Business Needs and Aligning Investments
Introduction

As mentioned earlier, the BEMs' primary responsibility is to help the business groups they serve define and manage a portfolio of productive investments in learning solutions. These learning solutions are not an end in themselves. Rather they are simply a means to enable the business to address important needs. So, if BEMs are to be effective, they clearly must understand how to help a business group identify, articulate, and prioritize its business needs.

But what does this really mean? Businesses are complex, and they have many kinds of needs. How can a business group know when it has developed a comprehensive view? How can it distinguish tactical needs from strategic needs?

Most of the time the L&D team as a whole spends with a business focuses on what is causing a specific performance gap and how they can reduce it. Accordingly, the industry has amassed a wealth of performance improvement models and methodologies (e.g., our personal favorite is the updated Behavior Engineering Model,[18] which lays out a useful catalog of root causes to help professionals troubleshoot poor performance).

For the BEM, however, a different question comes first, namely, "Which needs are worthy of attention?" *Most mistakes in identifying which business needs should receive which learning investments come from focusing too early on too detailed a level of conversation.* For example, a business leader might come to L&D to request a desired solution (e.g., "I want a two-hour course to communicate the following points...") or with what sounds like an appropriate need (e.g., "I am about to radically transform how our service consultants engage with customers."); the BEM might then follow up with a low-level "take the order" question before really validating what the need is and how L&D can help (e.g., "Sounds exciting. How much training will the service consultants need?").

In this chapter, we provide a systematic approach for business leaders and BEMs to identify, articulate, and prioritize business needs in a way that leads seamlessly into identifying appropriate learning investments.

Our approach is based on a particular notion of how L&D helps the business. When we say that L&D addresses business needs, what we really mean is that L&D helps a business group *improve its ability to execute*. This happens via a step-by-step chain of alignment. We find it useful to call out four separate levels in this chain, resulting in what we call the *Ability-to-Execute Alignment Framework* (see Figure 14).

This framework simply shows that the linkage between business performance and people performance is business processes. As a result, the way L&D *improves business outcomes* is through improving *business processes*, which it does by improving *people performances*, which it does by providing aligned, effective, and efficient *talent solutions*.

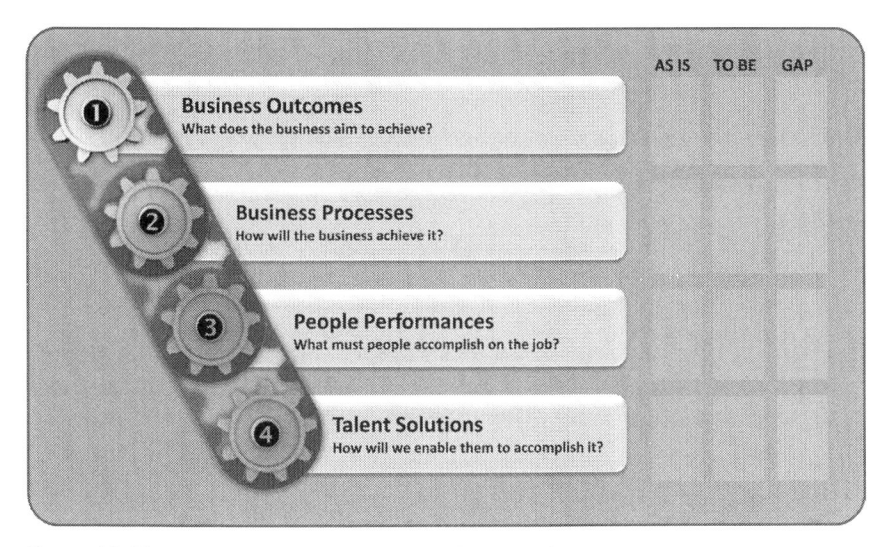

Chapter 4: Targeting Business Needs and Aligning Investments

Figure 14: The Ability-to-Execute Alignment Framework

When a business makes an investment in learning, it should be able to trace each link in this chain. Doing that requires it to identify the *improvement* required at each level. (If the business cannot trace the links or if it can but it is not convinced that doing each lower level will accomplish the next higher level objective, it is perhaps doing training that may end up generating some benefits, but it is *not* systematically investing in results. Note: For a useful explanation of the importance of clarifying the "as is" state versus the "to be" state, see *Zap the Gaps*.[19] For a useful distinction between training activity and training for impact, see *Training for Impact*.[20])

The Ability-to-Execute Alignment Framework

To clarify the framework, let's work through a simple example of how a BEM and business leader might use it to explore a business need. Ann is the head of the healthcare division of a large technology company. She is concerned about her ability to meet her target for revenue growth for next year. She thinks her team may need some new skills. Fred is the BEM who supports her. He uncovers this need during their regular quarterly check-in. Perhaps it arises in the form of a request for a solution, with Ann asking Fred if he can provide a sales training program. How would the framework apply?

Business Outcomes

Every business has some *business outcomes* that its leadership defines as "successes." Typically, these outcomes fall into three groups:

- *Achieving business goals*, such as goals for revenue, growth, and profitability;

- *Implementing strategic initiatives* that better position it to achieve its business goals, such as developing a presence in a new geography or centralizing a capability; and

- *Meeting operational objectives* that it views as instrumental to its business goals, such as lowering the cost of service calls or increasing win rates on proposals.

When Ann raises her concern, Fred first backs up to understand what business outcome is at issue. That's when he learns that she has a target of revenue growth for the next year of 15 percent and she is concerned she may only get half of that without change.

Business Process

The way businesses achieve outcomes is through business processes. These run the gamut from high-level processes, such

Chapter 4: Targeting Business Needs and Aligning Investments

as "define products," "manufacture products," and "repair products" down to fine-grained processes, such as "process purchase orders." Sometimes business processes are quite formally defined and monitored (as helpdesks and high-volume manufacturing processes tend to be for example), and other times, they are only informally managed.

After Fred and Ann identify Ann's desired business outcome, Fred will ask some follow-up questions to understand which business process is at stake and what kind of improvement to it is required. After some conversation, it may become clear that Ann believes that the issue has to do with the size of proposals. The division is doing fine in retaining customers and even upselling existing ones. It is also doing well in identifying prospects and in its win rate. However, it is not doing well on the deal size of its proposals.

The proposal process, like any business process, can be evaluated using a variety of metrics. To focus efforts to understand a need and move to solution, it's tremendously helpful to figure out just which ones are at stake. In this case, the metric that matters here is *deal size.*

At this point, Fred and Ann have identified that it is the *proposal process* that is at stake and, furthermore, that it is the one particular metric that requires improvement, *deal size.* Going further, Fred may learn that Ann believes that "*If we increase proposal deal size by 15 percent, then we will achieve revenue growth of 10 percent.*" This statement represents a projection about how much improvement in business outcomes will result from an improvement in the ability to execute. Just who is responsible for such projections varies as we move down the chain. Projections at this initial level about business outcomes fall squarely on the shoulders of the business itself.

People Performance

"People performance" captures what a target audience must do on the job. It goes beyond capability to what level of performance is actually achieved.

In this case, Fred may do some quick research to identify that Ann's top-performing salespeople achieve average deal size about 40 percent higher than average performance. He may further uncover that the key reason is that they create comprehensive solutions more frequently. The top-performers may propose comprehensive solutions 75 percent of the time while the average salesperson does so only 25 percent of the time. Fred may estimate: *"If we enable salespeople to propose comprehensive solutions 50 percent of the time, we will increase average deal size by 25 percent."*

This statement represents a projection of how much improvement in a business process metric comes from an improvement in people performance. The responsibility for such projections is typically shared. Frequently, L&D conducts the research and the business and L&D mutually ensure they are comfortable with their conclusions.

Talent Solutions

Along with the above analysis, Fred may put a solution on the table. He may have uncovered that top-performing salespeople are able to make comprehensive solutions because they:

Chapter 4: Targeting Business Needs and Aligning Investments

1. Ask a broader set of questions during discovery and

2. Develop a set of proven solutions, which they then rigorously reuse.

Working with the rest of the L&D team, Fred may identify a solution that the team believes will create the desired impact. He may propose to Ann, *"If we provide a library of proposals with sample comprehensive solutions (talent solution 1) and train technical salespeople on how to discover broader solution needs and define solutions based on the library (talent solution 2), we will enable salespeople to provide comprehensive solutions at least 50 percent of the time."*

This statement represents a projection of how much improvement in people performance will come from a talent solution. The responsibility for such projections falls squarely on the BEM's shoulders. This is a statement from L&D about the impact they believe they can make. (Note: This does not mean that the business is off the hook for the solution. The BEM will make the projection with a series of assumptions, e.g., the business will provide access to subject matter experts, part of the program will involve participants getting coaching from top performers on their next two proposals, and so forth. In Chapter 10, we speak about how these assumptions end up forming part of the "Results Contract" used to launch an investment.)

You may have noticed that we speak of "talent solutions" instead of simply "learning solutions." It is common for BEMs to help create integrated talent solutions by coordinating with HR generalists or others in the rest of HR. Such solutions may involve, for example, changing recruiting goals or incentive

The CEO's Talent Manifesto

plans. We consider such coordination as "par for the course" for BEMs. Of course, BEMs may also uncover the need for changes outside of HR itself (e.g., changing how a business process works or modifying a piece of enabling technology). We do not speak of "total performance solutions" because of a practical issue: actually driving them forward rarely falls within the BEM's purview. While a BEM can and should recommend such changes where relevant, actually chartering and executing them rarely forms part of the BEM's remit.

Documenting the Result: An "Ability-to-Execute Analysis"

To help BEMs and business leaders capture their thinking, it's useful to have a template. Figure 15 illustrates the format we use, which we call an "Ability-to-Execute Analysis."

Level	Item	Measure	Performance "As Is"	Performance "To Be" Target
1 Outcome	Revenue	• Growth	• 7.5%	• 10%
2 Process	Proposal Creation	• Deal size	• $32.2k	• $37.0k (+15%)
3 Performance	(Technical Sales) Create comprehensive proposals	• % Comprehensive	• 25%	• 50%
4 Solution	• (Information) Model proposal library • (Training) Discovery & solution definition			

Figure 15: An Example Ability-to-Execute Analysis

The BEM provides such an analysis for each business process gap. An extended example showing in depth how to use the Ability-to-Execute Alignment Framework and construct such analyses is available in appendix A.

The Pivot Point: Business Processes

The Ability-to-Execute Framework represents at the same time something old and something new. The concept of mapping out how activities support goals is of course something old.

Chapter 4: Targeting Business Needs and Aligning Investments

In particular, the Ability-to-Execute Alignment Framework is based on the work of Kaplan and Norton on strategy mapping.[21][22] Kaplan and Norton suggest that when businesses fail in their strategies, most of the time, the issue is poor execution rather than poor strategy. "Poor execution" includes, among many other possible causes, failure to identify and implement required changes to human capital. The Ability-to-Execute Alignment Framework refines the general notion of strategy maps for L&D by laying out the chain of causality through which L&D investments achieve business outcomes. This step-by-step chain provides "handrails" for business leaders and BEMs to use when planning learning investments, helping them make sure that they stay on track.

We particularly emphasize the second level of the alignment chain (see Figure 16). At this level, BEMs and business leaders focus on the business's ability to execute a *business process* (e.g., how a business group conducts customer service calls, identifies prospects, or selects suppliers or the like).

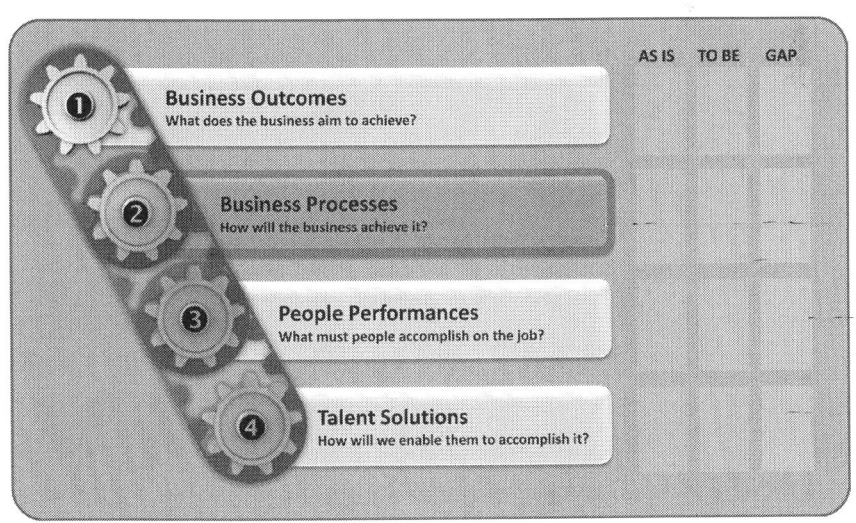

Figure 16: Business Processes are the Pivot Point in the Alignment Chain

This level provides a key pivot point in clarifying the chain of alignment. When business leaders and L&D get clear on what improvements they seek in a business's *ability to execute a business process*, they find it much simpler to know what improvements they should make at the lower levels of *people performance* and *talent solutions*.

Most of the performance consulting literature does not emphasize business process. It tends to skip from business outcome to performance. However, as Kaplan and Norton point out, "Just as you can't manage what you can't measure, you can't measure what you can't describe." If we want to improve sales, let's then improve sales skills. It clarifies the investment case to specifically call out the level of business process because it:

1. Allows the business to clearly "own" the link between business outcomes and business processes;

2. *Accelerates diagnosis* by more quickly focusing discussion. (Compare the range of people performance you might consider to address the issue "We want to improve sales" to the issue "We want to improve average deal size." The first launches into people performance starting with a business outcome, while the second starts from a business process measure. How many hypotheses can you generate for the first versus the second?); and

3. *Positions L&D to take its place as part of a proven approach to improving business outcomes.* Over the past thirty years, there has been a revolution, first in manufacturing and now services organizations, based on rigorous quality

Chapter 4: Targeting Business Needs and Aligning Investments

management of business processes.[23] Our perspective is that, at heart, L&D is simply one of the tools in the toolkit for enabling businesses to improve their processes.

Business leaders appreciate functional staff who understand their business, and they sometimes complain that L&D does not. An additional benefit is that BEMs can rapidly understand enough about business processes to allow them to *contribute* to the conversation of how to improve them. Imagine that Fred understands that Ann seeks to improve sales. Fred would like to narrow down the conversation to some hypotheses about which metric of which process is pivotal for Ann's goal. It would be ideal for him to be able to come prepared with a list of sales subprocesses, which they can both consider, e.g.:

- Generate suspects
- Identify prospects
- Qualify leads
- Identify needs
- Define solution
- Manage pricing
- Present proposal
- Negotiate contract

Imagine that Ann and Fred hypothesize that the "identify needs" and "define solutions" subprocesses are central to achieving Ann's goal. It would then be ideal for Fred to help further narrow the diagnosis by providing a set of measures for that process on which they could focus, e.g.:

- Number of suspects

- Conversion from suspects to prospects

- Conversion from prospects to qualified leads

- Conversion from qualified leads to closed sales

- Cost per lead

- Average deal size

- Pricing realization

In this way, Fred is collaborating with Ann to rapidly identify focused hypotheses for how they can make improvements. This is much the same kind of approach that the family doctor follows when creating a differential diagnosis. Given the business symptoms, which processes are likely at stake and which aspects of those processes are likely pivotal? And just like the family doctor, once concrete hypotheses rise to the top of the list, Fred can run some further tests to validate or invalidate them (typically by doing some performance consulting fieldwork).

Sound complicated? After all, the family doctor spent many years in medical school, and internship to prepare. In fact,

Chapter 4: Targeting Business Needs and Aligning Investments

Fred's task of identifying checklists to consider is simpler than you might think. Someone else has already done much of the homework! APQC (the American Productivity and Quality Center) has spent over a decade identifying a taxonomy of business processes and their measures. (They are now on version six.) APQC provides these resources at no charge:

- The Process Classification Framework, along with industry-specific versions for many common industries;[24] and

- Process definitions and key measures for dozens of the processes in the framework.[25]

The checklists Fred uses employ APQC's "Marketing and Sales Definitions and Key Measures." At the same time, while the Process Classification Framework provides a good starting point, it may not cover the particulars of your company's processes. Fred's checklists go beyond what APQC provides to include processes like "define solution," which may be found in most any primer on the end-to-end sales process. By starting with external resources like these, BEMs can accelerate their own understanding and bring to the table a framework that enables them and their business colleagues to adopt an engineered approach to conducting a diagnosis. Resource consumption and cycle time are often key process measures. Through doing such prep, Fred reduces the time required from the business and accelerates the cycle time of diagnosis.

The Ability-to-Execute Scan

So far in this chapter, we have described how the Ability-to-Execute Alignment Framework enables a business leader and BEM to target a single business need, align a learning investment, and document the results in an Ability-to-Execute Drill-down Analysis. The framework helps BEMs make intelligent decisions about where to direct discovery conversations regardless of the level at which they happened to start. The analysis captures the results, showing link by link how the potential learning investment will advance the targeted business outcomes. Many L&D organizations lack such a clear framework for targeting business outcomes and aligning investments. As a result, the learning investments they make provide unclear or inadequate business outcomes.

At the same time, *businesses do not suffer only when they go ahead with an investment that is not well aligned. They also suffer when they fail to make an investment that they should have.* BEMs help their business groups avoid this error of overlooking important investments too.

One way that BEMs help is simply by staying close to the business, walking the beat, and keeping an eye on levels of process performance and how people performance contributes to or detracts from it. However, BEMs also use a more systematic approach. Working with business leaders, they systematically scan the business group's major processes, understanding and prioritizing those that most require improvement. Having identified this "hit list," they can then apply the top-down Ability-to-Execute Framework to each item on it. We call this systematic approach the *Ability-to-Execute Scan*.

The Ability-to-Execute Alignment Framework moves *vertically* starting from business outcomes moving down to talent solutions. In contrast, the Ability-to-Execute Scan moves *horizontally* across the value chain of a business group's major processes.

Chapter 4: Targeting Business Needs and Aligning Investments

It helps business leaders and the BEM understand and prioritize where business processes most require improvement. From there, they can focus their effort on exploring the extent to which people performance and talent solutions may help with outcomes.

The scan starts with a simple high-level value chain that identifies the business group's major processes. For instance, for many business groups, this value chain suffices.

> Define It > Market It > Sell It > Make It > Service It >

Figure 17: An Example Value Chain

To conduct the scan, the BEM and business leader consider each business process in turn. To what extent is making changes to the process critical to the group's strategy? To what extent is the process performing well? Based on these questions, they complete a brief SWOT (Strengths, Weaknesses, Opportunities, and Threats) assessment for each process, focusing in particular on how well people performance supports current and anticipated requirements.

Let's consider an example, the advisory practice of an accountancy, Smith & Associates (this is the same example company used in appendix A for the detailed example of how to apply the top-down Ability-to-Execute Framework). Sally is the BEM who supports the advisory practice. She is conducting a scan with Jack, the managing partner for the practice. The practice has identified a key strategic outcome it wishes to create: becoming viewed as a thought leader in risk management. Such a strategy is likely to arise naturally in needs conversations. But how well are the group's other processes performing? To conduct the Ability-to-Execute Scan, Sally and Jack simply work through each major process. Starting with "define it," they discuss the key business process measures that Jack already uses to measure success. For instance, he may measure success by the percentage of revenue that comes from "new" services, meaning those less than three years old. They discuss Jack's target and actual performance. They may identify that Jack is running at 20 percent whereas his target is 25 percent. They rate this using a simple "High", "Medium", and "Low" rating scale, considering this performance to earn a low rating ("L"). They capture what they have said so far (Figure 18).

Business Process	Critical to Strategy?	Rating	Process Performance		
			Metrics	Target	Results
Define It	Yes	L	• Product Turnover	• 25%+	• 20%

Figure 18: Scanning the Results for a Single Process

They will then turn the conversation to consider how people performance can and should contribute to these business outcomes. What strengths, weaknesses, opportunities, and threats do they face in people performance for this process? They might identify that they have some industry thought leaders who form the bedrock of their approach, yet at the same time, they do not adequately tap into the ability of their entire staff to contribute. Jack feels this is an opportunity, as when the chance to contribute does arise, the staff involved find participating to be deeply engaging and rewarding. As a result, Sally and Jack might capture the SWOT shown in Figure 19.

Chapter 4: Targeting Business Needs and Aligning Investments

Business Process	Talent Performance			
	Strengths	Weaknesses	Opportunities	Threats
Define It	• Innovative leaders		• Few staff contribute • Can drive engagement	

Figure 19: The Talent Performance SWOT for a Single Process

Based on this SWOT, Jack and Sally might choose to dig deeper into how people performance can better support Sam's goals for new product development.

To conduct the full scan, Sarah and Jack simply repeat the same steps across the high-level business processes, resulting in Figure 20.

In completing the work, Sally may discover that the advisory practice also performs weakly in Service It, meaning ensuring that prior clients feel supported after engagements are completed. They fall well below industry benchmark rates in generating repeat business. She may learn that Jack believes that the root cause is that partners lack a systematic method to stay in touch with prior clients. Jack may realize that he never really considered this an issue that might be addressed through a talent solution. If Sally were to respond only to Jack's stated needs, it's quite possible this gap would never be identified.

This example illustrates how the Ability-to-Execute Scan helps BEMs and business leaders ensure they cover their bases when considering how learning investments can drive business outcomes. What this example does not illustrate is how the scan provides a context to both conduct discovery over time with a business and also work through making learning investments in an order that puts first things first.

The CEO's Talent Manifesto

Business Process	Critical to Strategy?	Rating	Process Performance		
			Metrics	Target	Results
Define It	Yes	L	• Product Turnover	• 25%+	• 20%
Market It	Yes	M	• Brand Recognition • Unsolicited Leads	• 75%+ • 6/month+	• 45% • 8.2/month
Sell It	Yes	M	• Sales • Closing Rate	• $12m/mo+ • 65%+	• $10.6m/mo+ • 72%+
Provide It	No	H	• Customer Sat • Engagement Margin	• 4.0+ • 55%	• 4.3 • 58%
Service It	No	L	• Repeat Sales	• 70%	• 45%

Business Process	Talent Performance			
	Strengths	Weaknesses	Opportunities	Threats
Define It	• Innovative leaders		• Few staff contribute • Can drive engagement	
Market It			• Consider external resources	
Sell It	• Seen as trusted advisors	• Strategic selling • No individual metrics	• Some partners at competitors dissatisfied	• 50% of partners past avg retirement age
Provide It	• Adaptable staff	• Avg tenure of staff growing		• Recruiting shortage?
Service It		• Lack of shared method		• Not viewed as priority

Figure 20: Example of a Completed Ability-to-Execute Scan

Chapter 4: Targeting Business Needs and Aligning Investments

In the example, Sally and Jack sit down one time to conduct the scan. In practice, they are likely to work together for several years. Over that time, Sally comes to learn more about the business, and, in parallel, Jack will evolve his goals. It may be that he does not actually track targets or results for some processes early on. His conversation with Sally may encourage him to begin to put them in place. Or it may be that "new news" arises that shows performance in repeat sales is better or worse than expected. The Ability-to-Execute Scan used over time provides Jack and Sally a tool that captures ground they have covered previously so that they can efficiently focus future conversations on what's new.

One risk of conducting an Ability-to-Execute Scan is that it might identify so many opportunities for learning investments that it leads to paralysis. After all, performance can always be improved and improvements will frequently lead to some beneficial change to a business outcome. Avoiding such paralysis is simple. Running a business is like owning a house. There are always many things that could be made better. The key is to focus on the most important few and work on those.

When a business leader and BEM have surfaced so many opportunities that they begin to feel paralyzed. Figure 21 can help in prioritizing them.

		Goal	
		Run the Business	Advance the Strategy
Rating	Red	Priority #3	Priority #1
	Yellow	Priority #4	Priority #2
	Green	No action required	No action required

Figure 21: Prioritizing Business Processes for Learning Investments

The CEO's Talent Manifesto

What this table says is that, absent other information, it's usually best to focus first on investments that will advance the strategy and only then on investments that will help run the business. Within those groups, it's naturally best to focus on where you are in the red than simply in the yellow.

With this approach in mind, it's perfectly reasonable for a BEM to decide with a business group to invest in just a few key opportunities at a time. Jack and Sally might agree to say, "For this year, let's just focus on the 'Implement the Strategy' ratings. Once we are in good shape with those, we can move ahead with others." The story of how they partner to help the practice leverage learning investments can unfold over a period of years.

The Ability-to-Execute Map

At this point, we have seen how the Ability-to-Execute Scan helps business leaders and BEMs scan horizontally across business processes to identify gaps in business outcomes and potential opportunities for people performance to contribute to improvements. We've seen how the scan can also help them decide when to dig into the opportunities they bring to the surface. We have also seen how the Ability-to-Execute Alignment Framework allows business leaders and BEMs to do the digging, enabling them to drill down vertically into the causes of a specific business outcome to ensure that, if they do choose to proceed with making an investment, it is tightly aligned and has clear and measurable outcomes associated with it.

All of this work provides significant insight and direction. At the same time, it also generates a lot of information. How can BEMs and business leaders keep track of their work? We ask them to capture the results in an *Ability-to-Execute Map*, which

Chapter 4: Targeting Business Needs and Aligning Investments

crisply summarizes their best thinking on which investments to consider and which to select. The Ability-to-Execute Map simply tracks:

> **TOOLS YOU CAN USE**
>
> We provide a template for the Ability-to-Execute Map

1. The Ability-to-Execute Scan and

2. The set of Ability-to-Execute Drill-down Analyses they have completed over time.

This map serves two purposes. It allows them to gradually develop a "body of knowledge" of how learning can contribute to the business, concisely reminding themselves of what they said before and what they have discovered since. More concretely, it provides the raw material from which the Learning Investment Portfolio and Value-Added Matrix developed.

The map is a living document. As business needs change, the BEM updates the map. As a BEM and business leader learn more about gaps and opportunities, the BEM updates the map. As new learning solutions are introduced to resolve old issues, the BEM removes the old issues from the map.

Maintaining the Ability-to-Execute Map is a constant part of the BEM's job. This chapter has made clear that BEMs cannot build a map from a single conversation with the business. What it probably does not make clear is that BEMs are constantly seeking to expand their understanding of the business and so refine their maps.

One of the ways that BEMs add value is by "keeping their antennae out" for what is happening in the business and noticing shifts, changes, and potential new needs that have not been recognized. For example:

- *Staff meeting*—When a BEM is attending a staff meeting with a business group, it may come up that the cost of quality is creeping up. Will the group form a new goal to bring it back down? To what extent are the processes and root causes understood?

- *After-action review*—When a BEM is reviewing results from an existing training solution, she or he may learn that the frontline employees now being hired have a different skill profile than those hired in earlier years. Is this impacting the business group's strategy of rapid expansion?

- *Watercooler conversations*—Looking at his or her business group's sales results, a BEM may see that the new product line is failing to take off. But last week, he or she happened to chat with a product engineer who was wildly enthusiastic about early customer pilot results from the product line. Is this simply a matter of giving it time, or is there a business problem?

Good BEMs are constantly on the lookout for ways to augment their understanding of their business groups' ability to execute. By constantly considering and integrating needs that have not yet been addressed, BEMs can help their business groups select the right targets for investments in learning.

Chapter 5: The Role of the Business Engagement Manager
Introduction

High-performing L&D organizations align their efforts to business goals, strategies, and operational objectives. Achieving "alignment" is no simple task. To do it, an L&D organization must:

- Understand just what goals, strategies, and objectives the business wants to pursue;

- Identify the changes in performance that are needed to achieve them;

- Determine reasonable and relevant targets for results;

- Determine which alternative learning solutions could achieve those results, and identify the trade-offs among them;

- Facilitate the business in choosing just which investments to make and solution options to employ;

- Evaluate actual results against targets; and

- Determine how to respond to results and optimize solutions as appropriate.

This is a complex list of tasks that needs to be worked through for each substantial investment a company makes in learning. And all of this work is in addition to actually executing the solutions themselves!

We have found that what enables L&D organizations to achieve strategic alignment is that they assign a small number of people the mission and primary responsibility to ensure it happens. These business engagement managers (BEMs) provide a bridge between what the business requires and the core capabilities that L&D can deliver. But what do BEMs actually do? In this chapter, we describe their role.

An Overview

A business engagement manager helps a company improve business outcomes. Each BEM serves one or more business groups, helping them define and manage a portfolio of learning investments, each of which is designed to achieve specific business outcomes that are aligned with the strategies, objectives, and priorities of the business. BEMs see themselves first and foremost as businesspeople who are in charge of organizing investments to achieve business outcomes.

The BEM provides a bridge between business leaders and L&D to facilitate the full lifecycle of a successful investment in learning. This cycle consists of a full Deming Cycle:

1. *Plan*—the initial identification of a business need worth addressing, the identification of performance changes

Chapter 5: The Role of the Business Engagement Manager

required to satisfy the need, the definition and selection of targets for success, and the selection of the desired solution option.

2. *Do*—The execution of the solution (including all that typically falls under the ADDIE model).

3. *Check*—The gathering of actual results and their analyses.

4. *Act*—Making recommendations for next steps where appropriate, to amend both the solution if required and the L&D system itself for continual improvement.

As the cycle indicates, BEMs make sure to "close the loop" on the investments the business makes so that business leaders remain clear about the demonstrated results they achieve from learning.

BEMs also help their business groups improve their skill at realizing value from their learning investments. Sometimes, business groups are convinced that only instructor-led training can meet their needs. BEMs help business groups understand the cost and value tradeoffs that underlie different types of learning solutions. Similarly, sometimes business groups feel that once they have approved an investment, they have done their job. BEMs help business groups understand how getting the right people into training, supporting application back on the job, and providing coaching can all increase value. BEMs help coach business groups to become as excellent in executing their learning investments as they have become in choosing them under A2B.

A Task Model

To enable their business groups to improve business outcomes through learning investments, BEMs perform three clusters of tasks.

Manage the Portfolio of Learning Investments
1. Understand the business: key objectives, strategies, processes and needs
2. Define & maintain a prioritized portfolio of investments in learning
3. Enhance the business's ability to select appropriate solutions

Manage the Relationship
1. Identify and support key stakeholders
2. Educate how to engage with learning
3. Increase ability to maximize impact

Manage Individual Investments
1. Charter new investments
2. Chaperone execution of solutions
3. Evaluate results & optimize solutions

Figure 22: The Business Engagement Manager's Key Tasks

These are the *ongoing tasks* that a BEM performs for a business group with whom the BEM has already developed a relationship and established a portfolio of learning investments. Chapter 8 describes the "getting started" process through which a BEM develops a relationship with a new business group.

As Figure 22 illustrates, the BEM's central function is to help the business groups define and manage a prioritized portfolio of investments in learning.

> **TOOLS YOU CAN USE**
>
> We provide a sample job description for a BEM.

To be effective, BEMs must manage their relationship with the business group as well as individual investments. BEMs perform these tasks as their primary role. Many L&D organizations have someone responsible for such tasks as just one component among several in a broader role which also includes responsibility for development or delivery. When the BEM does not spend the large majority of his or her time on these tasks (e.g., above 70 percent), alignment gets sacrificed. In such cases, alignment loses out to the "tyranny of the urgent" as the many day-to-day issues that crop up in development or delivery crowd out the longer-term, more important work of alignment.

Accordingly, just as important as what the BEM does is what the BEM does *not* do. For the BEM to be effective, it is important that driving alignment is the BEM's primary responsibility. When it forms the large majority of what the BEM does (and the primary focus on which the BEM is evaluated), achieving alignment does not get postponed "because of the job." Rather, it *is* the job!

Let's consider each of these tasks, starting with the central one.

Manage the Portfolio of Learning Investments

The defining problem of economics is how to support unlimited wants with limited resources. BEMs help their businesses address one corner of this problem, the corner that has to do with investments in learning. BEMs help their business groups become better investors in learning over time.

Understand the Key Objectives, Strategies, Processes, and Needs of the Business

BEMs align investments to performance. To succeed, they must obviously start by identifying the performance needs themselves. Therefore, BEMs spend significant time staying current with what is going on in the business and helping the business "look around the corner" to see where it has needs that could require learning support.

BEMs can sometimes find it confusing to sort out just when an investment is "fully aligned" (as can the business staff they support). After all, businesses are complex. They operate at multiple levels (e.g., company, department, unit…). At each level, businesses define objectives, implement strategies, build capabilities, and operate processes. How can BEMs know when they have really understood a need at the level they should? For example, imagine that in the past quarter, a BEM who supports the sales function in the company has identified three needs:

- The group is rolling out a new sales management application;

- The group is restructuring how it handles the midmarket; and

- The group is below target in selling add-on service contracts.

How can the BEM know whether he has helped the group define each need and understand just how "aligned" it actually is? To help keep it all straight, we have found that it's useful for BEMs to employ a framework for mapping the alignment between business priorities and needs and between needs and potential investments. To this end, we provide the Ability-to-Execute Alignment Framework in Chapter 4.

Chapter 5: The Role of the Business Engagement Manager

Define and Maintain a Prioritized Portfolio of Investments in Learning

Any business can create a never-ending list of things employees "should know" or capabilities employees "should have." To maximize returns from learning, a business must pursue a prioritized portfolio of investments that are aligned to what's most important to the business. BEMs help their business groups define and manage such a portfolio.

We have already covered the key tool BEMs use: the Learning Investment Portfolio. In Chapter 3, we described how L&D *facilitates the process* while the business *decides which investments to make*. BEMs provide the motivating force by collaborating with the business to:

- Illuminate what business needs exist and which can be supported through investments in learning;

- When specific investments are suggested, clarify whether and how they are aligned to business needs;

- Define relevant target results;

- Define a prioritized annual plan (in the form of the Learning Investment Portfolio and Value-Added Matrix).

- Assume accountability for the plan. Monitor results, and share with the business:

    ○ Monitor progress implementing the plan

- Report on actual results versus targeted results

• Collaborate with the business to refine the plan as needs change midyear, keeping it evergreen:

- Monitor how business priorities and timing evolve

- Identify and integrate new needs into the plan

Enhance the Business's Ability to Select Appropriate Solutions

Even after the business group has identified and prioritized needs, there are many reasons why it may stumble in selecting learning solutions to address them. Some business leaders may underinvest because they do not "believe in training." Others may insist on ineffective solutions because they feel that "we just need to tell 'em what they need to do." Yet others may insist on overly expensive solutions because "instructor-led training is what we had and it worked well enough." BEMs work with their business groups over time to help them make better choices about which solutions to use for which needs.

It's worth noting that this does *not* amount to "persuading the business to buy more training."

> BEMs are not concerned with the volume of activity they create. Instead, they are concerned with the demonstrated results they generate.

The way BEMs help is through education, coaching, and discussion over time. Like good coaches, they deal with the specifics

Chapter 5: The Role of the Business Engagement Manager

of the business groups they face. For example, if a stakeholder says one of these things, here is how a BEM might respond:

- *"I don't believe in training."*—A BEM approaches this situation as a performance consultant. What's the root cause? Is it lack of experience using training? Prior poor experiences where results were never made clear? Belief that "it never helped me"? Depending on the root cause, the BEM can then choose a course of action (e.g., highlight a compelling case in the business group where a learning solution could have dramatic effect and then share case studies of similar situations where learning solutions were implemented with demonstrated results).

- *"If we just tell 'em what to do, then they can do it."*—A BEM may construct a rapid pilot using two alternative approaches with two small groups to remediate a performance issue and share back evaluation results.

- *"Only instructor-led training is effective."*—A BEM may choose an area where the root cause of poor performance is lack of information or appropriate tools rather than skill. The BEM might construct a rapid pilot here to remediate the performance and, as above, let the results speak for themselves.

At the end of the day, however, the buyer decides. When working with key stakeholders, BEMs do *not* seek to take on the businesses' responsibility to choose which investments in which solutions they want. Instead, they understand that change takes time. So, they play a patient game, working to avoid wasted investments in the short term while building up the capability to make wise decisions over time. BEMs maintain the mantra of "L&D facilitates, and the business decides" and provide the data and experiences that enable business leaders to make increasingly better decisions over time.

Manage the Relationship

BEMs serve as the "single point of contact" for the business groups they serve. Each BEM functions as an internal account manager for the business groups he or she serves, ensuring that the business group and L&D work well together, that L&D is responsive to business needs, that status is transparent, and that issues are resolved.

Educate the Business about How to Engage with L&D

In interviews with business leaders we have conducted across businesses, we have found many who are simply unclear on how to engage with L&D. Most business leaders want a trusted advisor who can efficiently help them improve their business. However, all too often, business leaders do not know to whom to go for what, what kind of help L&D can actually provide, and how to use L&D effectively.

BEMs help their business groups engage more effectively in chartering and executing learning solutions. Besides the core work of understanding business needs and aligning investments, they also:

- Define an engagement model and share it

- Define a catalog of services that L&D can provide and share it

Chapter 5: The Role of the Business Engagement Manager

- Help develop subject matter experts who are comfortable working with L&D

- Educate the business on the responsibilities they must take on to generate the results they seek

Identify and Support Key Stakeholders

The squeaky wheel does not necessarily deserve the grease. BEMs do not identify the most important needs by sitting back and taking orders. Nor are the richest deposits of ore necessarily found closest to the surface. BEMs also do not identify the most important needs by spending time with those who are most enthusiastic about learning.

Instead, BEMs methodically identify the people in a business group who will have the largest impact on the value the group gets from learning, and then they systematically manage their relationships with these "key stakeholders." They spend perhaps 20 to 25 percent of their time "walking the beat" to keep current with their key stakeholders and their emerging needs.

In Chapter 8, we describe how BEMs define and implement what in sales is called a "strategic account management plan." This plan clarifies how BEMs should allocate their time by laying out answers to the following questions:

- *Who matters most?*—Identifying the key stakeholders in the group

- *What is their current behavior?*—Identifying what their current stances toward learning are and what kind of support they see themselves providing

- *What is their desired behavior?*—Identifying what stances and support are desired from them and how large a gap there is from the current state

- *What is the action plan?*—Identifying a pragmatic action plan for how to get from the "current" to the "desired" state

The "stakeholders" in this plan serve different roles: Some have business needs and can sponsor projects. Others have insight into organizational performance. Yet others can coach the BEM on how to support the organization.

When L&D has a smooth relationship with a business group, the action plan is usually little more than standard governance activities plus a series of "walking the beat" check-ins to ensure that the BEM stays abreast of breaking needs. In this case, the strategic account management plan simply helps the BEM be diligent about maintaining awareness. However, when a BEM is *new* to a group or the group *is not effectively using learning*, the plan gets more complex.

Increase the Business's Ability to Generate Demonstrated Impact

When business leaders charter, say, a new IT application, they may not be aware of the extra responsibilities they will need to take on to get value from their investment. For example, they may need to reengineer their existing processes, train users, spend money each year on maintenance, and so on. Similarly, when business leaders invest in learning, they may not be aware of the extra responsibilities required to maximize results. Many

Chapter 5: The Role of the Business Engagement Manager

leaders start with the simple assumption that once they fund training, they have done their part.

BEMs help business leaders understand these responsibilities and the consequences of carrying them out (or failing to). The three responsibilities that typically matter most are:

1. *Providing subject matter experts (SMEs)*: The most impactful learning solutions are usually those based on what is unique about a company. Such solutions require differentiated content, which must come from the business.

    BEMs educate business leaders on why access to SMEs is vital, and they help the business develop a cadre of SMEs who can be mobilized as required.

2. *Ensuring transfer to the job*: The most impactful solutions usually "follow participants home," requiring participants to apply what they have learned on the job under guidance from a coach (e.g., their manager, process experts, or high-performing peers). In contrast to "training as an event," such solutions systematically treat learning as a managed, end-to-end process. Although this approach improves results, deploying an end-to-end process is more complex than simply sending someone to an event. Typically, the key challenge does not lie in the complexity of administering the process (which is something L&D can do). Rather, it lies in ensuring diligence in follow-through and providing knowledgeable coaching (which are responsibilities the business must bear).

BEMs educate business leaders on the value they can receive from implementing an end-to-end process to ensure skills are applied back on the job and help business leaders set up a mechanism for taking accountability for application.

3. *Ensuring evaluation:* Business leaders should expect demonstrated results from their investments in learning. However, evaluation in L&D is perhaps most often observed in the breach. So, many business leaders have become used to "shooting blind" with their investments in learning. One reason why evaluation is neglected is that it is often "patched on" after a solution has been chartered rather than considered at the very initiation of a learning investment. This makes it difficult to pinpoint target results that are relevant, agreed upon, and practical to identify.

BEMs help business leaders set clear targets for success when chartering investments, educate business leaders on the need to follow through to actually gather evaluation data, and help business leaders define an evaluation plan that provides reasonable evidence of results for reasonable effort.[26] In the next chapter, we describe the approach BEMs use to establish the goals for a learning investment, which is the foundation on top of which the BEM forms the evaluation strategy for the investment.

Manage Individual Investments

BEMs are judged by the demonstrated results their groups achieve from their learning investments. To get results, BEMs go beyond simply defining the investment plan and waiting to

Chapter 5: The Role of the Business Engagement Manager

see how the investments play out. Like with a venture fund, they actively follow each investment through its complete lifecycle. They:

- *Lead* the chartering of new investments,

- *Chaperone* execution, and

- *Lead* the evaluation of results and optimization of solutions.

Leading the Chartering of New Investments

A business group cannot make wise investments in learning if its most important needs never get on the table. BEMs help business leaders ensure that important needs are considered. As the business evolves, BEMs "look around the corner" to explore where new business needs will arise and whether and how learning investments can play an important role in addressing them. To do so, they use the *Ability-to-Execute Scan* and the *Ability-to-Execute Alignment Framework*.

Similarly, a business group will not get the most value from its investments if it is not clear about what it seeks to accomplish. BEMs help business leaders ensure that new investments are appropriately chartered, with clear goals and targets, clear accountabilities, and enough depth of understanding of the need and solution for L&D to execute reliably.

To ensure that investments are appropriately chartered, after a need surfaces, BEMs:

- Clarify how that need is aligned. Which business outcomes are they seeking, and what is the gap? What business process is at stake, what measure requires improvement, and what constitutes success? What performances by which target audience will create that improvement?

- Clarify business sponsors' constraints up front. Where is the target audience located? Are there time constraints to get to market? Is it important to address some audience segments soon while others can wait? Are there other initiatives affecting the audience that we should try to integrate with (or simply schedule around)?

- Conduct needs assessments and, if needs remain unclear, use performance consulting to clarify them.

- Generate alternative options for solution, clarify their costs and pros and cons, and help sponsors choose. In some cases, the alternatives may offer trade-offs (e.g., "We can get the solution to market more quickly if we do X but will have a lower cost of ownership if we do Y. Either is reasonable although we suggest X. What would you prefer?").

- Ensure clarity on execution stating both what L&D and the business will do, including roles and responsibilities, effort levels, and time lines.

- Document and ensure consensus on the charter.

In Chapter 10, we provide a format, the "Results Contract," for documenting a charter that contains each of these elements

Chapter 5: The Role of the Business Engagement Manager

(Note: we have adopted this format from *Running Training Like a Business*.[27])

Chaperone Execution of Solutions

Once an investment has been chartered, it is then up to the specialists within L&D to take on the heavy lifting of implementing it. The Results Contract provides the L&D team with a high-level analysis and initial design from which to work. At this point, all of the core capabilities of the L&D organization are brought into play. If relevant, a deeper analysis is launched. Content is sourced or developed. Learning plans are defined and implemented on the learning management system. The learning solution is marketed and deployed. Instructors, managers, and/or coaches are trained in how to support the solution. Evaluations are performed.

The BEM's role during execution reflects a delicate balance. The BEM cannot afford to get drawn into doing or managing the project work. Otherwise, the BEM will suffer the "tyranny of the urgent" and lose the ability to focus on ensuring alignment. At the same time, the BEM will not generate the best results for the business if he or she simply "throws it over the fence" for execution.

We advocate that the BEM adopt a stance of "chaperoning" execution. This is the same stance that an account manager might take in a services firm. The BEM ensures that the L&D project team understands the goals and constraints of the business and that their work stays aligned. At the same time, the BEM also ensures that the business understands the inputs required from it to make the work successful and the consequences if these are delayed or not provided.

L&D projects, like all projects, hit bumps in the road. A new product can take longer to emerge from R&D than anticipated. A key SME or key instructional designer may unexpectedly leave the company. A project may grow or wane in importance as the business evolves. The pilot run of a solution may not go as planned. The BEM helps the project team and business collaboratively respond to such bumps in the road as they occur. As an account manager would, the BEM helps the business and L&D collaboratively work their way through them. The BEM ensures issues are raised back to the business when appropriate and that the L&D team does not lose the original motivation and vision for the solution in the hurly-burly.

Evaluate Results and Optimize Solutions

Even after the learning solution is in the field, the BEM's job is still not done. The investment has been made. But did it achieve the target results? For a solution that has been in the field for some time, is it still relevant and efficient?

Engineers know that even an error-prone system can routinely operate close to target if it has an effective feedback loop. BEMs implement that feedback loop, making sure that business leaders and L&D alike understand how well they jointly did against the targets they mutually set. The BEM:

- Identifies target results and an evaluation plan as part of chartering investments;

- Chaperones the implementation of the evaluation plan. Here, most of the inputs required come from the business;

Chapter 5: The Role of the Business Engagement Manager

- Compares results to targets and reports back;

- When results are not as anticipated, explores what changes might be appropriate and how to respond; and

- When results are as expected, explores which factors most contributed to success so they can become L&D "best practices".

Most of the time, learning solutions provide the targeted results or better. Sometimes, they do not. The BEM helps the business and L&D respond when results fall short. Beyond identifying what didn't work in the specific case, the BEM helps identify the weak point(s) in the L&D system that enabled the exception. By so doing, the BEM ensures that similar issues do not recur in other work.

Additional Capabilities BEMs Require to Succeed

So far, we have described what BEMs *do*, what an instructional designer would call their "functional competencies." To succeed, BEMs also need some supporting capabilities, or what that instructional designer might call their "behavioral competencies."

There are two such supporting capabilities that stand out among the others:

- *Business Acumen*—By "business acumen," we mean much more than "understanding how corporate finance works." BEMs must understand how their companies and the specific business groups they support create value. They must understand how the pieces of the business fit together so that they can see where the needs are and how improved performance can help the business increase value. We stress the importance of *business processes* as the pivot point in enabling organizational performance. BEMs must understand the role that these processes play in the business group and how the business outcomes of the group are driven by their business processes on the one hand and how those processes are enabled by the group's people capabilities on the other.

In Chapter 5, we explained what it means for a BEM to "understand" a business group. At heart, it means understanding what the group is trying to achieve, what its most important processes are, and how targeted improvements in performance can help it achieve specific business results.

- *Achieving Results through Influence*—BEMs lack position power. They may or may not have direct reports. In either case, they cannot force business leaders to invest in learning. If they have no L&D direct reports, they cannot force L&D project teams to follow their dictates. Instead, BEMs work through influence. They clarify how investments in learning can drive value, establish clear targets and goals, and ensure transparency on progress and results. They work with both the business and L&D to build commitment to business outcomes and overcome bumps in the road. To navigate such waters successfully, BEMs must be skilled in the consultative and soft skills required to achieve results through influence.

Section 2: Defining and Managing a Portfolio of Learning Investments

Starting with this section, we now dive deeply into the practices required to generate strategic alignment. As we have said, alignment is a continuum—you can be "tightly aligned" or "loosely aligned." As you consider how to improve alignment in your company, depending on your situation, you may find it practical to focus in on just one or two of the practices or instead to be more aggressive and launch a more comprehensive initiative. Feel free to browse the remainder of the book to explore just the practices that will add the most value to your company.

This section describes how to implement a governance structure that focuses on maximizing the performance of a portfolio of learning investments. As we have said, L&D's central task is to help the business define and manage an aligned portfolio of learning investments to remediate the targeted gaps in the business's ability to execute that matter most and thereby advance business outcomes. L&D collaborates with the business to create a portfolio in which:

- Investments are aligned to business needs, addressing any important gaps in the business's ability to meet its business goals, implement its strategies, and achieve its operational objectives.

- Investments have concrete targets for success that are relevant to the business leaders who sponsor them. Without such targets, L&D cannot ensure that it stays focused on the right goals, nor can it demonstrate its success at achieving what the business sought when it made the investment.

- The total level of spending reflects what the business actually needs and not, for example, what it happened to spend last year or what other companies in the industry happen to spend.

- The most important investments are prioritized, and low-value investments are eliminated.

- The portfolio is balanced according to how business leaders want to prioritize strategic versus operational and short- versus long-term investments.

Learning leaders and BEMs realize that business leaders must own the decision of which investments to make. At the same time, the decision is complex, so business leaders need the support of a partner who can facilitate the process. Thus, learning leaders and BEMs hew to the mantra "L&D facilitates, and the business decides."

The overview has laid out the pieces of the A2B methodology. Chapter 6 first summarizes how they fit together to enable the business and L&D to define an effective portfolio.

Section 2: Defining and Managing a Portfolio of Learning Investments

Chapter 7 then describes governance under A2B, including the annual planning process and quarterly reviews. This chapter describes roles and responsibilities and explains how activities flow over the course of the year. How do the business and L&D establish the investments to be made in the coming year? How do they review results? How do they adjust as business changes during the year?

Chapter 6: How the Pieces Fit Together: Information Flow under A2B

Introduction

Businesses are complex and, accordingly, so are the learning investment portfolios required to support them. In the course of generating alignment, BEMs can produce a *lot* of detail. Using A2B, companies can keep this work focused, making sure that all of this detail work directly improves the resulting portfolio. As we shift from the overview provided in the first section of the book to the implementation mind-set we take in the rest of the book, it's important to be clear about precisely how the pieces fit together. In fact, stepping back and looking at the big picture, the kinds of deliverables produced are not all that complex. A2B asks companies to generate four key deliverables. Figure 23 shows how these four pieces of the puzzle fit together.

The CEO's Talent Manifesto

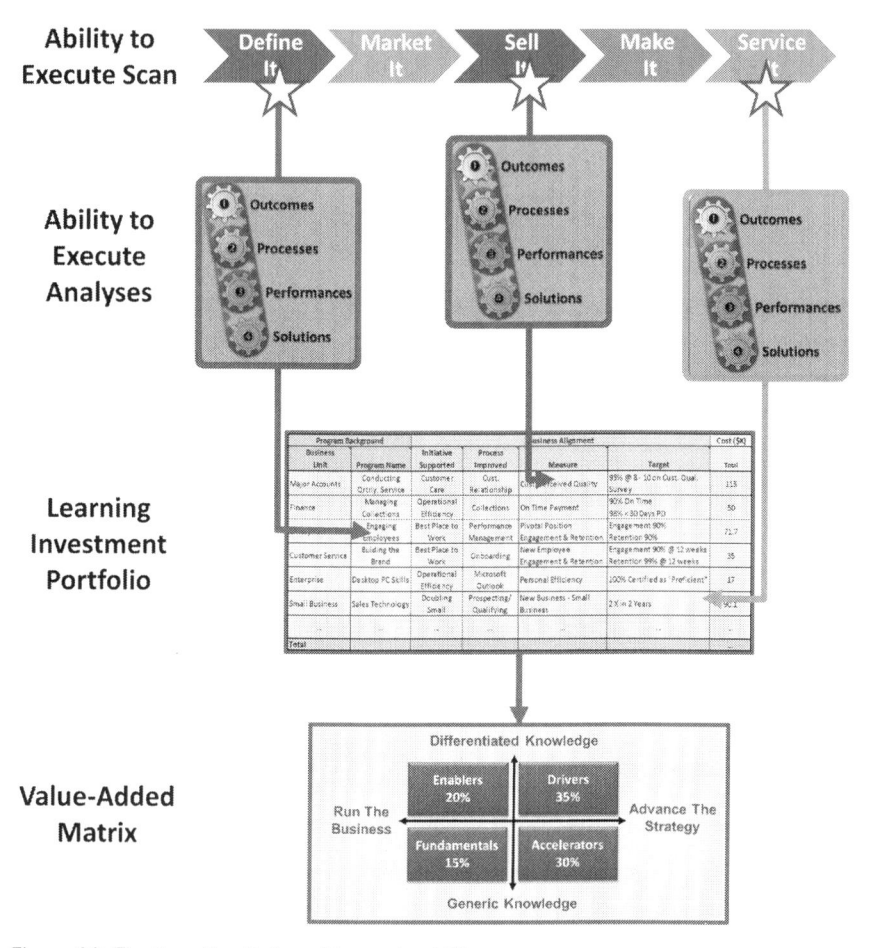

Figure 23: The Four Key Deliverables under A2B

Chapter 6: How the Pieces Fit Together: Information Flow under A2B

1. The *Ability-to-Execute Scan* produces a map of the business, which pinpoints and prioritizes gaps in its ability to execute (represented by the stars in the figure). When L&D lacks a top-down view of the business's ability to execute, it can miss major opportunities to contribute. The scan creates one and thereby ensures that no important business outcome or strategy is overlooked.

2. Each *Ability-to-Execute Drilldown Analysis* describes the specific chain through which a talent investment could help the business achieve a desired business outcome. BEMs use the Ability-to-Execute Alignment Framework to conduct these drilldown analyses on business needs as they emerge. These needs can come top-down from the scan or bottom up from ongoing interactions with the business. Sometimes "business needs" are loosely stated ("I have a need to improve sales performance") or not really at the level of business process performance ("I need my sales team to know the products better."). By putting each "business need" under the microscope of the framework, BEMs ensure that each individual learning investment specifically and concretely addresses a targeted gap in the business's ability to execute.

3. The *Learning Investment Portfolio* consolidates the drilldown analyses and summarizes which the business has selected. It provides "one line of detail" for each investment. Critically, this one line explicitly states the specific *business processes targets*, which the investment is to enable. This simple addition to a typical program plan shifts the focus from *activity* to *results*.

The CEO's Talent Manifesto

4. The *Value-Added Matrix* summarizes how investments are allocated across quadrants. The matrix provides business leaders with a broad view of investment allocation. In particular, this view helps them see whether they are sufficiently advancing their strategy and, conversely, challenge whether investments in running the business can be made more cost-efficient.

When a BEM and business leader are considering how to achieve a business goal, the information flow works top-down. The question might be, "What should we add to our portfolio so as to address the issue at hand?" In contrast, when a business leader is trying to allocate investment, the information flow works bottom-up. Of the specific investment opportunities we have in hand, which do we want to pursue now?

One warning—Because the figure shows a linear flow from scan through matrix, you may get the impression that BEMs actually follow such a clean, direct flow in their actual work. Well, sometimes. While BEMs do employ a formal planning process (described in the next chapter), the world is unpredictable and business evolves. So BEMs systematically "walk the beat" to stay abreast of changing business needs and keep these deliverables up-to-date.

The Ability-to-Execute Scan

The Ability-to-Execute Scan identifies the opportunities that a business group faces to advance the strategy and improve operations through improving talent performance (see Figure 24).

The scan looks at the major processes operated by a business group. It seeks to understand "as is" and target results. It then looks to see how improvements in talent could contribute. The

Chapter 6: How the Pieces Fit Together: Information Flow under A2B

scan does not attempt to be comprehensive and cover every performance gap in the business. Rather, it provides a way for BEMs and business leaders to follow the 80/20 rule and ensure that nothing of high priority gets left off the table.

Business Process	Critical to Strategy?	Rating	Process Performance Metrics	Target	Results
Define It	Yes	L	• Product Turnover	• 25%+	• 20%
Market It	Yes	M	• Brand Recognition • Unsolicited Leads	• 75%+ • 6/month+	• 45% • 8.2/month
Sell It	Yes	M	• Sales • Closing Rate	• $12m/mo+ • 65%+	• $10.6m/mo+ • 72%+
Provide It	No	H	• Customer Sat • Engagement Margin	• 4.0+ • 55%	• 4.3 • 58%
Service It	No	L	• Repeat Sales	• 70%	• 45%

Business Process	Talent Performance			
	Strengths	Weaknesses	Opportunities	Threats
Define It	• Innovative leaders		• Few staff contribute • Can drive engagement	
Market It			• Consider external resources	
Sell It	• Seen as trusted advisors	• Strategic selling • No individual metrics	• Some partners at competitors dissatisfied	• 50% of partners past avg retirement age
Provide It	• Adaptable staff	• Avg tenure of staff growing		• Recruiting shortage?
Service It		• Lack of shared method		• Not viewed as priority

Figure 24: The Ability-to-Execute Scan

An Ability-to-Execute Drill-Down Analysis

An Ability-to-Execute Drill-down Analysis fleshes out a single opportunity to make a targeted investment in learning (Figure 25). These opportunities may be identified through the scan or several other channels (e.g., walking the beat or quarterly governance meetings).

Level	Item	Measure	Performance "As Is"	Performance "To Be" Target
1 Outcome	Revenue	• Growth	• 7.5%	• 10%
2 Process	Proposal Creation	• Deal size	• $32.2k	• $37.0k (+15%)
3 Performance	(Technical Sales) Create comprehensive proposals	• % Comprehensive	• 25%	• 50%
4 Solution	• (Information) Model proposal library • (Training) Discovery & solution definition			

Figure 25: An Ability-to-Execute Drilldown Analysis

A BEM will create many such analyses for each business group. When the business decides to pull the trigger and act on one, it gets promoted into the Learning Investment Portfolio.

The Learning Investment Portfolio

The Learning Investment Portfolio summarizes the investments to be designed, developed, purchased, and/or delivered during the upcoming year (Figure 26). It provides line-item detail that business leaders require to decide which investments to make and how to monitor progress as the year proceeds.

Chapter 6: How the Pieces Fit Together: Information Flow under A2B

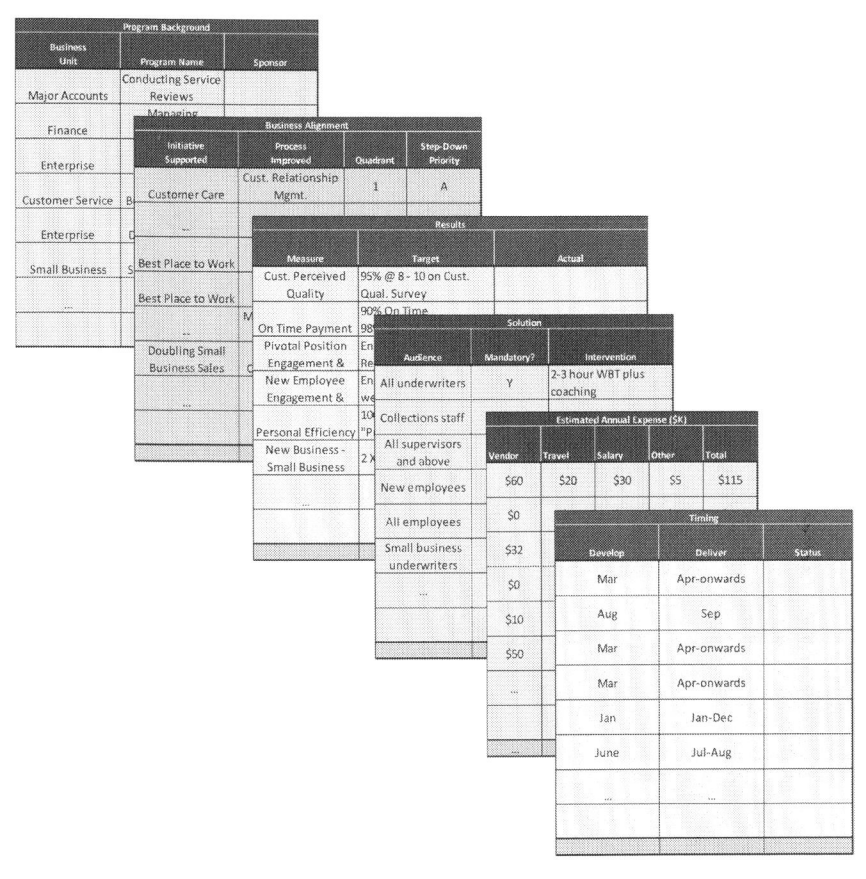

Figure 26: The Learning Investment Portfolio

121

The Learning Investment Portfolio identifies for each investment:

- *Background*—Which business group will be served? Who is the sponsor?

- *Business Alignment*—Is a strategic initiative being supported? If so, what is it? Which business process will be improved? Which quadrant of the Value-Added-Matrix best describes the investment? Is it a Driver, Accelerator, Enabler, or a Fundamental?

- *Results Targeted*—Given the business process identified, which output measure will be improved? Which metric and target will be used to evaluate results, and when will that be done? Later during the year as solutions are executed, which results are actually achieved?

- *Solution Highlights*—Which audience will be targeted? Will the solution be mandatory for the audience to complete? What will be the size and nature of the interventions employed?

- *Cost*—What is the estimated cost to implement? In many cases, it's helpful to subdivide cost into major categories that will be used in budgeting (e.g., the cost of salary and travel for L&D staff, the cost of external partners, the opportunity costs incurred by participating in the program, and so on).

- *Timing*—When will the solution be available? When will it be delivered?

Chapter 6: How the Pieces Fit Together: Information Flow under A2B

The Value-Added Matrix

Finally, the Value-Added Matrix takes all of the line-item detail in the Learning Investment Portfolio and organizes it using the four quadrant analysis of Drivers, Accelerators, Enablers, and Fundamentals (Figure 27).

This framework allows business leaders to ensure that they are allocating their investment optimally.

A Note on Evaluation

Many L&D organizations struggle with evaluation. A major reason is that they start thinking about it late in the process—after solutions have been chartered and when they are being executed. Evaluation thought-leaders appropriately advocate instead that it is best to build evaluation into the process from the start.[28] A2B helps companies follow this advice.

To see how, it's worth focusing on the "results targeted" field in the Learning Investment Portfolio. This field defines success metrics up front as part of the package the business "buys" when it decides to make an investment. The "results targeted" should be a measure of a business process that we want to improve, e.g., sales, quality, timeliness, cost, customer satisfaction, employee engagement, etc. Insisting on having clear target results ensures that real business needs are addressed. After all, if measures and targets cannot be identified, how important can the need be? It allows business leaders to compare the importance of benefits from different potential investments. It provides clear and concrete goals downstream for those who implement solutions. And, finally, it sets the stage for evaluation.

The CEO's Talent Manifesto

Differentiated Knowledge

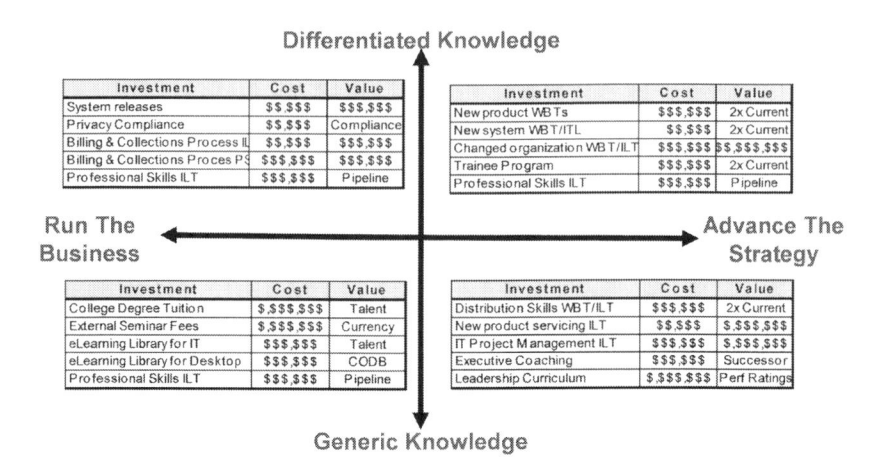

Investment	Cost	Value
System releases	$$,$$$	$$$,$$$
Privacy Compliance	$$,$$$	Compliance
Billing & Collections Process IL	$$,$$$	$$$,$$$
Billing & Collections Proces PS	$$$,$$$	$$$,$$$
Professional Skills ILT	$$$,$$$	Pipeline

Investment	Cost	Value
New product WBTs	$$$,$$$	2x Current
New system WBT/ITL	$$,$$$	2x Current
Changed organization WBT/ILT	$$$,$$$	$$,$$$,$$$
Trainee Program	$$$,$$$	2x Current
Professional Skills ILT	$$$,$$$	Pipeline

Run The Business ←————————————————→ Advance The Strategy

Investment	Cost	Value
College Degree Tuition	$,$$$,$$$	Talent
External Seminar Fees	$,$$$,$$$	Currency
eLearning Library for IT	$$$,$$$	Talent
eLearning Library for Desktop	$$$,$$$	CODB
Professional Skills ILT	$$$,$$$	Pipeline

Investment	Cost	Value
Distribution Skills WBT/ILT	$$$,$$$	2x Current
New product servicing ILT	$$,$$$	$,$$$,$$$
IT Project Management ILT	$$$,$$$	$,$$$,$$$
Executive Coaching	$$$,$$$	Successor
Leadership Curriculum	$,$$$,$$$	Perf Ratings

Generic Knowledge

Investment Allocation

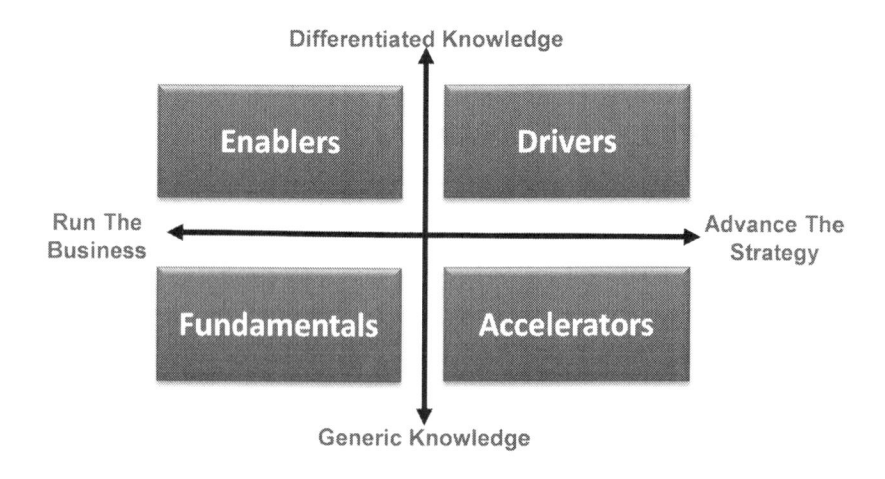

Differentiated Knowledge

Enablers	Drivers
Fundamentals	**Accelerators**

Run The Business ←————————————————→ Advance The Strategy

Generic Knowledge

Investment Summary

Figure 27: The Value-Added Matrix

Chapter 6: How the Pieces Fit Together: Information Flow under A2B

When business leaders and business engagement managers face the job of completing the "target" column, they know that those targets must be compelling if they are to warrant receiving investment. At the same time, they also know that, some months down the line, they will find themselves on the hook to demonstrate whether the targets have actually been achieved. Facing this double-edged sword up front when proposing an investment leads to very concrete conversations about what is possible to achieve—conversations in which the business and learning are completely aligned in their desire to find pragmatic approaches.

Chapter 7: Governance under A2B
Introduction

In the introduction, we saw how the A2B Methodology can enable business and L&D to collaborate to define a well-aligned portfolio of learning investments. Here, we focus on governance. What happens over the course of the year to define the portfolio? To ensure it remains on track as the business evolves? To provide business leaders with transparency and the opportunity to have input as the year proceeds?

We go in four steps, describing:

1. How to divide responsibilities between learning and the business;

2. How to allocate these responsibilities to roles;

3. How to conduct the annual planning process; and

4. How to perform quarterly updates.

This chapter describes how to implement A2B in a mid-sized to large company with a centralized L&D organization. Every company will need to adjust the approach to its own needs and structure. The chapter concludes with some thoughts about how to configure A2B for other common situations.

Establishing Responsibilities

Creating a high-value portfolio of investments requires collaboration. At a high level, the division of responsibilities is simple: L&D *facilitates the process* while business leaders *make decisions*. This is simply how any trusted service provider and its client divide responsibilities.

At the same time, do not underestimate what it takes to facilitate the process. Business leaders can find L&D decisions to be a bit confounding. When business leaders seek support from L&D, it may not be obvious to them when an outcome they seek requires a learning solution. When a learning solution is relevant, it only gets more complex as there are likely several alternative solution options and business leaders are probably unaware of the trade-offs among them. Most companies offer dozens, hundreds, or even thousands of learning solutions. So, sheer volume precludes business leaders from going into much depth except perhaps for a handful of the most important.

So, when we say "L&D facilitates the process," this means more than simply running some meetings. L&D must put in significant effort to provide business leaders with relevant information in condensed forms that are easy for business leaders to employ. That's what the Learning Investment Portfolio, Value-Added Matrix, and Ability-to-Execute Map are all about. They put performance gaps and learning solutions into a business context of priorities, investments, and results.

A2B provides for a clear division of responsibility between the business and L&D.

Chapter 7: Governance under A2B

Responsibilities Retained by Business Leaders

Business leaders hold the purse. They:

- *Set priorities*—Business leaders make investment decisions. This begins with determining when an investment might be appropriate and then how that investment will be prioritized versus other options.

- *Establish the total size of the L&D budget*—Business leaders determine how much in total to invest in L&D. To do so, they must take a broad view. Business leaders have multiple opportunities to invest in the business (e.g., R&D, marketing, IT, L&D, and more). Given the state of the business and the options to invest, how much L&D support does the company anticipate "buying" in the coming year? It's hard for business leaders to feel confident in their decision when they are not clear about just what they are buying. So, L&D should avoid offering abstract, top-down decision rules like "same as the industry average" or "10 percent more than last year." Instead, L&D should offer a concrete bottom-up analysis of the specific possibilities that exist to improve business outcomes through learning solutions (as expressed in the Learning Investment Portfolio).

- *Hold each other accountable for L&D investments*—Our experience is that the best way to get business leaders to manage their investments in L&D effectively is to get them to talk over their choices with each other. Consider your organization. Are there some groups that make great use of L&D investments and others that do not? How much does it help when the L&D team itself implores the laggards to, for example, do more careful needs analysis before launching programs, to reallocate investments more toward key strategic priorities, or to move away from treating training as an event and put more effort into ensuring skill transfer to the job? We see companies get better results when L&D organizes a venue where business leaders can, in essence, coach each other on how to make and manage appropriate L&D investments.

Responsibilities Retained by L&D

L&D provides expertise and facilitates the process. They:

- *Organize the process*—Business leaders respond well when they feel that they are given an appropriate level of control in a process they understand. L&D helps by providing a clear governance process for managing learning investments that clearly starts with business needs, offers transparency on alignment and results, and gives business leaders clear decisions and the data required to make them.

    In most organizations, the learning portfolio is large, consisting of more than a hundred (and sometimes more than a thousand) programs. Such a list is too disparate for business leaders to tackle directly. They need a framework that operates at a higher level to organize their choices. L&D helps business leaders manage this complexity by providing them with a concrete set of clear decisions to make along the way.

Chapter 7: Governance under A2B

- *Ensure that each important business need is considered*—Business leaders often do not have a clear view of which gaps in outcomes or process measures can be addressed through L&D. That's not their job. They can miss needs where L&D will be critical (e.g., "Gee, we never really thought about the training and performance support required to roll out that new engineering excellence initiative!"). And they can make the opposite mistake of asking for training where it cannot really help (e.g., "We need some training to tell our cashiers to provide better customer service!"). Like any service provider, L&D must ensure that relevant needs are proactively identified and false positives are gently put to rest.

- *Ensure that business leaders understand the potential business impact and cost of each proposed investment*—Across domains, business leaders select investments by considering how much benefit each can provide and how much each will cost. Business leaders should be reluctant to fund investments where either benefit or cost is unclear. Investments in L&D are no different. For each business need identified, L&D must ensure that business leaders are clear on the results a learning solution will generate and the cost required to implement it. L&D needs to work with the business to identify success metrics and then have the courage to put its neck on the line to commit to how much impact it can generate.

- *Ensure that every proposed investment is aligned to a specific business need.* We advocate a rigorously top-down approach to driving alignment using the Ability-to-Execute Framework. It is seductively easy for substantial spending to be targeted to "yesterday's" L&D investments that no longer address important needs. Training can be viewed as a perk and groups may be reluctant to part with their annual conference or training allocations. L&D must help the business identify how well spending is aligned to needs and recognize when it is dedicated to past learning solutions that are actually poorly aligned. The learning leaders must then confront business leaders with the choice of whether they wish to continue that spending—typically, they do not.

- *After investments are selected, close the loop on results*—All too often, the last discussion business leaders have about the results of learning solutions is when they charter a new project. L&D must educate business leaders on how to make good use of L&D. This requires L&D to take accountability for building business leaders' confidence that when they invest in a learning solution, they get the results sought (or understand why not). To do so, L&D helps establish concrete targets for results for each investment and then provides a feedback loop through which actual results are evaluated and compared to those targets. Of course, not every investment pays off. But for business leaders to have confidence, they must understand which do pay off and which do not and the reasons.

A Shared Responsibility—Getting Results

Of course, getting results is the end goal. The whole point of the A2B Methodology is to focus learning investments where they will generate targeted results that are pivotal to the business.

Chapter 7: Governance under A2B

So the question naturally arises, "Once an investment is chartered, who owns the responsibility for getting results?"

All too often, business leaders believe that once they have committed funding, they have done their part. The rest is up to L&D. Not so (See Figure 28).

> **The business and L&D must jointly own the responsibility for generating results from learning investments.**

Figure 28: Joint Responsibility for Results

L&D must contribute sound needs analysis and provide top-notch solutions at efficient costs. The business must provide subject matter expertise and support learning solutions once deployed. Just as the business and L&D collaborate to make the plan, so must they continue to collaborate when executing it.

That said, L&D remains squarely responsible for managing the process and providing transparency. This is what we mean by "closing the loop" above. If a sales training program for a new product under development is stymied by a lack of input from the business, L&D must make that clear (while—we hope—also helpfully seeking alternatives). If a coaching program does not actually result in team members getting sound coaching from participants, L&D must make that visible (while also exploring root causes and identifying corrective and preventative actions). Too many business leaders lack such visibility when things go south and so suffer from uncertainty about their learning programs. Uncertainty, in turn, breeds skepticism. However, once results become visible, shortfalls become less worrisome, as it is possible to systematically manage them. It's L&D's responsibility to manage the overall process, ensuring that the business is clear about its role and providing transparency on status and results.

Establishing Roles
Roles Required from the Business

Business groups usually organize two roles to carry out their responsibilities.

1. *Business Leads (one for each business group)*—A2B works in levels. First, each business group defines a set of investment options.[29] Then, in a company with centralized L&D budgeting, those outputs are integrated into a consolidated set of options. Each business group assigns a business lead, who works with the BEM assigned to his or her group to develop the group-level investment options and define the portfolio of learning investments. The business lead then collaborates with the BEM throughout the year to manage the resulting investments.

2. *A Learning Council*—The learning council actually makes companywide investment decisions. The learning leader forms the council, which is typically chaired by a senior business leader and facilitated by the learning leader. The council establishes the overall learning portfolio based on the group-level requests. In midsized organizations, the council usually includes the business

Chapter 7: Governance under A2B

leads themselves. In larger organizations, it may contain executives senior to the business leads.

Roles Required from L&D

L&D typically provides the following roles.

1. *The Learning Leader*—The learning leader oversees the process. She or he creates the organizational structure required to carry out A2B. This includes identifying business leads, forming the learning council, and staffing the BEM role. The learning leader manages the governance process and typically is the one to integrate the group-level investment options into a consolidated Learning Investment Proposal. She or he then takes the result and structures a set of management decisions for the council to consider and facilitates discussions with the council so that they can determine the "go forward" plan. Afterward, as the year proceeds, she or he runs quarterly updates with the council to provide visibility on progress and enable the group to react to changes as they arise.

2. *Business Engagement Managers*—Each business group is served by a specific, named BEM (although BEMs may serve multiple groups). The BEMs facilitate the process for the business units they serve. They collaborate with the business leads to define the group-level investment options and then, later, to manage the portfolio. They help identify needs, ensure alignment, structure solution options to address them, and prioritize potential investments.

3. *Learning Solution Architect*—When a business need arises, it is usually fairly clear to a BEM which options for learning solutions should be considered for addressing it.

To help BEMs, many organizations develop a predefined docket of solution types, representing their typical approaches to the learning problems their organization regularly faces. Many groups find it useful to assign an expert learning solution architect to create the predefined docket of solution options.

In some cases, however, this is not enough. When difficult cases arise, the learning solutions architect is available for consultation. The learning solution architect supports the BEMs by helping define and prioritize solution options for complex new needs.

And then in some of those cases, it will become clear that more intensive performance consulting is required to clarify the business gap, identify the performance gap, and assess the solution.[30] The learning solution architect has the time and expertise to roll up her or his sleeves and conduct this performance consulting.

4. *Evaluation Specialist*—Just as the learning solutions architect provides specialized expertise in solution design, so the evaluation specialist provides parallel expertise in evaluation. The responsibilities are the same: define the standard approach, be available for consultation on challenging cases, and be available for "heavy lifting" for special projects.

Chapter 7: Governance under A2B

Our experience has been that this role is typically less time-consuming than that of the learning solution architect and often can be filled by using external consulting support or developing this expertise in other L&D staff.

The Flow of Activities across a Year

A2B involves creating an annual Learning Investment Portfolio and then executing it, adapting it as appropriate as the year proceeds. Figure 29 illustrates typical timing.

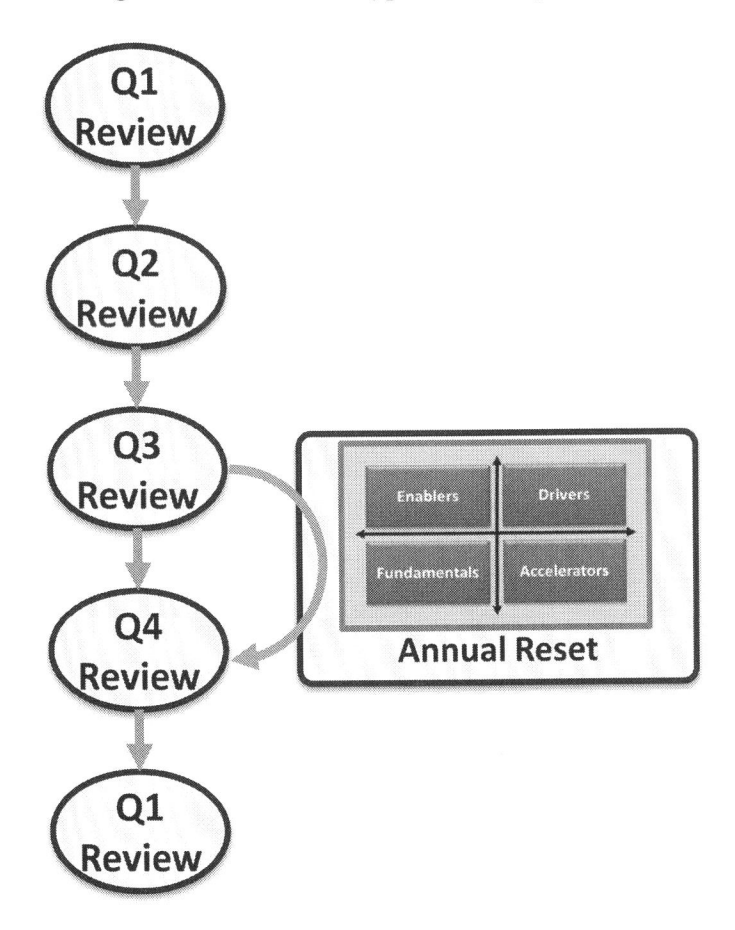

Figure 29: Timing of the Annual Process

137

The *annual planning process* results in a bottom-up reset to the Learning Investment Portfolio. It begins in the middle of the third quarter and is complete by the middle of the fourth quarter. This reset is based on the specific opportunities that the business faces to improve results through learning. Typically, much of the work for it has already been done by BEMs who have been "walking the beat."

After the Learning Investment Portfolio for the year has been defined, it is executed. However, business never stands still, and ongoing adjustments may be required. To provide transparency and manage progress, A2B provides for *quarterly reviews*. The reviews are more than status checks; their core goal is to validate that the business groups are, in fact, receiving value from the investments they are making.

This flow of activity is mirrored at two levels:

1. Within each business group, BEMs follow it with their business leads.

2. Across the scope of the company, the learning leader follows it with the learning council.

Annual Planning: Creating the Learning Investment Portfolio

Once a year, L&D and the business conduct a deep dive to reset the Learning Investment Portfolio. This process typically takes most of the late third quarter and early fourth quarter.

There are five steps to the process:

Chapter 7: Governance under A2B

1. Each business group defines a group-level Learning Investment Proposal.

2. The learning leader constructs a consolidated Learning Investment Proposal.

3. The learning leader helps the learning council set the Learning Investment Portfolio.

Note, in the following explanation, it may sound like each step is completed in a single conversation. And, in fact, that may be true for a mature organization that is used to the process and has had BEMs in place for some time.

For an organization new to the process, however, it is more typical for each step to be accomplished over several conversations. For example, in the first step, the well-prepared BEM will not only focus on the business group leader but will also do the spadework of engaging with line leaders to understand their priorities, objectives, and pains.

Step 1: Each Business Group Defines a Group-Level Learning Investment Proposal

The Learning Investment Proposal simply captures the plan that the business lead and BEM for the business group recommend. To create it, the business lead and BEM use exactly the same format as the Learning Investment Portfolio itself. The only difference is that the proposal is not yet approved and funded. It's the zero-base view of the learning investments the business would like to make and the results they would like to achieve in the upcoming year.

Ensuring New Needs Are Captured

If a company is to select investments that target the highest-priority business needs, the first step is simply to get those needs onto the table. This is done by working business group by business group and then consolidating the results.

Typically, this task is straightforward. After all, the BEM interacts with the business groups throughout the year. As we discussed in Chapter 5, the BEM continually maps each group's goals, strategies, and needs. So, the BEM is well aware of the business group's ability to execute and most of its needs. With this in mind, the "new work" is really only to ensure there is nothing new on the horizon. To do this, the BEM meets with the business lead and reviews the Ability-to-Execute Scan.

Successful BEMs go beyond simply asking the open-ended question "What are your new needs?" Instead, they help the business leads *articulate* their needs by stepping back and starting with the state of the business and the emerging plans for next year. Remember the Ability-to-Execute Alignment Framework? The BEM uses it to structure the conversation. Typical questions might include:

- Which strategies will be continued forward from last year?

- Are there new initiatives emerging?

- Are there any changes in how success will be measured? What will bonuses be based on?

- How are operations running? Is there pressure on quality? On costs? On accelerating product rollouts?

Chapter 7: Governance under A2B

- Will there be changes in key processes, technology, or organizational structure?

The BEM will also ask more specific versions of these based on the inside knowledge he or she has developed of the group's situation (e.g., "When we last spoke, it seemed like turnaround time for responding to new orders was becoming a concern. How has that evolved?").

The BEM creates an initial draft of the Learning Investment Proposal. To do so, he or she employs the Learning Investment Portfolio format and enters

> **TOOLS YOU CAN USE**
>
> We provide a guide to conducting this conversation.

any ongoing activities and already-planned investments. He or she then adds a new row for each new item. Given the previous discussion with the business lead, the BEM completes the "business need" and "targeted results" sections of those rows.

Identifying Solutions and Required Investment Levels

So far, the BEM and the business lead have worked through what changes are happening or will be initiated in the business, thereby ensuring that all important needs to improve the business's ability to execute are on the table.

Next, they identify appropriate investments for each new need. To do this, they work through the Ability-to-Execute Alignment Framework, identifying which people capabilities will be most critical to meet the need and which learning solution will best develop those capabilities. If the solution appears straightforward, they will capture it immediately in the investment plan by completing the "solutions highlights," "cost," and "timing" sections. More commonly, they will schedule a later session to further discuss the need. This gives the BEM time to do some homework on the need, identify solution options, and make a recommendation. For a description of how BEMs manage this process, see Chapter 10. As the business lead selects a preferred solution for each need, the BEM enters its description into the emerging Learning Investment Proposal.

Validating that Existing Investments Continue to Be Relevant

At this point, the BEM and business lead have finished considering new needs. Now, they revisit ongoing solutions or past investments in progress. To what extent are these still important? To what extent would it be useful to revisit them to improve results or reduce costs? If a solution had not been put in place before, would they recommend spending the money to put it in place now?

During this step, the BEM and business lead take a zero-based budgeting perspective to ensure that "carryover" investments are actually still important to continue.

Prioritizing the Recommended Investments

At this point, the group-level Learning Investment Proposal provides the full set of learning investments that the business lead and BEM recommend that the business invest in if budget were to be available. Each investment should pass the hurdle of being a good "buy" with a sound return for the business. At the same time, sufficient budget may not be available to support all desired investments. The proposal can (and likely does) include items that may not actually receive investment in the

Chapter 7: Governance under A2B

coming year. Companies tend to have so many opportunities to improve results through learning investments that not all financially worthwhile investments actually get made.

The challenge L&D faces is to find some practical way to enable business leaders to prioritize investments without overwhelming them by forcing them to get into the details of each and every one. To say the least, it would be difficult for a learning council to decide with confidence, for example, whether to prioritize investment recommendation #7 from finance over investment recommendation #12 from sales.

There are many ways one could organize the investment proposals to provide the learning council with a manageable set of decisions for business leaders. What we have found to be both simple and helpful is to use the notion of "step-down plans." Each business group creates "step-downs" for its proposal. The starting point is the full set of recommended investments. Then the business lead identifies reduced plans for various levels of cuts in spending. Typical step-down levels might be 85 percent and 70 percent.

While "the business decides" and so the business lead makes the choices, the BEM continues to facilitate the process, collaborating with the business leads to assign each item in the group-level proposal into one of three categories:

1. *Recommended under a major step-down*—This is the highest-priority category. We recommend this investment even if the budget could support only 70 percent of the total recommended investment.

143

2. *Recommended under a moderate step-down*—We recommend this investment even if the budget could support only 85 percent of the total recommended investment (but would deprioritize it if the budget were stepped down further than 85 percent).

3. *Recommended*—We recommend this investment (but would deprioritize it if the budget were to be stepped down).

Through creating step-down tiers, the business lead and BEM provide the learning council with a simple decision to make when it comes time to construct the integrated companywide Learning Investment Portfolio. What percentage of the total recommended budget would they like to support?

Each BEM conducts this exercise with each of his or her business leads. The *direct output* is a complete set of group-level Learning Investment Proposals that cumulatively cover all recommended investments in learning for the coming year with step-down priorities established. The *indirect output* is that the business retains ownership over the recommendations. Each item has been vouched for as a sound investment by the relevant business lead and its alignment to process improvement measures and the strategies and objectives they impact is clear.

Step 2: The Learning Leader Constructs a Consolidated Learning Investment Proposal.

The learning leader then integrates the group-level Learning Investment Proposals to construct a consolidated companywide proposal. It's important to restrict this to a simple mechanical task. The learning leader *does not make judgment calls*

Chapter 7: Governance under A2B

when doing the integration, as that would dilute the ownership of the business. L&D facilitates; business decides.

At the same time, the learning leader should review the results so as to serve as a clear-eyed advisor advocating appropriate investments. If a particular business unit appears to be under- or overinvesting, the learning leader can raise the observation along with relevant supporting data to help business leaders make decisions. For example, IT might be planning three major rollouts but only recommend a training investment for one. Conversely, IT might recommend training investments for all three and do so at a level dramatically above what benchmarks indicate is productive for similar rollouts in comparable organizations. In both of these cases, the learning leader adds value by serving as an advisor, noting the data, looking for opportunities, raising questions requiring validation, and providing benchmarks. At the same time, the business gets to make the final decisions of which needs it pursues and which solutions it buys.

To present the information, the learning leader prepares a packet for the learning council that contains:

- The Value-Added Matrix for the coming year (assuming the full investment plan).

- The supporting Learning Investment Proposal for the coming year (again showing the full investment plan and the step-down plans).

- The Value-Added Matrix and Learning Investment Portfolio from the current year.

Providing the historical data enables the learning council to make year-over-year comparisons. As the council considers their options, they are likely to want more detail than a simple set of top-line numbers. The packet provides both consolidated companywide information and group-level information. Typically, the learning leader does not provide the full set of Ability-to-Execute Maps, as that amount of detail would be unmanageable. However, he or she brings it to meetings for reference as needed.

Step 3: The Learning Leader Helps the Learning Council Set the Learning Investment Portfolio

Having shared the packet with the learning council, the learning leader then facilitates a strategic-planning / budget-setting workshop. The goals are to establish:

1. What level of investment in L&D is appropriate to make this year?

2. Are we allocating the investment appropriately between strategic versus operational needs and current (one to two years) versus future (three to five years) needs?

3. Are we allocating spending appropriately between business units?

The approach makes it clear to the business leaders what they get at each level of investment and that the decision lies in their hands. The approach avoids the problems of arbitrary decisions (e.g., "You get 5 percent more than last year") or inappropriate responsibilities (e.g., "We've given you the money. It's your job to make good use of it.").

Chapter 7: Governance under A2B

In some ways, this workshop can be anticlimactic. Given the level of homework and diligence that L&D put into helping the business articulate needs and investment options, it can be a quick conversation to select between the investment step-back levels.

At the same time, this approach provides the learning council with the type and level of information they require to make nuanced decisions. While the basic decision is to choose between investment levels, the council need not restrict itself to that. It may choose different levels for different business groups. For example, the council might decide that "Given that new product development is so critical for us right now, we will fund R&D at the 'full' level even though we are funding other groups only at the 85 percent level." The council might even get into

> **SIDEBAR**
> **CONVERTING UNBELIEVERS?**
>
> In many businesses, there are a few business leaders who "don't believe" in training. They may believe that apprenticeship is the only model that works, that training is the employees' responsibility, or have some other cause. But they choose to invest little in L&D. Can the A2B Methodology make converts of the skeptical?
>
> The short answer is "Well, maybe!" It should help you generate a group of great references: other business leaders in the organization. It should lead to skeptical business leaders being drawn into conversations in which they hear concrete stories about business-issue-driven training successes. However, at the end of the day, some people are just plain hard to change.

147

The CEO's Talent Manifesto

line-item detail. For example, one business leader might say, "I agree overall with setting funding this year at the 85 percent level. But I request that we also fund one item that does not make it on that list for these reasons. Can we agree to elevate that one item?"

Where this workshop tends to get interesting is in the way that business leaders hold each other accountable for the value of outcomes and the spending

> **TOOLS YOU CAN USE**
>
> We provide a guide for running this workshop.

needed to achieve them. When considering spending across units, business leaders may challenge each other on how they are using the organization's resources. Looking at the prior year's investment portfolio, why is the operations department spending so much on "run the day-to-day" training? Given the new products launching next year, should sales receive a higher level of investment than other groups? Each time these debates happen, they enable business leaders to learn from each other as they think through their decisions and explain their rationales. When these debates happen year after year, they gradually enable business leadership to build expertise in using L&D as a strategic investment.

The concrete deliverable from the workshop is an approved companywide Learning Investment Portfolio. This specifies the budget level and, possibly, some fine-tuning of which specific needs will be supported.

Chapter 7: Governance under A2B

At the same time, more than this concrete deliverable, the workshop produces ownership among senior business leadership of the investment portfolio which they helped create. They "get it" and see how the L&D function is taking pains to use the organization's resources wisely. This view of L&D-serving-as-business-partner can in turn lead to L&D earning the access it requires to produce peak results. At CNA, after Hilgart and his team implemented this approach, the business engagement managers found themselves being invited to business leaders' monthly and/or extended staff meetings to which they had not been privy before. They had earned a seat at the table.

Conducting Group-Level Quarterly Reviews

Once the Learning Investment Portfolio is agreed upon, the work then turns to executing it, adjusting as necessary through the year. A useful approach to doing so is to provide for quarterly reviews. Just as the annual planning happens at two levels, so too does the quarterly review: first BEMs conduct reviews with each of their business leads and then the learning leader conducts one with the learning council (Figure 30).

BEMs find that the group-level quarterly reviews are high leverage. They consume little time. But they provide a critical opportunity for L&D to demonstrate value and ensure that it remains aligned. The real key to success in conducting them is straightforward: be prepared.

The CEO's Talent Manifesto

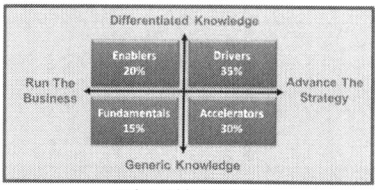

Value Added Matrix

	Differentiated Knowledge	
Run The Business	Enablers 20% / Drivers 35%	Advance The Strategy
	Fundamentals 15% / Accelerators 30%	
	Generic Knowledge	

Learning Investment Portfolio

Investment	Cost	Value
New product WBTs	$$$,$$$	2x Current
New system WBT/ITL	$$,$$$	2x Current
GM Development Program	$$$,$$$	$,$$$,$$$
CEO Leadership Forum	$$$,$$$	Successor
Leadership Curriculum	$,$$$,$$$	Perf Ratings

Business Group Update

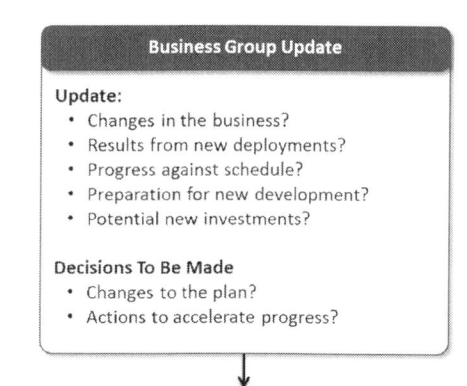

Update:
- Changes in the business?
- Results from new deployments?
- Progress against schedule?
- Preparation for new development?
- Potential new investments?

Decisions To Be Made
- Changes to the plan?
- Actions to accelerate progress?

Learning Council Update

Update:
- Progress against schedule?
- Changes to plan with business reasons?
- Effect of changes on budget?
- Spotlight issues?

Decisions To Be Made:
- Take action on any progress shortfalls?
- Revisit changes to plan?
- Accept budget changes or identify offsets?

Figure 30: Agendas for Quarterly Reviews

Goals

The typical goals for a group-level review are twofold:

1. Alignment

   a. Understand key changes in the business and ensure that the Learning Investment Portfolio remains aligned as the business evolves during the course of the year.

   b. Determine whether the level of funding remains appropriate—whether the business group requires additional investment or can make do with less.

Chapter 7: Governance under A2B

2. Accountability

    c. Review progress and address open issues

    d. Share recent evaluation results or other key news about L&D

At the same time, these goals shift depending on the particular context of a business group. For example, in a group

> **TOOLS YOU CAN USE**
>
> We provide a guide for running a quarterly review for a business group.

where a new leader has come on board, most of the time may go toward understanding the leader's priorities. In a group where the BEM believes the group relies too much on instructor-led training, some time may go toward a show-and-tell of alternative approaches. In a group where the most important learning program has fallen way behind schedule, time will go toward addressing that.

Agenda

Group-level reviews are led by the BEM and must involve the business lead. Other attendees, either from the business or from L&D, may be invited for part or all of the review.

The agenda for a review tends to be straightforward.

1. *Goals for the Day (5 min)*—The BEM summarizes the goals of the review and the agenda.

2. *Update on the Business (10 min)*—The BEM asks if there is any significant "new news" about the business. It's best for the BEM to be prepared and to lead off with what the BEM has already learned and then ask for validation or additions. The goal here is not to do a deep dive on how to support new needs with learning solutions right away but simply to validate that the assumptions on which the Learning Investment Portfolio was originally made remain appropriate. If there are changes to be made, they will be noted and discussed in detail later.

3. *Review of New Results (10-15 min)*—If solutions have run their course and have evaluation results, the BEM shares these. The BEM talks through actual versus target results and summarizes proposed future actions, if any. At this point, the BEM is typically only summarizing decisions that have already been taken. This is because when solutions are executed and results come in, the BEM facilitates a separate after-action review and explores whether additional action is appropriate. These decisions are reported in the quarterly review.

4. *Progress Update on Solutions under Execution (10-15 min)*—The BEM walks the business lead through progress on solutions under execution. The BEM proactively raises action items and open issues for the business while addressing questions, comments, and suggestions that the business lead raises. If the BEM is to be seen as a credible business partner, she or he must behave as an honest broker, impartially representing both good news (e.g., some positive evaluation results from a recent

Chapter 7: Governance under A2B

rollout) and bad news (e.g., a delay in development for a new learning solution).

5. *Preparation for Solutions about to enter Execution (5–10 min)*—The BEM summarizes solutions that are about to move into execution. The key question is: "Does this remain the right investment at the right time?" Given how business needs evolve, some projects will be postponed or cancelled. Best to identify this before starting. The second question is: "Is the business prepared?" The BEM helps ensure that the project is lined up to begin smoothly.

6. *Discussion of Potential New Investments (Optional, 10 min)*—The BEM and business lead discuss whether the plan remains aligned and whether it would be useful to modify it. The BEM returns to any new business needs raised in the business update part of the meeting. If there are surprises or more than one or two changes (which is unlikely), the BEM may need to ask for separate time to discuss them.

7. *Reflections (5 min)*—The BEM asks the business lead for open-ended feedback. Is L&D engaging with the business appropriately? Are the learning solutions being provided relevant and effective? Are there any other concerns or issues that the business lead would like to address?

8. *Close (1 min)*—The BEM thanks the business lead and summarizes the next steps.

Preparation

To get ready for a quarterly review, the BEM prepares three items:

1. *Updated Learning Investment Portfolio*—The BEM updates the plan, highlighting what has changed since the last review so that it stands out. Most changes are status updates to particular investments as solutions work through design, development, implementation, and evaluation. Some changes are new investments or strike-outs as the plan is adjusted on the fly to reflect evolving business needs. The BEM shares the updated plan in advance of the review.

2. *Agenda*—Using the draft above, the BEM prepares an agenda for the review. Earlier, we noted how the goals for a review may vary from "typical" based on a business group's context. Needless to say, the agenda should likewise vary to match the actual goals the BEM sets for a review.

3. *Docket of discussion points*—Reviews typically last an hour, and the time goes by quickly. To make the best use of it, the BEM prepares a specific set of discussion points. These generally follow the agenda. See the toolkit for a detailed checklist of issues to consider when determining discussion points.

Follow-Up

A word on maintaining strict discipline. It builds the confidence of business leaders when BEMs are impeccable in their professionalism. The BEM should get the materials to the business

Chapter 7: Governance under A2B

lead in advance of the review. Similarly, the BEM should provide minutes within twenty-four hours. We will take it for granted that the BEM maintains a similar level of professionalism throughout the other interactions we describe in the book.

The key parts of the minutes are the next steps. If the review was concluded with open issues (e.g., a potential new business need to be explored, a piece of surprising feedback to be investigated), the BEM should also define next steps to pursue these. That can be as simple as getting the next meeting on the calendar or including in the minutes the next action the BEM will take.

Conducting the Company-Level Quarterly Review

The learning leader holds the company-level quarterly review after the group-level reviews are held. The idea here is that business leads get the opportunity to have input on status for their individual business groups before the learning council reviews the integrated effort.

A useful side effect of this approach is that it allows for company-level investment decisions to get escalated. In companies that fund L&D centrally, it is typical that during the year, one group will have a new need and want investment beyond what their group was initially allocated. When this happens, it's often also the case that some other group actually requires less investment so money can be redirected. In other cases, additional investment is called for. It is useful to see what emerges from the business group reviews to see what the company as a whole faces.

The CEO's Talent Manifesto

For the most part, a company-level review is similar to a group-level review. The goals, preparation, conduct, and follow-up are all alike. However, there are a few differences:

- *Less detail*—A group-level review tends to get into operational detail, but the company-level review typically remains at the strategic level.

- *Decisions taken about new investments or investment trades between groups*—When unplanned investments are required, the golden rule of business engagement applies: L&D facilitates, and the business decides. To be a good partner, the learning leader provides options and a recommendation. But the learning council is responsible for making the choice about whether and how to fund such requests.

- *Increased focus on "continuing education" for the participants*—The learning council provides a rare forum for business leaders to discuss with each other how they leverage learning. Accordingly, a wise learning leader uses each meeting to introduce a key issue or raise a recent success story. The idea is to leverage the meetings to provide a focused bit of continuing education for the participants on how to take advantage of learning to improve the business.

- *Integration with the broader talent management plan*—In many companies, HR as a whole is actively working to move beyond tactical HR to supporting the business strategy.[31] In such companies, the specific relationship between L&D and HR can vary widely and evolve rapidly. If the L&D investment plan is not tied into the broader talent management plan in some way lower down in the process, it can be useful to review it at the company level.

Adjusting A2B for Your Company

This chapter has described how to implement a governance process that ensures learning investments are targeted to pivotal gaps in a company's ability to execute. We have focused on how the process might work in a midsized to large company with a centralized L&D organization. Your organization might differ. How might you adjust the process?

The short answer is "whatever makes sense in your context," short of violating a few nonnegotiables. The core of the process includes:

- Each business group is served by a business engagement manager dedicated to ensuring alignment. The BEM is the engine that drives the process. Unless the BEM is in place and has the time and expertise required, the process will not work.

- Each business group identifies a business lead who is similarly responsible for ensuring alignment.

- Each business group shares its results with the other groups. The learning council (containing the business leads or someone farther up the business chain of command) convenes to review and discuss them.

- The format used provides for each investment to have target results. L&D counts up the frequency with which each group's investment plan has actually defined these.

Some of the changes we have seen include:

- *Decentralized approval*—In companies that have decentralized funding for L&D, the process may not require the learning council to actually make the decisions. Rather, the decisions may be made at the group level.

- *More levels*—In most cases, it suffices to have the two levels of business group and then the whole company. For large companies, there may need to be a third more detailed level to capture information for specific departments or units.

- *Additional dimensions for categorizing results*—We recommend categorizing investments using the two dimensions of strategic versus operational and differentiated versus generic. At the same time, your company may want to cut the investment data in additional ways. For example:

    ○ *Near- versus long-term*—One company was concerned about the extent to which it was making appropriate near-term investments to achieve one- to two-year goals versus longer-term investments to prepare it to achieve its three- to five-year goals.

    ○ *Skill category*—Another company was concerned about the extent to which investments were being made in leadership versus technical versus professional skills. While this categorization may not be very helpful for many organizations, the point is that it is easy to add columns to the "business alignment" segment of the plan to be able to summarize the data in additional ways relevant to your context.

Conclusion

We've seen A2B provide L&D with a way to confidently collaborate with business leadership to target learning investments and improve the business's ability to execute. The approach gives business leaders a clear framework for how to think through investment decisions in a way that aligns with how they tend to think of investments in general. It gives both business and L&D clear targets for success with joint responsibility for achieving them.

Section 3: Managing Your Relationship with a Business Group

Business engagement managers enable their companies to generate demonstrated results from their investments in learning. They interact with business leaders not as "providers of training programs" but instead as "managers of investments in learning solutions." They become emotionally invested in the business groups they serve and continually seek ways to help them grow and prosper. While their stock-in-trade is learning solutions, they bring an "outside-in" perspective, focusing on the results to be achieved more than the internal elegance of the work.

BEMs help business groups define and manage a portfolio of learning investments that generate demonstrated results. To be effective, they must have a deep understanding of the business groups they serve along with the business goals, strategies, and operational objectives those groups establish. They think business first, considering learning solutions as instrumental tools that can be used to help improve business results. BEMs seek to be viewed over time as trusted advisors who help leaders make better use of investments in learning year in and year out.

The CEO's Talent Manifesto

Clearly, BEMs must develop effective working relationships with the business groups they serve. This section describes how. It begins with a chapter on how to strike up a relationship with a new business group. It then describes how to sustain a relationship with a business group over time.

Chapter 8: Building Your Relationship
Introduction
Chief learning officers want to "earn a seat" at the executive table. BEMs likewise want to earn a seat at the table within the business groups they serve. There is a simple litmus test you can use to tell whether a BEM has built a good relationship with a business group: does the BEM regularly get invited to the business leader's meetings? When the BEM gets this literal "seat at the table," it means that the business leader sees the BEM as a helpful resource, a member of the team who can help the group achieve their goals.

Imagine you have just been awarded the opportunity to serve as a BEM or have been given another business group to serve. How should you get started? How can you earn your seat at the table?

Overview of a Phased Approach
BEMs typically serve multiple business groups, helping each to realize demonstrated results from their investments in learning.

When a BEM begins to serve a new business group, it might take six to nine months to come up to speed and earn a seat

The CEO's Talent Manifesto

and then another twelve months for the BEM to fully hit his or her stride working with the business group. This is enough time to work through the annual planning process at least once (and likely twice) and for the business to see how L&D follows through and closes the loop. In our experience, during this time, BEMs work through four major phases in building their relationship with a business group:

1. *Prepare*—Do your homework on the group.

2. *Launch*—Form your initial connections, and learn enough about the business to be able to be helpful.

3. *Establish*—Build a reputation of being capable and helpful.

4. *Sustain*—Maintain and solidify your position over time through continually adding value.

In this chapter, we discuss how to prepare, launch, and establish. In the next chapter, we describe how to sustain.

Phase 1—Prepare

As BEM, you provide a bridge between a business group you serve and L&D. To be effective, there is some basic background about the business group you will need to have.

You can consider yourself "prepared" when you understand the business group from four distinct perspectives:

1. *What is the group's work?* What does the group actually do at a basic, concrete level? To find this out, spend time

Chapter 8: Building Your Relationship

with frontline staff. Here, you are not trying to perform any sort of detailed task analysis, much less become proficient in the actual work. Rather, you only want to understand enough about the work to begin to develop instincts about how learning can support it. You want to understand what the key jobs are, how people interact with each other, their core performance strengths, and some of the key barriers they face to delivering top-notch performance.

2. *What results matter?* You want to understand the way management evaluates the group's business performance. If it is a sales function, are pipeline metrics key? If it is a manufacturing function, are labor productivity and quality rates the priorities? To get educated, spend time with the finance person for the group. Spend time with the quality management person, if there is one. Get the management reporting for the past couple of years and work through it. You want to understand what metrics are used, current levels of performance, and how the business has been trending.

3. *Who is your target audience?* Get the organization chart, and understand how the group is divided into job roles. If they exist, review the job descriptions so you understand the roles for each audience. Get the basic demographics of each audience: how many in each role, what backgrounds do they have, what level of turnover do they experience, and how fast is the group growing? These numbers will help you estimate training volumes later.

The CEO's Talent Manifesto

4. *What is the strategic direction?* Each business group will have some set of goals it is pursuing. How has the group evolved over the past three to five years? What is hot this year? Are there major initiatives planned for the next one to two years?

Your goal with this homework is to rapidly develop a broad-based perspective. You are not attempting to become an expert and should retain a humble attitude about your level of knowledge. You simply want to make it efficient for business leaders to communicate with you.

In Chapter 4, we introduced the Ability-to-Execute Map (shown again in Figure 31). As you work through your homework, document what you find; create a first version of the map by identifying how business objectives map to strategies/initiatives and how strategies/initiatives map to business processes. Of course, it will be incomplete…but it will give you a basis to refine over time.

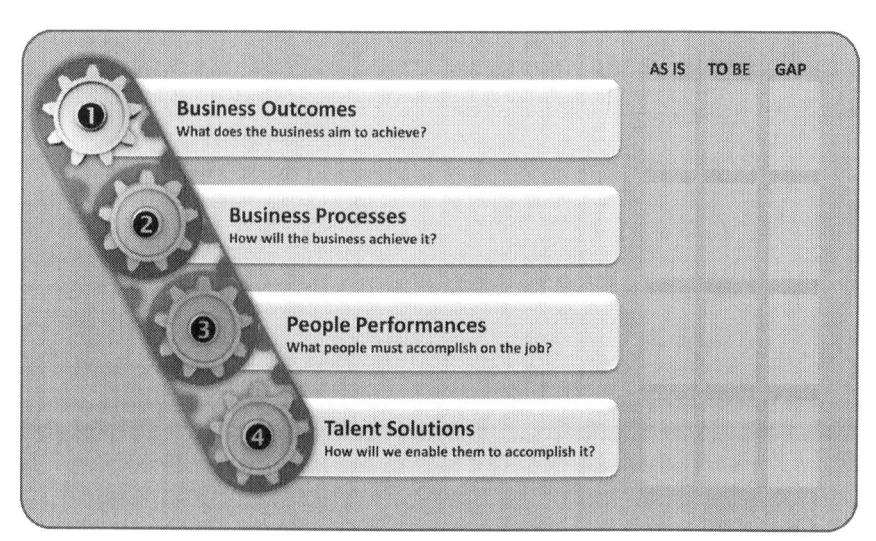

Figure 31: The Ability-to-Execute Alignment Framework

Chapter 8: Building Your Relationship

Using a framework like this enables you to clearly map out the links between a business unit's strategies, its key processes, its key "people performance" requirements, and the key talent-management processes (including learning and development) that support performance.

Beyond preparing you for success, documenting what you find using a framework creates a strong impression. By working rapidly and purposefully to understand the business and employing a simple framework that will serve as a touchstone over time, you present yourself as a person who is proactive, willing to work hard, and focused on the business.

It is important to work through the "prepare" phase quickly. If you do not get out into the field rapidly, you may start out on the wrong foot with the business thinking of you as a reactive order-taker instead of a proactive partner. So, you might spend up to two weeks in "prepare." If there is more you would like to do, follow up later in parallel with proceeding onward to the next phases.

Phase 2—Launch

In this phase, you begin to engage with the business. Having done your homework, you are prepared to hold fruitful conversations. Still, to be realistic, the goal of these conversations is not yet to actually add much value to the business. That does not come until the next phase. Rather, you want to lay the groundwork for a solid relationship.

As you make your initial connections, you'll have a unique opportunity to ask open questions and ask business leaders to take a step back. It's important to use the opportunity well.

That's why you will do your homework beforehand, so that you do not require so much education that business leaders will see your initial conversations as unwarranted overhead.

This phase, like "Prepare" before it, is rapid. You can expect to spend one to two weeks in it.

Conduct Learning Effectiveness Discovery Interviews

Ask to interview the business leader and perhaps three to five of his or her reports to understand how you can best support their group. The goal here is to get context that will enable you to serve the business effectively. The "big three" questions you want to resolve are:

1. What are the important issues facing the business today?

2. What people performance issues are pivotal? Where would improving people performance have the largest impact on the business?

3. What are the business leader's expectations for support from learning? To what extent have those expectations been met historically?

During these interviews, you want to establish yourself as someone who thinks first about the business and only then about how learning solutions can help. Keep the Ability-to-Execute framework in mind, and use it to ensure that wherever the conversation begins, you walk out understanding business issues.

At the same time, what you want to accomplish with the interview may differ from how the business leaders you interview

Chapter 8: Building Your Relationship

have previously interacted with L&D. Because of prior expectations (or urgent needs), a business leader may want to talk about new solutions ("You know, some training we need is…") or issues with existing solutions ("You know, we really have an issue with the service technician onboarding program"). Acknowledge these issues, but do not allow the interview to become diverted to them. Rather, schedule separate time to do a deep dive with the appropriate personnel.

If you are new to the BEM role overall, you may feel that it's your job to use this opportunity to "sell" the business on some training. Not so! Sure, if an urgent need arises, certainly ask for separate time to explore it. But do not feel pressure to hunt for needs that are not apparent or to suggest changes to the way things are now. Keep your focus on simply understanding the current state of business needs and business issues. Starting in these interviews, you establish yourself as a trusted advisor focused on serving the business by helping it identify and manage worthy learning investments. Jumping to solutions or focusing early on what may later turn out to be low-priority needs won't help.

First impressions do count. Since this is the first real work that the business will see you do, it's important that your professionalism is impeccable. Much of this is simply being disciplined in your discussions. Have a clear agenda. Do not exceed your allotted time. Send a thank-you note after each interview summarizing your key learnings. Share back a synthesis after you have completed your round of interviews. It's critical to demonstrate that you understand the value of the time that you ask for here. By demonstrating such professionalism, you convey that you use it respectfully.

Develop a List of Key Players to Start an Initial "Strategic Account Plan"

One of the most important decisions you will make will be where you invest your time. You will need to balance between long-term and short-term needs. You will need to balance between serving existing relationships and making new ones. It's worth being explicit about this critical choice.

We suggest you define an explicit plan for who your "key players" will be. A "key player" is simply someone who can significantly help you as you work to help the business group. Typically, this is because the key player can:

- Sponsor significant learning projects,

- Influence those who can sponsor projects, and/or

- Provide unique insight into business needs

Note, a "key player" is not the same as a "friend" or "ally." In fact, one of the risks a BEM faces is to spend too much time with friends who may be enthusiastic about L&D but who do not really have the ability to advance it in support of the business.

When you select someone as a key player, it means that you intend to build and maintain a relationship with him or her. Each BEM can manage relationships with perhaps ten to fifteen key players.

Later, your list of key players can evolve into a full Strategic Account Plan, which you will use to help evolve the business group toward more and more effective usage of learning. To

Chapter 8: Building Your Relationship

start, however, it's great progress to simply summarize who you believe will be key players and the most important features of each:

- Name and title

- Role that you would like him or her to play

- Current level of understanding of and support for using L&D to improve business performance

- Goals and actions for the next quarter

The Strategic Account Plan provides a convenient place to capture your evolving list of key players. We understand that as you get started, you may not actually know a lot about the key players you have selected and, in fact, you may find that your list stretches and shrinks as you establish your position. But soon you will find that you will settle down into a routine of managing your key players among the ebb and flow of specific business needs.

One reason why you keep your number of key players limited is so that you can realistically maintain your relationship with them over time even when other work needs to get done in parallel. We describe how to "walk the beat" to stay in touch with your key players in the next chapter.

At the same time, it's useful to realize that you will find opportunities to support the business via managing learning investments sponsored by people who are *not* key players. In their book *Strategic Business Partners*, Robinson and Robinson draw

The CEO's Talent Manifesto

a useful distinction between "sustained clients" (the "key players" we speak about here) and "project clients" (whom you may serve on an ad hoc basis as specific needs arise).[32] For example, the business group may roll out a new software application. While the project manager may not be an ongoing key player, she or he may be someone you collaborate with first to scope the learning needs the rollout will require to be a success and then to implement the required learning solution. After the rollout has happened, you may then not maintain a sustained relationship.

Establish Expectations about How L&D Engages with the Business and the Services It Can Provide

Unlike the tasks above, this one is not always required. If you are replacing a prior BEM and are working under a well-established set of processes with a group that has a successful history of engaging with L&D, no need. If not, however, it is helpful to educate business leaders on how to engage with L&D.

A good place to start is by holding a set of "chalk talk" meetings with your key players to go through your organization's engagement model. Just as you asked for time from people to learn about the business as you did your homework, so too you can ask for time from business leaders to take them through a walkthrough.

> **TOOLS YOU CAN USE**
>
> We provide an example PowerPoint deck explaining the engagement model.

Doing the walkthrough is a helpful foundational activity that sets some initial expectations. At the same time, you should

Chapter 8: Building Your Relationship

realize that it is a bit like "teaching by telling." We know that people learn best through experience. So, you can expect your educational task to unfold over time through your day-to-day work. As you take on new projects or respond to requests, you can expect to continually need to educate the business about how they can most productively engage L&D and, in turn, what L&D will require from them to maximize success.

Phase 3—Establish

When you are new, the business will be unclear on what value you can bring. Depending on the relationship they have had with L&D in the past, they may be downright skeptical or consider you an order-taker to be called in only when a specific training need has already been specified.

In this phase, your goal is to demonstrate that you can add value by interacting as a business partner. A partner is someone emotionally invested in the business's success and concerned to continuously find ways for it to grow and prosper. Over your first six to nine months, you want to grow a relationship in which the business welcomes your contributions and comes to rely on your expertise. During this time, you are seeking to establish initial "proof points" of three specific capabilities that are required:

1. *You think "business" first and "learning" second.* One concern that the business may have is that you are there to "sell more training." In point of fact, your perspective should be that you are neutral on this. Training is expensive, and it's hard work for L&D to provide great service. If there is no need where learning can make a major impact, your company should avoid unnecessary

The CEO's Talent Manifesto

investment. At the same time, learning has often proven vital to helping business succeed. You want to help the business identify the extent to which it has such needs. You always come at this from the perspective of what's important to the business.

2. *You are a team player who brings an independent perspective.* Another concern that the business might have is that you will be a drain on their time. When you participate in business meetings, it is tempting to consider yourself an "observer" and limit yourself to asking discovery questions more or less directly linked to training needs. Going down this path will lead the business to label you as a narrow, functional specialist. It is wiser to view yourself as part of the management team for the business, even though only informally. You should seek to understand issues outside of training and training needs and be able to contribute to business conversations. If you take this stance, you will be able to provide helpful insight since you bring a perspective that straddles the line between being inside the business and outside of it. And you should show a willingness to put forth efforts that go beyond strict learning initiatives to prove out your usefulness.

3. *You can help the business identify new ways to apply learning that can increase alignment, raise impact, and/or reduce costs.* A final concern that the business may have is that "the old way" for chartering learning investments worked well enough and that the role of BEM is unneeded. Over the long haul, the role will demonstrate its value. It is helpful to establish "early wins" that pave

Chapter 8: Building Your Relationship

the way for long-term success. This could mean, for example, helping the business articulate performance issues that might not have been recognized before, eliminate ways of training that are not working, or conduct some quick evaluations to determine whether some existing training is, in fact, having an impact.

The way to establish these points is not by simply claiming them but rather by demonstrating them. You seek ways to engage with the business that allows you to continue to deepen your knowledge while establishing these points. Following are four types of activities that can help you do so.

Execute the Day-to-Day Work

In most cases, you will have ongoing core L&D work to do. Some programs will need to be developed, others deployed, and yet others evaluated. Issues will arise requiring attention (the L&D team may want your help mobilizing a subject matter expert, the business may be concerned about how a class is going, and so on).

A fundamental way you will establish yourself is by professionally managing the learning initiatives that are underway. Your exact role may vary, but it is critical that you actively form a bridge between the business and L&D. You advocate for the interests of the business within L&D, and you educate the business on what is required from it for its investments in L&D to bear fruit.

At the same time, it's also important not to become consumed by the project work of the moment. This work tends to be more instrumental and tactical than strategic. Focusing on it alone is unlikely to help you develop a clear view of how L&D can best contribute to the business or enable you to further develop the relationships you require with your key players. You need to do it and do it well, but it alone is not enough.

Participate in Reviews and Strategy Sessions

Obviously, you can serve your business groups better if you understand their strategies and progress against them. Most business groups have some mechanism for managing their strategy and tracking their progress. This can be through regular staff meetings, periodic strategy reviews, and/or an annual retreat for example. Clearly, you want to earn a seat at these meetings. How can you do so?

The first answer is simply to ask. Explain your desire in terms that stress the value to the business. After all, it's a win-win if you participate, as it will provide a low-effort way for business leaders to get to know you while also saving them later from having to educate you from the ground up. But at the same time, everyone knows that larger meetings are less productive than smaller ones. If you act as a passive observer, the proverbial lump on a log, you may not be invited back. For you to keep your seat, you will need to go beyond "just attending."

So, seek to add value. Again, doing homework is critical. Given the goals of an upcoming meeting, how can you prepare so you can bring something potentially useful to the table? Can you bring some past experience or outside benchmarking about how other organizations dealt with issues under discussion? As you are establishing yourself, continue to go the extra mile.

Chapter 8: Building Your Relationship

A separate way to add value is to offer to use your independent perspective more directly. Many people selected to be BEMs have excellent facilitation skills. Would it be helpful to the business to have an independent facilitator run a specific session?

Proactively Identify Opportunities for L&D to Contribute

As described above, it's helpful to find some early wins, some concrete ways to improve how L&D contributes to the business as you move ahead. At the same time, it's also important to pick your shots. You want to demonstrate that you are a thoughtful professional, not a loose cannon. So, it's helpful to find one or two specific opportunities *and make sure that they are well conceived.* For example, if a business group is running an expensive program that consumes much of their L&D budget, you might do some gentle exploration first to validate that the program is adding value and that it is operating efficiently. If there is a major strategic thrust, you might explore what new people capabilities are required and whether the organization should plan for training.

Your task while you establish yourself is not to try to close every gap or optimize every investment right away. Rather, it is to find some places to make useful progress. These can become early success stories, earning you the right for future work.

Summary

It can seem daunting to take on the role of business engagement manager for a new business group. How can one human bring both business and learning expertise? How can one person stay on top of the connections between strategy, operations, people performance, and learning solutions? How can you avoid getting so deeply entwined in creating and delivering solutions that you maintain the bandwidth to manage relationships with the business and the overall learning portfolio?

This chapter has provided a primer on how to come up to speed. The BEM role certainly offers a compelling and challenging opportunity for those who want to create business impact through learning. By using the ideas in this chapter as guideposts, you will soon be helping your business groups do so.

Chapter 9: Sustaining Your Relationship
Introduction

BEMs help the business groups they serve define and manage a portfolio of investments in learning. The investment plan for the year is defined during the annual planning process. Does this mean that the BEM simply supports execution for the rest of the year?

Not so.

Companies continually learn, and their plans continually shift. One new product is late to market. Another wildly exceeds expectations. The sales strategy needs to be tuned. It's turning out to be surprisingly hard to get manufacturing quality up to desired levels. For L&D to help the business, it must remain aware of shifts in direction and changes in priorities.

Therefore, successful BEMs are careful to keep their feelers constantly out to understand changes in the business. Certainly, the formal quarterly reviews that BEMs run as part of governance help (see Chapter 7). However, BEMs mostly identify changes before those reviews and use the reviews themselves to decide on actions to take based on what they have learned (e.g., charter a new investment).

In this chapter, we describe how BEMs can sustain their relationships with the business groups they serve. We focus on how they can constantly sense new opportunities and risks. Once the BEM has "sensed" a change, he or she can then systematically manage it as discussed in the section on managing individual investments. In keeping current, the key issue that BEMs face is *access*. They cannot simply ask for weekly meetings with business leaders to ask "What's happening?" It is all too easy for business leaders to see time spent talking with the BEM as *overhead*. So a core principle of the approach we discuss is that BEMs must consistently *provide value* from interactions.

We call what BEMs do to sense change "walking the beat." BEMs use a two-pronged approach to walk the beat:

- *Top-down*: The BEM systematically identifies with whom to touch base and what to discuss by maintaining a Strategic Account Plan.

- *Bottom-up*: As they work through the day-to-day of managing learning investments, BEMs continually insert "sensing" questions into their interactions with others.

The Top-Down Approach
The Foundation: Maintaining the Strategic Account Plan

The business groups that BEMs serve will usually contain thousands and sometimes tens of thousands of employees. As BEMs strive to stay current, with whom should they invest time?

Chapter 9: Sustaining Your Relationship

One answer is "the leadership." This answer is correct—but it is not complete. The time BEMs will get with business leaders will not be sufficient to keep fully current. In addition, leaders may themselves not be aware of performance issues that could call for learning support. BEMs must canvass a wider span of people to stay aware of change and bring a credible voice about the causes of performance issues.

Another answer is "those who are interested in L&D." Again, this answer is incomplete. Within any company, there will be some groups that welcome learning support and others that do not. Such dispositions do not always correlate with where learning has the largest opportunity to generate value. Since the BEM's job is to demonstrate value, he or she should invest time where there is opportunity, not necessarily where a BEM is most welcome.

> TOOLS YOU CAN USE
>
> We provide a template for a Strategic Account Plan.

When BEMs walk the beat, they do not go in with a blank slate. Rather, based on their work to date, they understand where the business group's major needs are as well as which areas they have not yet probed. Like a talent scout for a sports club, the BEM has a fair picture of the talent gaps his or her business group faces. Think back to Chapter 5 where we discussed how the BEMs capture their current understanding in the Ability-to-Execute Map. Their work is to maintain and refine that understanding over time.

When determining where to invest time walking the beat, a BEM should focus on whoever will most help refine the Ability-to-Execute

181

Map. We realize this advice is abstract. The challenge is that we have not yet discovered any simple rule to identify just who such people are across companies and business groups. Instead, BEMs need to think through their situations to identify whom to consult and what to ask of them.

In the last chapter, we saw how a new BEM can use a Strategic Account Plan to come up to speed on a business group. The BEMs should use the same tool to systematically direct their ongoing "sensing" activities. In this chapter, we describe how a BEM should maintain the Strategic Account Plan. The idea here is simply for BEMs to systematically make good use of their time while also consistently creating focused and purpose-driven conversations with the business.

BEMs should sit down once a quarter to plan out how they will spend time walking the beat. They can start by identifying where the Ability-to-Execute Map most requires validation or refinement as shown in Figure 32.

Questions
Identify *key questions* to pursue

Sources
Identify *whom* to ask

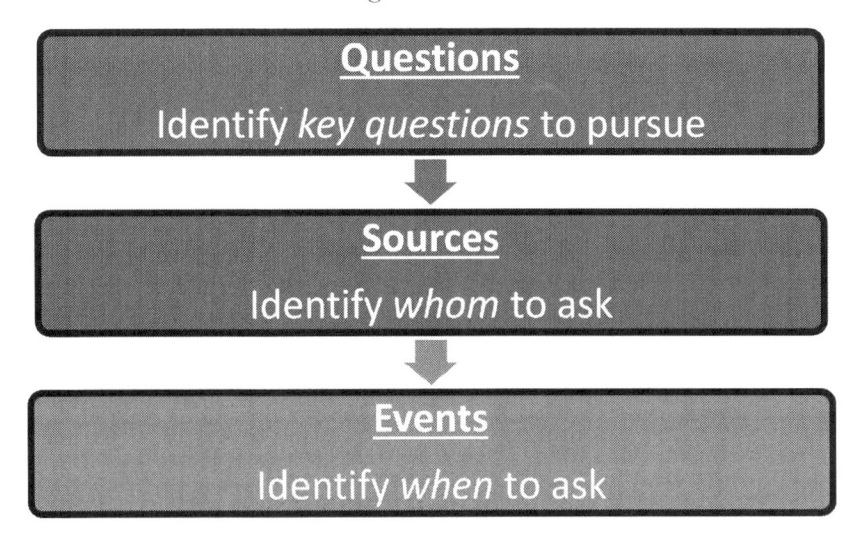

Events
Identify *when* to ask

Figure 32: Planning Where to Spend Time "Walking the Beat"

Chapter 9: Sustaining Your Relationship

The Strategic Account Plan simply helps BEMs keep track of progress.[33]

Identifying Key Questions

We have said that the BEM must provide value from each interaction. If the BEM simply wanders the halls asking "What's new?" and "Does that mean you need some training?" then most of his or her interactions will fail to generate value. A BEM requires a better way to ensure interactions are productive.

The place to start is by identifying important unknowns. The BEM generates a list of questions which, if answered, are likely lead to changes in the group's Learning Investment Portfolio. Conveniently, the BEM already has such a list underway. In Chapter 4, we discussed the Ability-to-Execute Map. When starting up a relationship with the business group, the BEM creates this map, including:

- Business outcomes

- Business processes

- People performances

- Talent solutions

The BEM has already laid out the most important items for each layer, as well as how the group measures success for each item and how well each is performing. When creating it, the BEM also identified some key "unknowns." Here, the BEM revisits the mapping to consider the unknowns in a more systematic way. It's useful to look for three types of questions at each layer:

1. *Holes*—A BEM will never have a completely comprehensive mapping. Here, the BEM considers what is unknown. Are there processes the BEM should understand? Is the BEM aware of status against the key strategies? How likely is getting more information to lead to changes in learning investments?

2. *Opportunities*—A business group will rarely see all the ways in which learning investments can help them achieve their goals, much less see them far enough in advance to mobilize support without a last-minute rush. Here, the BEM tries to imagine ways that the business group could be aided by investments in learning. This is an entrepreneurial activity, trying to spot an opportunity others have not seen. Perhaps the group has identified that the technical support team should raise its scores. They may even have considered training for frontline team members. Have the skills of supervisors been considered? In a professional services business group, perhaps margins are down. What are the most critical decisions that most impact margins? If the BEM can identify what they are, then it will be clearer whether learning support would lead to better decisions and higher margins.

3. *Risks*—When a company executes its strategies, it faces risks. One of them is that people will unexpectedly require new skills as they put the strategy into place. For example, a business group that is accelerating product development may find that its market researchers are struggling to analyze the new markets they are targeting. Here, the BEM tries to identify progress against key

Chapter 9: Sustaining Your Relationship

strategies and which key performances might impede success. Are these potential risks actually materializing?

Identifying Whom to Ask

The previous step produces a set of important unknowns that the BEM intends to explore over time. The way the BEM explores is almost always to ask someone. So, the next step is generally pretty straightforward: determine whom to ask.

The danger in this step is that the BEM shoots too high. It is almost always easiest for the BEM to target a senior business leader. However, that means consuming the time of the senior leader. This is not a place to prioritize the BEM's convenience over judicious use of business leaders' time.

Instead, it's more productive for the BEM to invest the extra energy required to maintain a network of contacts and strive to get questions answered at the lowest level feasible so as to use the overall organization's time the most efficiently (and earn kudos from senior leaders for being consistently well-prepared for conversations with them). For example, imagine the business sets the goal to improve customer satisfaction in technical support. The BEM wants to explore to what extent improving the coaching skills of supervisors would help. To do so, instead of just raising the question to the head of technical support, it would be better to speak to a couple of tech support representatives first.

Identifying When to Ask

The preceding two steps represent most of the "science" of top-down sensing. This step represents the "art."

The simplest route at this point would seem to be the most direct one: the BEM has a set of questions and sources to resolve them. The BEM could just set up time with each source. However, this route, used too often, can lead to relationship disaster. "Gee, this is the third time this year you have asked for time to ask these exploratory questions. So far, nothing has come of it. Why don't you wait until you have something concrete to ask me next time?" The last thing the BEM wants to happen is for people in the business to see him or her as a hanger-on who continually consumes time to "stay informed" but who does not seem to produce any real action much less results based on that information.

Here, the BEM looks to identify the least intrusive means possible to get the questions answered. For example, from less to more intrusive, some common methods include:

- *Get invited to a business meeting where the answer will be discussed anyway.* For example, a BEM might be concerned about the release data of an application for which L&D will provide end-user training. She or he might ask to be invited once a month to the project team status meeting.

- *Insert the question into a meeting that is happening anyway.* For example, a BEM might want to explore whether improving the coaching skills of technical support supervisors would improve customer satisfaction. The BEM might be involved in a project already to provide training to frontline representatives. He or she might find time during a break or after a meeting that ended early to ask, "By the way, I know that the business leader

Chapter 9: Sustaining Your Relationship

wants to improve customer satisfaction this year. How do supervisors help their teams improve satisfaction? What do the best ones do? What kind of support do supervisors get so most can act more like the best?"

- *Insert the question into ad hoc hallway conversations.* One of the advantages of being systematic in identifying your priority questions is that it makes it easier to take advantage of unexpected opportunities to get them answered. So, if the BEM above finds him- or herself walking from the car to the office with the head of technical support, he or she may be able to insert a question along the way (e.g., "I saw that our customer satisfaction scores have not yet increased. I was wondering about that. I don't think we do much training of supervisors in that group. To what extent do you think that we might accelerate improvement if we improved their skills in coaching for customer satisfaction?"). While such conversations are typically too brief to provide satisfyingly meaty answers, they give directional information and can open doors to more substantive discussion. For example, the head of engineering might well reply, "Gee, I hadn't really thought about that. You know, why don't you go do some digging with some managers?" Having such a stamp of executive support even if it just gives the BEM permission to explore can help a BEM accelerate such work.

- *Schedule a lunch or coffee break.* People in the business understand that BEMs need to stay in touch. If you can be careful with their time and don't ask too often, they will generally make it available. A good technique is to explicitly ask for "touch-base" time but look to schedule it during lunch or over coffee. When you adopt this tactic, it's important to go beyond simple "What's new?" questions. Rather, bring one or more substantive and specific questions to each meeting. "Gee, I had this idea about coaching in technical support that I wanted to bounce off of you."

- *Include it in the quarterly review of the investment plan.* The BEM meets with business leaders quarterly as a matter of course to review progress against the investment plan. When there are open questions, this is a sensible time to raise them. The constraints are that since this meeting is with senior business leaders, the BEM should come to it well prepared, raise questions that are only at a senior level, and limit the number of questions. The BEM can perhaps raise two or three unexpected questions during the meeting, not a dozen.

- *Schedule a meeting specifically to address the question.* Even with diligence, it won't always be the case that you can get your questions answered in low-overhead ways. For questions that will be seen as important by the business and for which getting answers in a timely way is obviously important, there's nothing wrong with asking for a formal meeting specifically to address the question. If the BEM is thoughtful about exhausting other avenues before going down this path, the meetings that actually result will be clearly useful and productive.

When you learn of new opportunities, make sure to help the business group feel good about how they have helped. Let them know that their inputs did result in action so they know that you are following up on the ideas they have raised to you. As you proceed, give credit back. Your contacts should be rewarded for making the investment to help you do your sensing work.

Organizing the Work

Making this top-down approach to sensing effective takes *work*! Periodically, the BEM needs to refresh the set of questions to be pursued and how to pursue them. It can be helpful to schedule time to organize the work. For example, a BEM might:

- *Quarterly*, spend an hour to rebuild the set of questions from the ground up.

- *Monthly*, spend a half hour to identify which questions remain open and decide whether to adjust the plan for getting them answered.

- *Weekly*, review which questions are open, which are not, and which the BEM plans to address during the week.

The Bottom-Up Approach

Through the top-down work, a BEM can stay abreast of much of what develops in the business groups he or she serves. At the same time, no one can know what he or she doesn't know. So, a successful BEM complements structured top-down sensing with bottom-up sensing. This involves two actions: a) maintaining a set of relationships with stakeholders who will contact the BEM when unforeseen changes or needs arise and b) continually using the day-to-day work to seek opportunities to generate value.

Maintaining Relationships

As part of the BEM's Strategic Account Management Plan, the BEM identifies a set of key stakeholders in a business group. These can play different roles. Some might be sponsors; others might be coaches; yet others might be good sources of information. As part of the BEM's ongoing work, he or she should retain relationships with these stakeholders.

A BEM might maintain relationships with twelve to fifteen stakeholders over time. As a rough guideline, to keep the relationship alive, the BEM should find some useful way to spend time with each stakeholder *at least* once a quarter. What that turns out to mean in practice is that the BEM will usually find him- or herself having coffee or lunch or otherwise meeting with one or two stakeholders each week.

With the key stakeholders, the BEM can explicitly ask permission to seek their time on a regular basis (e.g., "To ensure we meet your needs, it would really help if I could check in with you once a quarter or so. Would it be OK with you if we try that out and see if it's helpful?"). At the same time, even if the BEM is given permission, it's useful to keep in mind that the permission is always only provisional. If the BEM does not make good use of the time, the stakeholder will withdraw it. So, the BEM must be sure to have something for each meeting which the stakeholder will see as value-adding to the business group if not the stakeholder directly.

During sessions with these stakeholders, the BEM can and should step back and ask broad-based questions like, "What's going on in the business? What is the new news?" However, this is *not* the place to start. Rather, the BEM should start with a couple of concrete "work items" that he or she would like to cover before stepping back to the big picture. Doing so ensures that the discussion gets some concrete work done even if there is no new big-picture news. And that, in turn, leaves stakeholders with faith in the BEM that the BEM is making thoughtful use of their time.

Continually Seeking Opportunities

The final method of sensing is at once the simplest and yet the hardest. Simply, the BEM should retain an entrepreneurial mind-set throughout all dealings. If the BEM is in a meeting reviewing results for a line training program, were there case stories that indicated there might be a way to get the same effect but with a simpler solution? Were there case stories that indicated an unrelated need that the team had not yet identified? If the BEM is in a staff meeting, did someone raise a topic that he or she did not understand (and therefore could not determine whether learning support would be appropriate)?

A BEM can accomplish a significant amount of sensing simply by noticing such potential opportunities "in passing." While this sounds easy, it requires discipline. To pull it off, the BEM must maintain a mind-set that should be familiar at this point: the BEM should continually keep the Ability-to-Execute Map in her or his head, map what she or he hears to it, and identify gaps or surprises. At the same time, this must happen in the midst of whatever the actual work of the moment is. Accordingly, to be effective, the BEM must make it a *habit*.

Section 4: Managing the Lifecycle of a Learning Investment

Most of this book explains how a BEM collaborates with a business group to define and manage a portfolio of learning investments that are aligned, efficient, and produce demonstrated results. In this section, we focus on how a BEM delivers value from a single investment. We assume that the BEM has already defined an appropriate portfolio and is effectively managing his or her relationship with the business group. What happens when a new need arises?

In short, the BEM assumes accountability for the *full lifecycle* of a learning investment as shown in Figure 33. In L&D, we are used to thinking of lifecycles in terms of the "ADDIE" model (which contains steps for **A**nalysis, **D**esign, **D**evelopment, **I**mplementation, and **E**valuation). Certainly, the BEM's accountability includes the steps in ADDIE. But it goes beyond it. From the BEM's perspective, the lifecycle of a learning investment can be viewed as a sandwich. ADDIE fills the middle layer, but the BEM has responsibilities both beforehand and after.

The CEO's Talent Manifesto

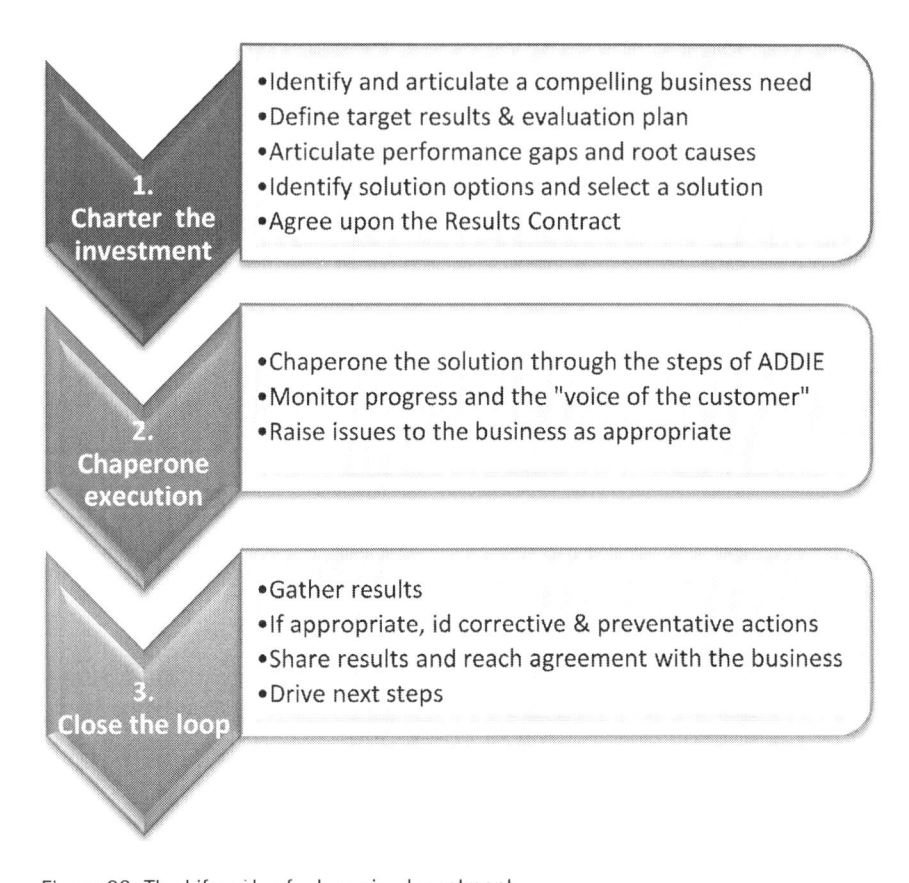

1. Charter the investment
- Identify and articulate a compelling business need
- Define target results & evaluation plan
- Articulate performance gaps and root causes
- Identify solution options and select a solution
- Agree upon the Results Contract

2. Chaperone execution
- Chaperone the solution through the steps of ADDIE
- Monitor progress and the "voice of the customer"
- Raise issues to the business as appropriate

3. Close the loop
- Gather results
- If appropriate, id corrective & preventative actions
- Share results and reach agreement with the business
- Drive next steps

Figure 33: The Lifecycle of a Learning Investment

Initially, the BEM helps *charter the investment*, setting it up for success by ensuring it is well-aligned and has clear targets. BEMs spend much of their time identifying and prioritizing the most important business needs and chartering solutions to address them.

Then the BEM helps *chaperone execution*, covering the traditional ADDIE steps (of **A**nalyze, **D**esign, **D**evelop, **I**mplement, and **E**valuate). Here, the BEM serves as an account manager linking the business and L&D. He or she makes sure that the

Section 4: Managing the Lifecycle of a Learning Investment

project stays on track, provides the business with visibility on progress, and ensures that L&D in turn understands the business's point of view.

Finally, the BEM *closes the loop* to identify what the company has learned through the project and its results and then makes sure that it takes appropriate action based on the lessons. Sometimes, this can mean revisions to the learning solution itself. In other cases, it can mean articulating and disseminating best practices for how to approach other investments.

Chapter 10: Chartering an Investment
Introduction

We use the term *chartering* for the process of moving from the initial discovery of a business need through launching execution of a well-aligned solution. The BEM becomes aware of business needs through the formal annual planning process and through the ongoing informal process of "walking the beat." Once a business need has been identified where learning *might* add value, the BEM then helps the business identify the extent to which it *really would* and then determine whether the business *should* invest in it given competing demands.

To do so, the BEM helps clarify how well the need is aligned to goals, strategies, and operational objectives. The BEM helps size the need and determine the extent to which learning can in fact address it. The BEM identifies a solution and then ensures clarity on the key items required to launch execution: results, roles, the evaluation plan, and timing. Throughout this work, the BEM collaborates with a group of stakeholders who have varying perspectives on the business need and predispositions toward learning, bringing the group toward a confident decision.

The output of chartering is a Results Contract, which captures the clarity the BEM has achieved. This Results Contract provides a touchstone for both execution and closing the loop, reminding the group of stakeholders what they set out to accomplish and what they committed to contribute.

Keeping Your Eyes on the Right Prize

BEMs come from L&D. Should they actively seek to expand its use? This raises a confusion that is easy for BEMs to fall into. Does the BEM win only when he or she makes a sale? Does success mean earning the right for L&D to provide some training?

Yes, BEMs help expand the use of L&D. But it is not because they "win" when L&D gets an orsder. Rather, it is because they help a business make a productive investment.

The bottom line for the BEM is simple: help the business make investments in learning that generate demonstrable business value. Success is not generating *training activity*. The BEM does not care if marketing specialists get sent to a two-day course. The BEM cares that the consumer products company increases Gen Y market penetration.

It is all too easy for BEMs to take up the concept that they should "promote training." When this means working hard to help a business understand its needs, that's great. But when it means taking chances on poorly thought-through investments, the BEM does L&D a disservice. If it's not yet clear whether training can in fact help, should the BEM err on the side of recommending it? Or if a business leader directly asks for some training, shouldn't the BEM make sure to provide it? No and no.

Chapter 10: Chartering an Investment

It helps for BEMs to take the long view. BEMs are best able to generate value when they earn the privilege of being viewed as trusted advisors by business leaders, who will do so when they experience demonstrated success. Well-chartered investments produce strong results and so make next year's collaboration with the business easier than this year's. Poorly chartered investments do not produce demonstrated results and so make next year's collaboration more difficult.

What this means is that the BEM certainly adds value by getting high-impact, well-aligned investments approved and into execution. But the BEM also adds value by helping the business avoid making poorly-aligned investments. The way the BEM does both is the same: by generating clarity about the business case. *Clarity* is what counts, not steering the work toward a predisposed preference to provision some training. Once the right needs are on the table, let the cards fall where they may.

The BEM as Proactive Facilitator

One way to view the BEM's role during chartering is as a business analyst who helps the business clarify the case for a potential investment in learning. This view focuses on the conceptual work required to create the case. It is certainly accurate, and most of this chapter is dedicated to describing how a BEM works through the steps and milestones involved. At the same time, this view is incomplete. It implies a level of orderliness about the work, which can understate its true complexity.

A complementary and equally accurate view focuses on the multiple stakeholders that the process often involves. Under this view, the BEM serves as a proactive facilitator who helps manage the hopes, predispositions, concerns, and perspectives of these stakeholders so that they understand and buy into whatever business case emerges. Let's take an example. Imagine the chief marketing officer of a consumer products company wants the marketing staff to better target Gen Y. This provides a clear strategic direction, but the CMO may be skeptical that training can help achieve it. In contrast, the HR generalist responsible for the marketing talent pool may see a lot of potential value but be most concerned with getting a clear and concrete statement of just what that value is and how it can be evaluated. A product manager brought in to contribute a business perspective may simply be reluctant to release his marketing people for yet more training. And a marketer consulted because she has proven effective at reaching Gen Y may feel the real problem has to do with incentives and not skills at all.

In short, when BEMs explore a need, the stakeholders with whom they engage all bring their own concerns to the table. They will not buy into the emerging business case until those concerns are at least acknowledged and, we hope, addressed. The BEM may take a wide variety of steps to address them. For the CMO, the BEM may share a case study and walk through some example training. For the HR generalist, the BEM may engage finance to construct a financial projection. To identify the cause of the performance gap, the BEM may request additional time from a broader span of practitioners so as to do a more complete performance analysis.

As BEMs proceed, they cannot presume that the stakeholders are engaged and eager to offer their time to work through the

Chapter 10: Chartering an Investment

process. Instead, they must *gain permission* to use their time and then, as they use it, *build* commitment to the process. As a result, BEMs' day-to-day work in chartering a learning investment can feel as much like herding cats as it does like an orderly march through the analytic work of developing a business case. As BEMs proceed on the analytic work, they constantly consider the stakeholder network. Is the group ready to move to the next step in the process? Have the right people been brought to the table given the progress made so far? Should the BEM continue with the exploration or instead step back to provide some proof points of how training has helped in analogous situations? What is the right-sized action to ask for next? Is it better to ask for a quick telephone conversation with a proficient performer to explore root causes or instead a more systematic survey of a larger sample of the target audience?

In the rest of this chapter, we focus on the conceptual work of building the business case. At the same time, we do not wish to minimize the complexity of the dance required to nurture a potential investment.

Step-by-Step

To charter an investment, the BEM moves through seven steps:

1. Identifying and articulating a compelling business need

2. Defining concrete targets for results

3. Defining how target results will be evaluated

4. Identifying the required performances

5. Identifying the gaps and root causes that block success

6. Identifying solution options and selecting the solution

7. Creating the results contract

If the investment is approved, the process produces a Results Contract and moves into execution. At the same time, the process can terminate at any point if the BEM and the business identify that the business case is not compelling enough to warrant proceeding.

Step 1. Identifying and Articulating a Compelling Business Need

The process starts with BEMs helping their business groups identify where learning investments are required to achieve their goals, strategies, and operational objectives. Prior chapters have already discussed much of the mechanics. BEMs identify business needs through two "funnels":

1. They run a formal planning process, the governance process discussed in Chapter 7.

2. They informally "walk the beat" as discussed in Chapter 9.

As potential business needs arise top-down or as BEMs become aware of performance gaps that could represent important business needs, they ensure that they are well-aligned by using the Ability-to-Execute Alignment Framework as discussed in Chapter 4 (shown again in Figure 34).

Chapter 10: Chartering an Investment

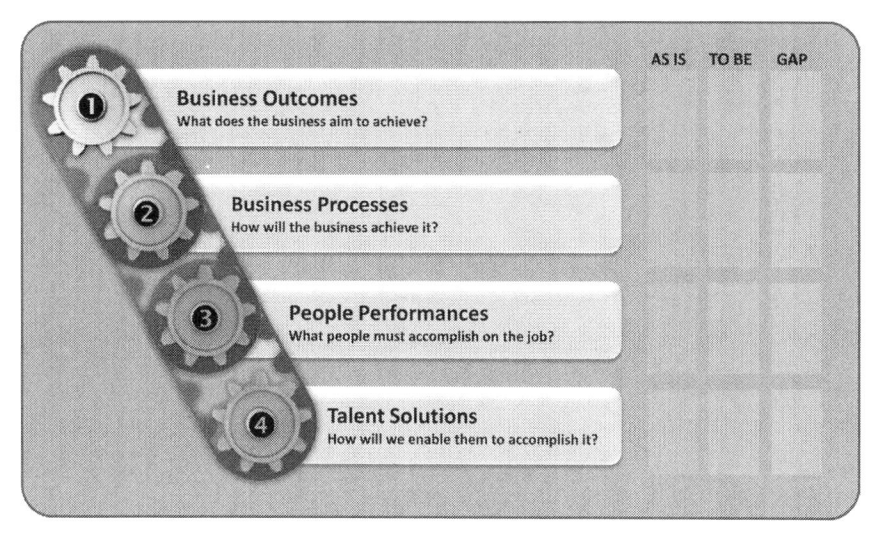

Figure 34: The Ability to Execute Alignment Framework

The level of effort involved in identifying a business need ranges from "it fell into my lap" to significant patient exploration. There are three major cases.

Case 1: The Business Makes a Well-Aligned Direct Request for Learning Support

This is the simple case. Imagine it's time for annual planning in a company that sells enterprise software. The head of sales says to his BEM:

> Our major initiative is that we are seeking to double the amount of business we generate through our channel partners. To do this, we are changing our fundamental channel strategy. Instead of trying to recruit as many channel partners as we can, we will focus on the ones who themselves focus on the particular target markets we serve the best. We expect to eliminate over half of

> our existing partners. We will then invest much more heavily in the ones we retain to help them grow. As they expand, they will need to upskill existing personnel and bring on new ones. Part of our investment will be to help them develop their personnel. So, we want to make a major expansion in the channel training we provide starting next year. Can you help us determine what's required?"

The head of sales has presented the BEM with a major business need that appears to require a major learning investment. As this example illustrates, sometimes a BEM is off and running with a clear charter and enthusiastic business support from the first conversation about a need.

Case 2: The Business Makes a Poorly Aligned Direct Request for Learning Support

In contrast, now imagine it's time for a quarterly learning investment review in a bank. The head of the retail banking business group says to her BEM:

> Besides what we've discussed, I also have a new need. We need to increase revenue from new products. So I would like to give my product managers a two-day course on innovation.

Here, it sounds like the head has a real business need. But the linkage between the need and the request is far from clear.

To proceed, the key tactic is for the BEM to create the space required to systematically explore the need without actually

Chapter 10: Chartering an Investment

committing the business to launching training. So, the BEM can acknowledge the request and ask permission to explore the need ("It sounds like you have an important need. To make sure we do what is most useful to you, can I ask a few questions?").

Given the muddy linkage, the BEM cannot tell whether learning support is actually required or not. So, it's a mistake to either "take the order" since that may result in a low-value solution or to disparage the need ("Well, I see that you are asking for training. But it doesn't make sense for us to provide it unless there is a clear performance need!"). Rather, the BEM should take the responsibility to proactively explore the need.

Case 3: The BEM Proactively Identifies a Potential Need for Learning Support

Let's go back to the annual planning at the manufacturing company. Imagine that the head of sales does not make a direct request for learning support. Instead, perhaps in response to a question from the BEM about plans for the coming year, he simply mentions:

> Our major initiative is that we are seeking to double the amount of business we generate through our channel partners. To do this, we are changing our fundamental channel strategy. Instead of trying to recruit as many channel partners as we can, we will focus on the ones who themselves focus on the particular target markets we serve the best. We expect to eliminate over half of our existing partners. We will then invest much more heavily in the ones we retain to help them grow.

The conversation starts in a great place with a major business strategy. But the head of sales is not (yet) thinking about learning support. What the BEM does in this case is gently explore the strategy to see whether learning support will actually be required. So, the BEM might ask, "To what extent do we know what is preventing those partners from growing today?" and then "To what extent do the partners have the capabilities required to grow? To what extent do they need deeper or new capabilities?" If such discovery questions indicate that the people capabilities or partners may be critical, then the BEM can ask permission to explore the need.

Step 2. Defining Concrete Targets for Results

Many companies make learning investments without setting concrete targets for results. This lack of targets creates an unproductive fog. Business leaders who are not clear on what they are getting are less likely to invest in learning. Some "have the faith," but many do not. An L&D development team that is not clear on what outcomes they must achieve is less likely to provide the most efficient solution. How much performance improvement is enough? Then, once a solution is provided, both business leaders and L&D have a hard time deciding whether and how to optimize. If you don't know what you are shooting at, it's hard to know if you hit it.

In contrast, setting concrete targets has a remarkably productive clarifying effect. They serve as a form of currency between business leaders and L&D providing welcome clarity to both. The rule for setting targets is simple: they must clearly address the business need and the business sponsor must agree that achieving those targets is well worth the required investment. The specifics of course vary widely.

Chapter 10: Chartering an Investment

Throughout this book, we have described the value of using *business process measures* as targets. The following table lists some examples.

Business Process	Measure	Target
Sales agent productivity	Proposal volume	3.5+ proposals/agent
Call center inbound calls	Customer Service Rating	95%+ of interactions rated 8+
Managing collections	On-Time Payments	90%+ payments on-time
Service engineer onboarding	Time to proficiency	90%+ certified w/i 4 months
Sales agent legal compliance	Compliance certification	100% certified

Figure 35: Example Business Process Measures and Targets

Looking at this table, you will notice that, for most of the targets, *L&D cannot generate the result by itself.* You may wonder how L&D can commit to such a target. For instance, consider the first line in Figure 35, which represents a company that has determined it needs to reduce its cost of sales by growing sales agent productivity. It has set a target to raise sales agent productivity from 2.5 to 3.5 proposals per agent per month within two years, an increase of 40 percent. If you are the BEM exploring this need, you may be convinced that many agents currently lack critical skills. Based on initial interviews, you may have learned that:

- Agents waste time on low-probability leads because they do not know how to prospect and qualify opportunities.

- The current sales tracking system forces them to spend an average of 30 percent of their time on administrative activities.

207

- The incentive system drives them to focus much more on nurturing existing clients than seeking new ones.

Given all of the barriers to improvement, how could L&D possibly commit that investing in learning will raise productivity 40 percent? You may be confident that if those barriers were removed, results would at least meet the target. But you know that learning by itself cannot address all of the barriers.

The key insight here is to realize that BEMs create value by generating clarity. You can make your assumptions clear. A business leader who wants to achieve a goal must balance and integrate various ways to achieve it. The business leader needs some way of judging which bets to place. A BEM might stay in the comfort zone by saying, "Gee, I see there are skills gaps but there are so many variables that I couldn't possibly tell you how much of an impact it would make to close them." But this does not really help the business as it forces the business leader to then make that judgment. With such a response, the business leader will probably categorize the BEM as a functional specialist who is unhelpfully squeamish. Then the business leader will probably underinvest in learning because he or she will discount its value as having a high risk of uncertainty.

In contrast, if the BEM were to make a reasonable back-of-the envelope calculation and state some assumptions, then the business leader can make a judgment call. For example, in this case, a successful BEM might pull together a proposal such as this:

- Salespeople spend limited time developing new business. Our initial assessment shows that salespeople spend

Chapter 10: Chartering an Investment

only about 30 percent of their time on new business, while they spend about 40 percent on existing customers and the remaining 30 percent on administration.

- Reduced time calls for changes in the sales administration process. This is broad-based, requiring changes to how sales managers behave, what reporting salespeople are required to provide, as well as the software we use to track sales.

- Reallocating time from administration to new business could readily raise time on new business by 50 percent. If we could halve the time spent on administration and reallocate that to new business, that would increase time on new business from 30 percent to 45 percent, an increase of 50 percent.

- Salespeople must be incented to spend time on new business. Simply providing more time is not enough. Incentives drive salespeople to invest in current customers. So, incentives would need to be modified.

- More time on new business is part of the answer, but better skills are required too. The variance in productivity across salespeople in prospecting and qualifying is substantial. If we were to remediate the current lack of prospecting and qualifying skills, we believe that we could make each minute spent 33 percent more productive. We'll talk about what's required to achieve that level of improvement.

- If we combine 50 percent more time on new business with a 33 percent increase in productivity, the net result should be a doubling of new business. We therefore think the goal of 40 percent is achievable if we: a) change the administration system; b) change the incentive structure; and c) implement a learning solution.

The key to such a proposal is that it lays out some simple working assumptions that enable a business leader to make an informed choice. Along the way, the BEM adds value by structuring the thinking. In this example, the BEM has put a spotlight on key areas that the business leader may not have been aware of (e.g., the amount of time salespeople spend on administration). In turn, the BEM has made a commitment for L&D, in this case to improve productivity per minute of sales effort, as measured by number of proposals produced.

At the end of the day, the BEM, with support from the rest of L&D, must be prepared to make such commitments. While this entails risk and can be uncomfortable, no one is better placed than L&D to estimate the business impact that L&D can have. Business leaders must balance what they can gain from, for example, implementing new systems, hiring more staff, investing in L&D, or changing incentives. To do so, they must ask various specialists, "What can you do for me?" Answering in terms that are meaningful to business leaders (e.g., "I believe I can improve productivity per minute spent by 33 percent") helps them make their choice. Answering in technical terms that don't map to results does not (e.g., "We can get all salespeople through a two-hour course within three months. We will cover the following performance objectives…").

One word of caution: As the BEM works through the process of chartering an investment and setting targets, it is not required

Chapter 10: Chartering an Investment

that the BEM commit prematurely. During an initial conversation, the BEM can probe to identify desired targets. In this example, the head of sales might state, "Our target is that we want to raise sales productivity by 40 percent." At this stage, it's valid and appropriate for the BEM to do the legwork to identify feasibility. That's when the BEM might come back with a response like the sample above. Being willing to make a commitment is not the same as being willing to make an *uninformed* commitment. Since L&D will be judged by whether it meets the commitments it makes, it's important not to have unfounded confidence.

One approach to make the call on just how much to commit is for the BEM to make a "best guess" and then to reduce the committed level by a confidence factor. For example, the BEM in the case above might have the conversation shown in Figure 36 with the learning leader while defining the commitment.

Effective BEMs make sure to remain transparent with their business sponsors about what's possible even though it can be tempting for them to stretch. Remember, the goal is not to "make a sale" but to "define the business case with clarity." For example, in the case above, it might be that L&D has long believed it could impact sales performance but has not yet had the opportunity to try. Given its lack of experience, it might not be so confident in its abilities and so knock down its commitment substantially. In such a case, the BEM might say to the business lead, "We do see a lot of opportunity. But as you know, we have not yet implemented learning solutions for this group, so we are uncertain about what we can achieve. We are confident that we can improve productivity by at least 20 percent and think it could be much more than that." In turn, the business leader

The CEO's Talent Manifesto

might decide not to make the investment. *That's okay.* Risky investments with moderate returns are not the wisest way to spend money. There are enough ways for investments in learning to generate results that L&D does not need to go out on a limb to promote low-performing or unduly risky ones.

Learning Leader: "So, we need a target for improving sales productivity. How far along are you?"

BEM: "There appears to be significant variation in the current system, which leads to waste. The two most pressing examples are that there is no guidance on how to prioritize 'suspects'. And there are no standard templates for proposals so they take salespeople a long time to create."

Learning Leader: "OK. If salespeople were better able to prioritize, how much wasted effort could they eliminate?"

BEM: "We heard stories about salespeople routinely taking sales all the way through to proposal, then finding out that the prospect was in no way ready to invest that much in a solution. So qualifying was a problem too. Between saving 20% of their time from not pursuing low-probably suspects and another 15% by eliminating prospects that aren't really qualified, rough estimate, maybe up to a third of their time in new sales."

Learning Leader: "Sounds good. Now, how about providing better templates and tools for creating proposals. What effect could we get from that?"

BEM: "Well, they seem to only spend about 20% of their time actually creating proposals. We could probably cut that by a third too, so another 5-10%".

Learning Leader: "Good too. That totals about 40%. How confident are you in these numbers?"

BEM: "Really pretty confident, actually. We have done similar sales skills in other groups and had similar results. And while we haven't provided templates and tools for creating proposals for this group, we have done something similar for creating service warranties. So we have some bona fides."

Learning Leader: "OK, so we're actually pretty confident. So, how about we knock 20% off of our number. That would have us committing to about a 33% increase. Comfortable with that?"

Figure 36: Example Dialog to Define a Commitment

Chapter 10: Chartering an Investment

When the key reason not to make an investment is risk of the unknown, instead of simply giving up, a BEM can explore experiments to eliminate the unknowns. For example, imagine the sales force ran an experiment in which they asked three highly productive salespeople to each coach three average salespeople on prospecting and qualifying for a month and the result was that the average salespeople raised their productivity 25 percent. Would that build confidence that a formal learning solution could achieve similar results? By offering to organize and evaluate such an experiment, the BEM can clear the fog around potential results and so help the group achieve its business goals.

One final word on concrete targets: In this section, we have focused on the key targets that a BEM establishes with a business leader to evaluate whether an investment achieved what was intended. *While these form the foundation of the agreement with the business, they are not the only targets that L&D will set.* Instead, L&D should also set and evaluate targets along a series of dimensions in addition to business impact, including time-to-market, participant feedback, transfer to the job, cost per participant, and so on. Without such additional targets, L&D cannot ensure that it is providing efficient and effective solutions. A full discussion of evaluation is beyond the scope of this book. We recommend *The Training Measurement Book* by Josh Bersin.[34]

Step 3. Defining How Target Results Will Be Evaluated

In serving as a reliable partner, L&D will report back to the business the extent to which the promise was met and the targets were hit. To do so, L&D must put in place some mechanism to get the data required. In many cases, L&D can simply report back data that the business itself generates.

Once concrete targets are set, figuring out how to collect the data is usually not a difficult proposition. It is important to address up front, however, for several reasons:

- *It can affect which specific targets are picked.* In the previous example, L&D is really planning to affect sales productivity per minute on new prospects. However, the metric the BEM offers is proposals per month. Why? One reason is that the metric is closer to what the business leader cares about. While this metric does not isolate specifically what L&D contributed (as opposed to the impact of incentives or other changes), at the end of the day, if the metric is hit, the business will be satisfied. However, another reason might be proposals per month are already tracked, so the data come for free. Only if the target is missed will more detail be required…and in that case, the extra work required to isolate the impact of L&D can be taken up. But why create extra work in advance?

- *It clarifies roles and responsibilities.* As part of chartering an investment, the BEM identifies who will do what to execute the solution. Since business process measures usually form the core of the evaluation and come from the business, it's particularly important to clarify who will provide them. Business leaders, appropriately, do not like to be surprised with their teams being asked to do unexpected work. By chasing down the evaluation plan up front, the source of the support required is made clear from the start.

Chapter 10: Chartering an Investment

- *It avoids territoriality later.* Business groups can be reluctant to share their data with L&D, particularly when they are not used to doing so. Involving the relevant staff up front so that they understand the need and know that the need is supported by business leadership paves the way later to actually obtain the data when required.

Step 4: Identifying the Required Performances

Learning improves business results by improving performance. To charter a learning investment, the BEM must identify, at least at a high level, which performances are to be improved.

The outcome of this step is a clear and succinct statement of the performance capabilities the learning solution will develop. For instance, in our sales example, the statement of required performances might be along the lines shown in Figure 37.

	Performance	Monthly Target
1.	Use research tools to identify suspects	50+
2.	Use the prioritization framework to select prospects	20+
3.	Establish appointments with prospects	12+
4.	Conduct initial conversations with prospects	10+
5.	Qualify prospects and produce proposals	3.5+
6.	Pursue proposals and close new sales	1.5+

Figure 37: Example Performance Outcomes

Much has been written about how to conduct performance analysis and craft performance objectives. For more on this, we recommend *Preparing Instructional Objectives* by Mager.[35] This step is usually quite rapid and is based on a simple task analysis of the performance at hand.

215

Step 5: Identifying the Gaps and Root Causes Blocking Success

We believe that more money is wasted in L&D because of a failure to align solutions than any other cause. After lack of alignment, what's the next largest source of waste? We believe its lack of prioritization. Many companies employ an overly simplistic approach to how companies use training to achieve a list of performance objectives. Once they have identified a list of required performances, they say "Let's take each one and train people how to do it." This bottom-up approach leads to "mile-wide, inch-deep" training that fails to account for levels of difficulty—what is easy, what is hard—and what really blocks success.

Having identified the desired performances, we are still not yet ready to move to solution. Rather, we have only understood the behavioral endpoint we wish to achieve, having shifted from a business goal to a performance goal. We do not yet understand the distance we must cover to actually enable those performances. At this stage, the BEM must take the additional steps of identifying the gaps between target and actual performances and their root causes.

For example, in our sales example, it could well be that most salespeople already succeed in steps #1 (identifying suspects) and #3 (setting appointments and conducting initial conversations). If so, no additional work is required there. It could also be that they know how to do #2 (prioritize suspects), but they are unconvinced that the prioritization framework is sound and find it an awkward, unduly, and time-consuming process. So, they intentionally don't use it. And it's only in step #4 (qualifying prospects and producing proposals) where they

Chapter 10: Chartering an Investment

lack the skills required. Until a BEM uncovers such gaps and root causes, he or she cannot help a business group construct a solution that is either effective or efficient.

Here, the BEM sits in the sweet spot of performance consulting. For BEMs who come from L&D, this is usually old and comfortable ground. However, for BEMs who come from the business, this is where they must develop the new skills required. For such BEMs, there are a variety of robust frameworks for how to conduct performance consulting, and many L&D organizations have defined their own approach. For example, one good reference is *First Things Fast* by Rossett.[36]

In performance consulting, one first *identifies gaps*—that is, where actual results fall short of target results. This step is typically concrete and quick. Then one determines root causes—that is, why individuals do not routinely generate target results. While eye-openers can come from both steps, it's usually the second step of identifying root causes where the most new insight is generated.

Most of us are too ready to attribute performance gaps to lack of skill or, conversely, to attribute to training more power than it actually has. It's important to be careful and systematic so we can draw out the argument step-by-step:

- To achieve a *required performance*, we must eliminate a performance gap.

- To eliminate a *performance gap*, we must remediate its root causes.

- To remediate a *root cause*, we must implement a solution.

217

Perhaps the trickiest part of this chain is in identifying the root causes. To do this, it helps to bring to bear a catalog of types of root causes. Many exist. Our personal favorite is the *Updated Behavior Engineering Model* by Roger Chevalier, which builds on work by Thomas Gilbert (Figure 38).[37]

Chevalier also provides a useful cause-analysis worksheet for thinking through and documenting how various root causes contribute to performance gaps.

Now, doing a really thorough job of performance consulting can require substantial effort. The question at this point is "how much is enough?" Unfortunately, there is no hard-and-fast answer. The real answer is "enough so that the business and L&D can charter a solution with confidence that it will achieve the target results for the estimated investment." In practice, we have seen the level of effort being bimodal. In most cases, BEMs who are knowledgeable about a business group report that the effort required is only a couple of days or less. In some cases, though, such an initial exploratory investigation is not sufficient to clarify which performances are really critical, which gaps exist, and/or the root causes driving them. In these cases, a deep dive is required and the BEM should be reluctant to plow ahead with proposing a solution. How can the business be confident of results? Instead, the BEM should seek an initial step to clarify the problem via a performance consulting study. In our experience, such studies are primarily required when tackling audiences who have received little support previously or for processes that are relatively new. In practice, few business needs are both large enough to make it worth conducting a special study and yet unclear enough to require one. So a business group will likely find it requires at most one or two such studies per year.

Chapter 10: Chartering an Investment

Environment		
Information	**Resources**	**Incentives**
• Roles and performance expectations are clearly defined; employees are given relevant and frequent feedback about the adequacy of performance. • Clear and relevant guides are used to describe the work process. • The performance management system guides employee performance and development.	• Materials, tools and time needed to do the job are present. • Processes and procedures are clearly defined and enhance individual performance if followed. • Overall physical and psychological work environment contributes to improved performance; work conditions are safe, clean, organized, and conducive to performance.	• Financial and non-financial incentives are present; measurement and reward systems reinforce positive performance. • Jobs are enriched to allow for fulfillment of employee needs. • Overall work environment is positive, where employees believe they have an opportunity to succeed; career development opportunities are present.

Individual		
Knowledge & Skills	**Capacity**	**Motives**
• Employees have the necessary knowledge, experience and skills to do the desired behaviors. • Employees with the necessary knowledge, experience and skills are properly placed to use and share what they know. • Employees are cross-trained to understand each other's roles.	• Employees have the capacity to learn and do what is needed to perform successfully. • Employees are recruited and selected to match the realities of the work situation. • Employees are free of emotional limitations that would interfere with their performance.	• Motives of employees are aligned with the work and the work environment. • Employees desire to perform the required jobs. • Employees are recruited and selected to match the realities of the work situation.

Figure 38: The Updated Behavior Engineering Model

Step 6: Identifying Solution Options and Selecting the Solution

Once the performance analysis (gaps and root causes) is on the table, it's time for the BEM to provide a set of solution options for the business to consider, typically along with a recommendation.

Determining Whom to Bring to the Table and How to Organize a Solution Team

In most cases, once the performance analysis is complete, the BEM can simply move ahead with a learning solution. However, sometimes life is more complex. Driving required performance could potentially require changes in training, compensation, recruiting, enterprise IT systems, business processes, and on and on. When the business is more than just a learning solution, how can the BEM mobilize the right people? Who takes which responsibility?

The first step is for the BEM to ensure buy-in from the business to at least explore broader solutions. A business leader may not initially appreciate the complexity of the performance need and may see the BEM as overcomplicating the problem.

After that, the BEM ensures the right people are brought to the table. This can be a challenging balancing act. In most cases, it is difficult for the business itself to organize a broader solution. The business leader likely neither has the bandwidth nor the expertise required to engage specialists from multiple support functions, go through discovery and solutioning with each, and then integrate the results. Instead, it would be ideal from the business leader's perspective for someone to play the role of "solution architect" to pull together a total solution. At

Chapter 10: Chartering an Investment

the same time, it is not typically realistic for the BEM him- or herself to play this role, particularly when there are changes required to IT systems or business processes, as IT and business staff are unused to working under the direction of L&D.

BEMs will not add value or earn the trust of the business if they simply step back and restrict themselves to focusing solely on the learning elements of the solution. Successful BEMs work hard to bring together some team structure that is both pragmatic and addresses the need. While the specifics vary by company and even by particular need, we have seen this as a default position. When the solution requires:

- *Learning elements*—The BEM manages these directly.

- *Other HR elements*—The BEM collaborates with HR to determine one lead voice to the client. The BEM and HR ensure their solutions are tightly integrated.

- *Elements beyond HR* (e.g., IT systems, business processes)—The BEM asks the business to take the lead in inviting appropriate staff to join the solution team. The BEM supports this process through, for example, briefing these staff on the discovery work done to date and sharing information about intended L&D or HR solutions. The BEM offers to support the effort as the full team sees best.

In some cases, the performance analysis may show that there really is not a meaningful need for learning support at all, even if the business leader has requested a learning solution. When this happens, it's possible for BEMs to feel like they have "lost" a promising opportunity. Not so. The BEM's job is to help the business. Throwing money and L&D time at low-value opportunities is a waste. Identifying where low-value training solutions can be avoided provides value just as implementing high-value ones do. So, when this happens, BEMs should simply follow the data, provide what support they can to the solution that does emerge (if *some* solution is needed, albeit not a learning solution), and move on.

Defining the L&D Solution Options

Typically, BEMs will simply define the L&D solution options themselves. The goal here is to provide the business with a small set of options, each of which is optimal under some set of trade-offs. For example, what would be the best solution if the business leader were to prioritize time-to-market above all? How about effectiveness? How about cost-efficiency?

To develop options, BEMs will need to consider:

- *Types of components*—To what extent will different intervention types play a role in the solution? Will there be assessments, training, job aides, coaching, and/or other components?

- *Delivery modalities*—To what extent will interventions be synchronous or asynchronous? Group, manager-led activities or self-study?

- *Job transfer support*—How will participants practice what they have learned on the job and demonstrate success? How will they receive coaching while they do so?

Chapter 10: Chartering an Investment

- *Off-the-shelf, customized, or custom development*—To what extent will the interventions require custom content development? What can be reused from prior efforts, and what must be new?

Rating the Options

As a good business partner, the BEM does not simply provide business leaders with a list of options and say, "You choose." Instead, as a learning expert, the BEM guides business leaders through the options, helping them structure how they think about them. A simple way to do this is to create a table that summarizes the options and provides key rating criteria.

Unfortunately, many L&D organizations do not do a good job of providing rating criteria. Often, the only hard fact offered about alternatives is how much direct cost L&D itself will incur to provide a solution. To provide a robust picture, the BEM offers a broader set of rating criteria. A minimum set might include:

- *Development Cost*—Total cost for development, including costs for vendors, L&D staff time, business staff time for subject matter experts, and travel.

- *Delivery Cost*—Total cost for delivery, excluding participants, including costs for vendors, L&D staff time, business staff time for facilitators and coaches, and travel.

- *Participant Cost*—Cost of time off the job for participants plus travel costs. (This can run 1.5 to 3x the development and delivery cost.).

- *Rollout Time*—The time required to prepare for and launch the training for the first "batch" of participants.

- *Level of Risk*—Level of risk that the solution option will not succeed, either because of development struggles, ineffective design, lack of transfer support, or other. When this risk is medium or higher, the BEM also identifies specifically what the risks are.

Beyond these "standard" criteria, a BEM may also include others when they are relevant to the business need at hand. For example, if a business leader advocates face-to-face training for a large-scale application rollout, the BEM may also choose to include "completion time" as a criterion to highlight that although a virtual solution may take longer to roll out, it will be quicker to deliver to the full audience.

Responding to the Business Sponsor's Desired Solution

Business leaders are an opinionated lot. It's often the case that a business sponsor has not only raised a business problem but also suggested a specific solution as well.

When such a solution is one that L&D sees as optimal under some set of priorities, there is no issue (e.g., "Yes, a one-hour webinar followed by manager-led assessment is what we would suggest if rapid rollout is your key priority.") The suggested solution simply becomes one of the solution options, and everyone moves on with selection. However, what should the BEM do if he or she does not believe the business leader's suggested solution fits in the optimal set?

Chapter 10: Chartering an Investment

While it can be tempting to leave it out "for the business's own good," this is not the appropriate choice. Since the business leader has already suggested the option and *since the business leader owns the decision*, the BEM does not have the privilege of taking the business leader's initial preferred option off the table. Instead, the BEM should simply provide an honest accounting of it. If the business leader's suggested solution has some simple fixes that will significantly improve it, the BEM may also wish to add an improved version of it to the set of solution options as well.

Selecting the Solution

The key to actually selecting the solution to pursue is to keep in mind that L&D facilitates and the business decides. So, the BEM shares the solution options with the business leader and helps him or her frame the decision logic of how to choose among them.

Most BEMs find that when they prepare thoroughly and provide business leaders with a small, thoughtful set of options along with a clear recommendation, the business leaders usually follow their advice. After all, business leaders know they are not experts in L&D. When BEMs are able to act as trusted advisors, business leaders may challenge them to understand the depth of their thinking. But when that thinking then proves sound, business leaders are more likely than not to take the advice.

Step 7: Creating the Results Contract

Having reached this point, the business leader and BEM have become clear on the business case for making the investment. It's important to document this progress to ensure everyone is on the same page as well as to share the decisions made with the project team.

At the same time, the business may well assume that at this point, they have made their contribution. Unfortunately, it's usually not the case that L&D can simply take the bull by the horns and drive the result by itself. Rather, it will require subject matter experts, coaches for job transfer activities, communication support, and other forms of support from the business. To ensure that everyone is clear about what is required to implement the solution, it's imperative that the BEM think through the commitments that L&D and the business will each take on to execute the envisioned solution.

In *Running Training Like a Business*, Adelsberg and Trolley introduced the notion of a "Results Contract." We have adopted that concept here and, as the final step of chartering an investment, recommend that BEMs get sign-off on a Results Contract. The Results Contract summarizes the:

> **TOOLS YOU CAN USE**
>
> We provide an example format for a Results Contract.

- Business need

- Targets for success

- Target audience

- Performance need

Chapter 10: Chartering an Investment

- Solution to be provided

- Responsibilities of L&D and of the business to implement it

- Time line

- Evaluation plan

The Results Contract is the key pivot point in the life of an investment in learning between chartering and execution. All of the activity leading up to it is identifying where and how L&D can generate business value. Downstream from it is execution.

A Note: Building the Infrastructure to Make the Process Efficient and Reliable

We have now walked through the process of how a BEM charters a learning investment. There is some simple infrastructure that the L&D organization can provide to help facilitate the process.

In an IT shop, the work of chartering a solution might be carried out by someone titled "solution architect" or the like; this person spends most of her or his time thinking about system design. BEMs instead spend most of their time thinking about solving business problems. It's unrealistic to expect them to be top-notch learning solution architects along with all the rest of their responsibilities. So, to do the work, they require design support.

To a great extent, the support they require can be "canned." In particular, it's useful for the L&D organization to develop canned standards for three areas:

> **TOOLS YOU CAN USE**
>
> We provide an example format for design architectures.

- *Design architectures for common learning problems*—Most companies face the same kinds of learning challenges repeatedly. It builds comfort for everyone if types of solutions that have been proven to work before are reused. How does the company develop product sales knowledge? How does it handle new complex analytical skills? How does it support a new methodology? A new application rollout? How does it handle new compliance requirements? Such standards also help drive useful innovation since once there is a standard, it's easier to figure out how to systematically improve upon it.

One cannot expect a standard to give "the answer," but it can go quite far. For example, if you have a standard for an ap-

> **TOOLS YOU CAN USE**
>
> We provide an example format for costing standards.

plication rollout, you will need to adjust it depending on the size of the target audience, the complexity of the rollout, and the patterns of who uses the application when. At the same point, it's much simpler to tweak an existing design approach than to approach each problem from the ground up.

Chapter 10: Chartering an Investment

- *Costing standards*—Costing can be somewhat of a prognosticator's art. How much time will it take us to develop a thirty-minute webinar? A three-day face-to-face class? This process can be made efficient and consistent through developing a simple rate card. Often, the rate card includes cost elements broken down into development and delivery. Those categories are then broken down further, for example into vendor cost, internal L&D cost, and time required from the business for subject matter experts or coaching support.

- *Evaluation standards*—When BEMs charter an investment, they define targets for success that are relevant to the business sponsor and reflect the actual business results that the business sponsor seeks. Typically, this means that BEMs establish Kirkpatrick Level 4 targets. In addition, however, the evaluation plan will also include other targets beyond those meant for the business sponsors. In most cases, but not all, the BEM will want to identify whether participants found the training engaging and relevant (level 1). For compliance or certification, typically passing a test of knowledge, judgment, or performance is the result sought (level 2). For most training, understanding whether participants have applied the skills learned and how they performed is warranted (level 3). At the same time, not all types of evaluation are useful for all types of programs (e.g., levels 3 and 4 are generally not useful for compliance training). Evaluation standards identify: (1) which levels are to be used with which types of solutions; (2) which methods and technologies are to be used to collect and evaluate

The CEO's Talent Manifesto

the data; and (3) how the data is used for each project and in summary form.

Beyond this canned support, it's helpful for BEMs to have access to senior instructional designers who can play the heavy-hitting role of "solution architect."

> TOOLS YOU CAN USE
>
> We provide an example format for evaluation standards.

Most opportunities do not require such support, but when the standard infrastructure combined with the BEMs' own capabilities are insufficient, it's helpful to have one or more specialists named who can coach them. At the same time, when BEMs bring in such support, they do not relinquish their role to ensure that solutions address the business need and that they are presented in a way that enables the business leader to make a good decision with confidence. Expert solution architects can fall in love with their solutions and can tend to describe them using L&D jargon. When BEMs involve a solution architect, they should carefully review the options generated from the perspective of the business leader and be prepared to explain them in nontechnical language using that perspective.

Similarly, there will be times when the evaluation standards do not fit a particular project. In such cases, it can be helpful for BEMs to have access to an evaluation specialist. Few L&D organizations have the level of demand to call for an architect-level evaluation specialist (as opposed to someone to operate the established evaluation system). So, it can be more economical in addition to providing better depth of expertise to use an external consultant.

Chapter 10: Chartering an Investment

When Problems Arise...

As in any partnership, from time to time, problems will arise as the BEM partners with a business group to charter learning investments. Here are some of the most common issues we have seen and approaches for resolving them.

There Is Insufficient Budget Available to Support a New Need

While it's useful to create annual learning investment plans, it's a mistake to believe that they describe what will actually happen during the year. The plan ensures that a roughly appropriate level of investment is made with the right balance between strategy and operational objectives and long- and short-term objectives. The plan makes sound trade-offs given what is known about needs and options when it is developed. And then business moves ahead. During the course of the year, some initiatives will be delayed. Other products will receive a surprisingly warm reception by customers. Unexpected problems in execution will surface.

As a good partner, L&D must evolve the support it provides "at the speed of business." This means that it can expect that new needs will surface during the course of the year. These new needs should go through the same kind of prioritization thinking that was employed when creating the plan, and the business may then choose to support them. As in the annual planning process, this is a decision to be *facilitated* by L&D but *made* by the business.

Once budgets are set, however, where does the money come from? In a company that employs a centralized model for funding, it's helpful to think about the three concentric circles

The CEO's Talent Manifesto

shown in Figure 39 which represent three types of decisions to be made.

1. Within the Business Group

2. Within the Existing Plan

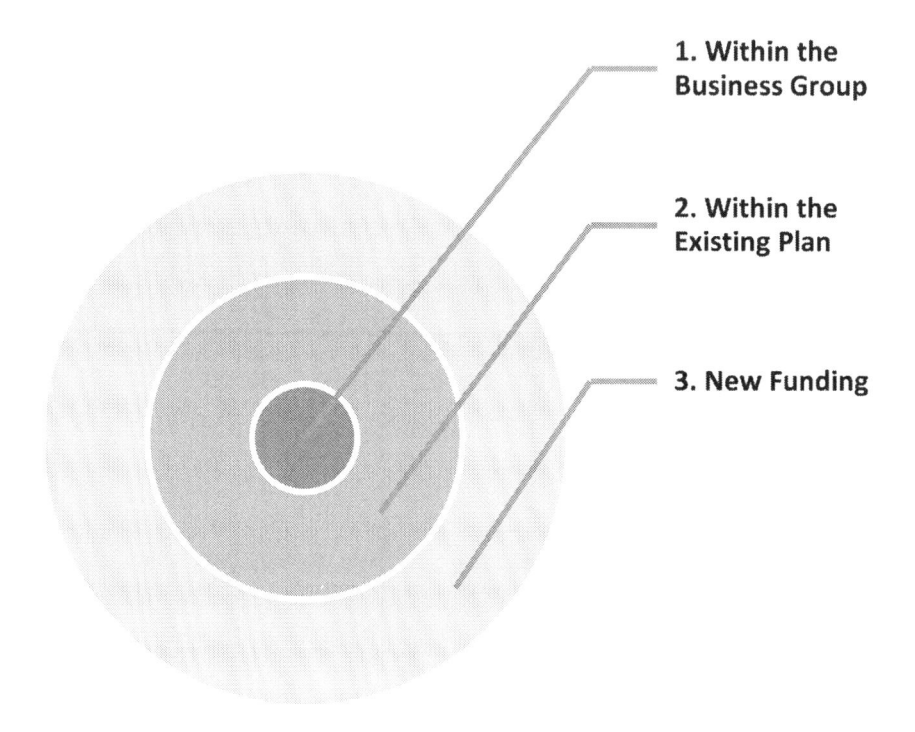

3. New Funding

Figure 39: Alternative Sources of Funding

An L&D organization typically provides dozens or hundreds of solutions. At any given time, when an unexpected need pops up, there is likely to be another forecasted need that has either been delayed or disappeared or for which a solution could be postponed without undue damage.

Circle #1—Within the Business Group: When a new need arises within a business group, the first stop is to check within the investments already in the plan for that group. Is there a change that the business leader in that group is comfortable making to provide funding for the need? Or would the business leader

Chapter 10: Chartering an Investment

advocate to his or her peers that his or her group receive additional L&D funding? When making this decision, the business leader can choose between: a) reallocating funds from a project that has been delayed or cancelled already; b) proactively choosing to delay a project until the next fiscal year; or c) proactively choosing to cancel a lower-priority project.

Circle #2—Within the Existing Plan: If the business leader believes that new funding is appropriate, it may be possible to balance off against a business group that is unlikely to consume its target budget for the year. This is a conversation for which L&D can play the matchmaker, identifying the other business group and facilitating the conversation. If both business leaders agree, the new investment can be made simply by involving the two business leaders.

Circle #3—New Money: If no such second business group can be found, it becomes a matter to be escalated. A typical approach would be to raise it in the next quarterly review of the learning council (see Chapter 7). The council can decide whether to pare someplace or to allocate new funding.

In our experience, most new needs can be handled in the first step itself, within a business group. Relatively few go to the full learning council. It's worth remembering that while the business makes the decisions, L&D facilitates. So the BEM makes this process efficient by actively framing the choices and putting specific options on the table. If the business lead wanted to fund it from the current plan for his or her group, what would be the three best choices for how to do so? If L&D wanted to be a matchmaker to find a business group that could spare budget, what would be the three best choices for that?

233

A Business Leader Brings L&D in Late for a Rollout

While there are a variety of approaches meeting short-time-line needs, they are not always the best approach to take. And, like any operations shop, it is difficult for L&D to support large, unexpected needs. How should L&D react when faced with a large need at the last minute?

The basic answer is simple. As a business partner, L&D should help the business as best it can. While this may not be to the same degree as if L&D had earlier warning and it can cause uncomfortable scrambling, this is a chance for L&D to demonstrate flexibility and willingness to support the business.

However, when such a case occurs, it points to a weakness in the relationship between L&D and the business. If the BEM is fully engaged with the business, how could it be that such a need went undetected and undiscussed until so late? While the project team puts their shoulders to the wheel to help the business, the BEM and learning leader should understand how not to let a good crisis go to waste. Why was the BEM not aware? What can be changed? This is a chance to explore and refine the Strategic Account Management Plan for the business group (discussed in Chapter 8). Is the BEM cultivating enough stakeholders? Is the BEM covering new initiatives in the quarterly reviews?

A Business Leader Wants to Pursue a Low-Value Need or Use a Low-Value Solution

Business leaders who have not previously worked with BEMs may be used to "ordering up" their training. We have said that "L&D facilitates and the business decides." Does this mean that the BEM must support such decisions?

Chapter 10: Chartering an Investment

Not really.

The BEM works to ensure demonstrated results from investments in learning. When an investment is headed down an unproductive path, the BEM should try to redirect it. It's like being in the passenger seat when a driver is headed toward an ice patch he or she doesn't see. You tell the person...but you don't grab the wheel.

For example, your L&D organization might have a playbook for common types of learning needs. Perhaps your playbook includes post-training, on-the-job application activities. However, a business group does not want to support them. This is likely to undermine results. So you work with stakeholders to see if you can get the activities incorporated. A helpful guide for how to do this work is *Getting to Yes*, which provides a principled approach to conducting negotiations.[38]

All the same, if you have applied your best influence skills and the answer remains "no," you neither can nor want to force the business group to adopt your views if they are not ready to believe in them. What you can and should do is to take the long view. Treat the answer not so much as "No, we will never do this," but as "No, we do not wish to do this for this particular investment." Seek to let the evidence speak for itself over time. (Of course, to do this, you will need to make sure to implement evaluation so that the results are clear!)

For example, you may be supporting a business leader who is new to the organization. That leader may wish to provide some training to the group. From your perspective, the training seems to be poorly thought through. Perhaps the business leader wishes to promote selling behavior and wants to use SPIN Selling although your organization has organized around Solution Selling. Perhaps he or she wants to train everyone and you think that a more targeted audience would be appropriate. New business leaders often want to make a cultural shift and see training events as one part of their change strategy. If so, you can afford to be flexible so long as you also treat it as an exception.

In short, the BEM seeks to help the business group make better investments over time. This can sometimes take two or even three years for some business leaders. While BEMs should argue the case when a business leader pursues what the BEMs consider a poor investment, BEMs should also consider each investment one play in a larger game. It's rare that a business leader will really insist on suboptimal approaches over the long haul. After all, business leaders generally want results and they know they are not experts. If you can demonstrate you clearly hear their goals and offer them options and you can explain which options you recommend and why, they will mostly follow your lead.

Chapter 11: Chaperoning Execution
Introduction

During execution, the BEM ensures that L&D and the business execute in a timely way with quality, assess the resulting impact, and make relevant adjustments as they go. In essence, the BEM's role is to keep the work on track…even when the tracks shift.

Depending on the nature of the solution, the BEM's work may involve overseeing a complex project. During execution, the full force of the L&D organization may be brought into play. With the Results Contract in hand, the L&D team has a high-level analysis and initial design from which to work. It then works through the ADDIE steps. If relevant, a deeper analysis is launched, leading to these being refined. Vendors are identified and engaged. Content is sourced or developed. Learning plans are defined and implemented on the learning management system. The learning solution must be marketed and deployed. Instructors are trained. Deadlines are set, and progress managed.

Depending on the rate of change in the business, the BEM's work may also involve adjusting to new information. A well-chartered learning investment represents a projection made based on the information available at the time. When you read a stock prospectus, there is always a big caveat that historical results do not necessarily indicate future returns followed by a list of the risks involved in buying the stock, so too when making an investment in learning.

BEMs are not responsible for doing any of this work. At the same time, they do not sit aside while it is done. Instead, they remain accountable for the value originally conceived being delivered or expectations being reset based on what has been learned.

This chapter describes the BEM's role during execution. Now, L&D organizations usually excel in execution. It's what most do best. Accordingly, this is our shortest chapter. Our goal here is to clarify the unique role of the BEM and what it means to remain accountable for the value generated while not being responsible for actually doing the work.

The Role of the BEM during Execution: Account Manager

In the last chapter, we said that during chaperoning, the BEM acted as a *consultative salesperson* to "herd the cats" while working step-by-step to clarify the business case for an investment. During execution, the BEM takes on a different role—that of *account manager*.

An account manager is a role from the world of professional services used when clients buy high-value services often on a recurring basis from a provider. For example, enterprise technology companies tend to provide an account manager for major customers. In the learning industry, custom-content development companies generally provide account managers for

Chapter 11: Chaperoning Execution

recurring customers. Management consulting firms also tend to provide account managers, albeit in the high-powered version of consulting partners.

Account managers ensure successful execution and customer satisfaction. To do so, they take on three responsibilities:

1. Ensuring project governance

2. Relationship management

3. Servant leadership (this category includes a veritable grab bag of ways BEMs pitch in to help projects succeed by stepping up to whatever issues they may face)

Ensuring Project Governance

BEMs stay on top of projects in execution. To do this, they ensure that the project has a governance system that gives transparency to both the BEM and the business about project status.

"Governance" sounds complex, but, in fact, this tends to be the most straightforward of the BEM's responsibilities during execution. L&D organizations evolve systems of ensuring projects stay on track. They may use weekly status reports and biweekly check-ins. They may conduct design reviews or run pilots and so on. For the most part, BEMs simply use whatever system has been put in place.

Successful BEMs do think through the governance system to make sure it gives them visibility on what they care about for a project. Generally, they consider five key aspects of the project:

1. *Vision*—If the BEM has done a good job in chartering, the initial vision for the solution should be clear. As the project winds its way through analysis and design, however, teams can lose sight of the vision. BEMs, who do not get involved in the hurly-burly, retain the initial vision and ensure that it only changes in ways that advance the results desired.

2. *Voice of the Customer*—As the project proceeds, the BEM checks in with the business to assess whether they are happy with the emerging solution and the progress being made.

3. *Health of Working Relationships*—The BEM assesses whether the joint project team is working effectively. L&D projects can have complex structures. The largest have members from the business, from L&D, and from several vendors. Frictions and gaps can emerge. The BEM spots such gaps and helps the L&D team manage them.

4. *Progress Versus Plan*—The BEM assesses whether the project is meeting its milestones and whether it has appropriate contingency plans if not.

5. *Risk Management*—The BEM helps the team assess the major risks to success and determine how they will assess, avoid, or mitigate them. For example, if a project uses a new design approach, what is the plan for piloting? If a project is for a new application under development, what happens if development is delayed? If a project requires the new virtual classroom technology,

Chapter 11: Chaperoning Execution

what is the plan for proving it out? Project teams tend to keep their heads down on the work immediately at hand. The BEM helps them "look around the corner" to think through problems that may arise later.

As mentioned, most project teams already provide suitable governance structures. The place where BEMs tend to be able to add the most value is in the last area: risk management. Here, BEMs think through what could make the project fail and ensure that the team has a way to work around it. Project teams can be overly optimistic that risks will not materialize. BEMs can provide a more realistic perspective that helps them sidestep issues or run simple tests to highlight them early enough to cope with them.

What this means in practice can vary widely. For the most part, it means the BEM monitors, participating in major review events and checking in informally with project participants from both the business and L&D. Depending on the scope, duration, and risk of the execution, this "monitoring" work can also include one or more of the following:

- Asking for and reviewing change management plans and readiness reports

- Asking for and reviewing customer satisfaction surveys

- Following up to understand issues raised in status reports or informal conversations

- Providing positive encouragement and recognition when activities are on track or improved

- Attending pilot events

Over the course of execution, the BEM monitors progress to ensure that the solution stays aligned as it moves through its lifecycle. L&D teams produce new products. Like entrepreneurial ventures, they learn as they move forward and sometimes should "pivot" from their original vision. For example, a team working on product sales training may discover that the sales team requires sales tools as much as sales training. Or a team working on leadership development may find that the goals for success that were established when the investment was chartered are not viewed as relevant by the target audience. A successful BEM ensures that when such new lessons are learned, teams stay aligned. Just as venture capitalists sometimes need to make difficult decisions with their investments, so a BEM can collaborate with a business group to choose to redirect, expand, or in rare cases even cancel a project.

Relationship Management

BEMs typically serve as the most senior "accountable person" from L&D for a project. While the project team will have day-to-day accountability, it is the BEM who helped charter the project and who was the one who provided the Results Contract and the commitments it contains.

BEMs stay in touch with the business during the execution of the project. This "staying in touch" itself typically consists of three elements:

- Attending key events (e.g., major status meetings or reviews)

Chapter 11: Chaperoning Execution

- Informally checking in occasionally to see how key stakeholders are feeling about the project.

- Responding when the relationship between L&D and the business seems to be unwinding.

When the business and L&D staff on the project team start to develop trouble working together, the BEM tends to get directly involved. This can take many forms. It can happen when the business does not produce the subject matter experts required when required, the subject matter experts believe that the team is slow coming to grips with the content they provide, or the sponsor has concerns about the solution design as it is being implemented and feels the team is not being responsive to those concerns. Whatever the cause, when the integrated execution team begins to break into "us" versus "them" camps, the BEM mediates to restore harmony.

Servant Leadership

BEMs are accountable for results. Their names are associated with the Results Contract. They have every motivation to want projects to succeed. And so, they go out of their way to ensure that they do. As a result, when a project is at risk, BEMs will take on all kinds of work to help it succeed.

This is simply what any good general manager will do when he or she is accountable for results. BEMs give each particular project the support it needs to succeed. Some projects run like clockwork, and the BEM is barely involved. Other projects struggle to get the subject matter experts they need, and BEMs engage heavily with the business to get SMEs mobilized. Yet other projects fail to develop compelling designs, and BEMs engage heavily with the L&D team to challenge and motivate them.

As long as the project is on track, the BEM remains on the sideline, allowing the joint project team to carry on. However, when issues arise, the BEM begins to take a more active role to provide directly or mobilize whatever support might be required for success. Some BEMs can be control-oriented. *The fact that an issue arises does not mean that the BEM takes on leadership of the project.* Instead, the BEM serves as a manager-of-managers, helping the project team to succeed. This can encompass diagnosis to help the project team understand the issues and identify options for resolving them; it can include coaching or bringing in new resources, and a wealth of other issues.

When Problems Arise…

It's a given that some projects will run into trouble. The BEM should therefore expect to invest time in helping the business and L&D work their way through resolving project issues. Maybe a vendor has turned in shoddy work. Or maybe the sponsor does not like how the details of the suggested instructional design have evolved. Or then again, maybe the project is simply falling behind schedule.

The BEM seeks to have the project team manage issues directly. But when they become serious, the BEM helps the project team work them out. This becomes a generic management process of resolving whatever the issue may be. For example, what should the BEM do if the subject matter expert that the business has offered is not giving time to a project? A thorough treatment of how to handle such issues is beyond the depth of

Chapter 11: Chaperoning Execution

this book. However, as a simple model, the BEM can consider three general paths for resolution:

- *Address the issue directly*—The BEM might have the project manager talk directly with the subject matter expert to understand the reason why the SME is not providing time and work to resolve it.

- *Provide an alternative*—The BEM might use his or her connections to locate an alternative SME.

- *Escalate*—The BEM might take the issue to the business sponsor and request help.

Chapter 12: Closing the Loop
Introduction

After a learning solution has been implemented and the evaluation has been completed, the BEM is still not yet done. The final phase of managing a learning investment is to *close the loop* to identify what the company has learned from the project and its results and then make sure that it takes appropriate action based on the lessons.

To close the loop, the BEM:

1. Reports back to the business on the results.

2. Identifies what optimizations, if any, should be made to the learning solution. This includes corrective actions if the anticipated results were not realized.

3. Identifies what best practices, if any, should be learned from the effort and folded back into future projects. This includes both new ideas uncovered during the project and also preventative actions to avoid pitfalls experienced.

4. Provides recognition for those who earned it.

The key event in this phase is an after-action review, which the BEM facilitates with business leaders.

Reporting Back on Results

We have spoken about BEMs seeking to create a virtuous cycle in which business leaders invite them to the table because they have experienced the value L&D can provide, BEMs charter wise investments, those investments pay off, and the cycle repeats. At the heart of this cycle is the notion of a promise and a clear payoff. Chartering is where BEMs make the promise. Closing the loop is where the payoff is made clear. For BEMs to nurture the virtuous cycle, they must make the payoff clear to business leaders.…*It's not just that L&D provides some amorphous sense of value; it's that L&D routinely provides demonstrated value in the specific terms that the business sought when they chartered an investment.*

The conceptually difficult work in reporting back on results is front-loaded. It's during chartering that the business and L&D establish targets. So, while actually gathering the data can take some work, it's really just a matter of diligence for the BEM to gather and report back on them.

In many companies, business leaders have grown used to not seeing results reported back. So, when results are not strong, BEMs can be tempted to skip this step. Just as it is short-sighted for a BEM to try to "sell" an investment up front when there is not a strong business case, so also is it shortsighted for a BEM to try to soft-pedal results when they fall short of targets. Of course, business leaders gain trust when they see their investments pay off. Surprisingly, they can build even more trust when results are not achieved but they see that their partner

Chapter 12: Closing the Loop

has shown good faith during execution and then proactively considered how to do better.

Most business leaders are used to placing bets with incomplete information. They understand that not all those bets will pay off as planned. When considering whether to make future investments, perhaps the most disturbing aspect for them is simply being unclear whether past investments have paid off. While it is certainly unhappy when prior bets do not pay off, the key is whether the bet led to *learning* in the system. Are future bets also likely to fall short? Or has the company learned something so that shortfalls are less likely in the future. When they see L&D making good use of shortfalls by improving how it functions, it makes the next bet that does pay off feel even better.

From the perspective of the L&D function, it's worth acknowledging that there is a fair degree of art involved in executing learning solutions. Investments do not always achieve the results envisioned. Taking a quality perspective, this means that L&D is something of an error-prone system. As mentioned earlier, engineers know that even an error-prone system can routinely operate close to target if it has an effective feedback loop. It is the BEM's job to implement the feedback loop so that L&D can eliminate the issues that cause shortfalls over time.

Optimizing Solutions

Many L&D investments produce programs that are run repeatedly over time (e.g., a call center onboarding program). Such recurring programs accumulate over time and can end up consuming most of the L&D budget. Given the seemingly never-ending stream of work that L&D organizations face, it can be all too easy for a BEM to consider such programs as "known quantities," which are under control and therefore do not require further attention.

This is a mistake. Such recurring programs offer low-hanging opportunities for L&D to increase value. Consider how other functions operate. Each year, manufacturing works to increase quality and reduce costs by, for example, making the product easier to assemble, eliminating slow-downs in the process, and eliminating the causes of defects. Each year, product management works to make its products more appealing by introducing new features that its customers want while getting rid of aspects that make products awkward to use. *So too should L&D work to drive continual improvement to make sure next year is better than the last. One key way is by ensuring programs are optimized over time.*

When considering a recurring program, the BEM starts by thinking through options for improvement offered by three basic questions:

- *How can we increase results?* Even solutions that meet their targets can be improved. And improved results are almost always worth more to the business than shaving costs. So, the BEM starts here. A typical way to consider this question is by considering the gap between "proficient performers" and "actual graduates from the solution." There is always a gap; no learning solution converts every participant into a completely proficient performer. How could we eliminate, say, half of the gap?

Chapter 12: Closing the Loop

Would more on-the-job mentoring be important? A better job aid? A change in how work is actually staged?

- *How can we reduce costs?* Here, the BEM seeks to reduce the *total cost* of the program. This can include ideas to optimize the delivery expense of the "solution as currently envisioned," like using less expensive delivery partners or rearranging instructor travel schedules, which would reduce the cost to L&D itself. However, in most cases, by far the largest opportunities lie not in the cost for L&D to provide the solution but rather in the cost to the company for participants to consume it. So, the primary source of ideas that typically matter most have to do with revisiting delivery modalities. Are there portions of the solution that employ face-to-face delivery that we can shift to virtual classroom delivery? From training to performance support?

- *How can we simplify execution?* Finally, the BEM considers how to make the solution easier for participants to consume and easier for L&D to provide. As more solutions move toward "learning as a process" rather than "training as an event," solutions do tend to get more complex. Ironing out the process for how prework gets assigned, how managers of participants learn about their role in the process, how experts from the business are nominated to participate in coaching sessions, and so on help improve participant satisfaction and reduce the number of fire drills over time. Besides such fine-grained refinements, shifting delivery modalities can make large changes in complexity. For example, over the past several years, many technology companies

The CEO's Talent Manifesto

have moved toward using virtual labs accessed over the Internet so that instructors do not need to go through the hassle of setting up classroom computers with software test beds before each session.

The net result from this work so far is a grab bag of ideas. The BEM then takes the grab bag and makes it into a recommendation for the business. Sure, there are lots of ideas that we *could* pursue. Which should we? Here, BEMs act very much as they do when chartering a new investment. Their role is to facilitate a decision by the business. To do it, they put a clear structure on the table (e.g., a prioritized short list of options to consider) and make a recommendation.

In many cases, the recommendation may be "no action." That's fine. By going through the process above, BEMs give the recurring program the moral equivalent of an annual checkup. It's not a bad result for the doctor to come back after your annual checkup and give you a clean bill of health.

For solutions that recur over long stretches of time (e.g., leadership development), this becomes a regular review done quarterly or semiannually. With such solutions, BEMs should resist the temptation to view the learning solution as a "finished product." Instead, it's more helpful for BEMs to adopt the mind-set of an agile project manager and view it as a continual "work in progress." Here, learning professionals can take a lesson from technology professionals. In information technology, project teams have come to realize that the waterfall model of development is overly rigid and fails to produce the best product with the least effort. Instead, using an agile model of iterative development achieves more for less. When a company invests

Chapter 12: Closing the Loop

in learning solutions that require large ongoing expenses or consume significant time from participants, adopting this agile mind-set pays dividends. By continually refining a solution based on its actual performance and the actual issues in its execution, a project team can efficiently provide higher results and lower costs.

Identifying Best Practices for Future Use

Great innovations are grounded in real problems. One of the best ways for L&D to innovate is to start by considering the actual problems that occurred during a project and also the ways the project team worked around them. It's not just "what broke?" but also "What did the team do that worked particularly well?"

When considering a project, BEMs determine whether ideas that come from the project experience should be promoted to be "best practices." For example, the team may have used an external subject matter expert for the first time. Did that work? The team may have handled the pilot in a new way or involved different people in setting the targets for success.

Given the number of solutions that L&D implements, the BEM should not expect every project to produce new best practices. At the same time, by systematically harvesting those best practices that do happen to arise, the BEM helps L&D grow more mature year by year and thereby advances the mission of helping the business get more value for its investments.

Providing Recognition

Implementing solutions can take significant and sometimes heroic efforts. Large projects consume months of effort from

The CEO's Talent Manifesto

subject matter experts, facilitators, and L&D staff alike. Once the solution rolls out, it is easy for them to feel a letdown. We put in effort…and then what happened?

The BEM ensures that those who contributed to projects are recognized. This can happen in many ways ranging from a simple email to their boss recognizing their contribution to a party with awards. The recognition typically does not come from the BEM him- or herself, but instead, the BEM simply facilitates making it happen. Effective BEMs make sure contributors are recognized because they understand that projects are not one-time events. BEMs are responsible for the effectiveness of a *portfolio* of the solutions and so want to ensure that the system that produces them gets stronger and stronger over time. Providing for recognition is simply one way to support the system.

Conducting the After-Action Review Session

Way back when an investment was chartered, the key deliverable produced was the *Results Contract*. The analogous deliverable when closing the loop is the *Results Report*. Whereas the Results Contract lays out what was expected from a learning investment, the Results Report lays out what was achieved.

> **TOOLS YOU CAN USE**
>
> We provide an example Results Report.

The Results Report provides draft answers to three questions:

1. What were the *results* compared to targets?

Chapter 12: Closing the Loop

    a. What were the target *business results*? What were the actual results? How did they differ?

    b. What were the expected *costs and rollout schedule*? What were the actuals? How did they differ?

    c. What *ancillary information* did we learn about the solution? For example, what were the results of pilots? Of participant evaluation scores?

2. What *changes*, if any, should we make to the solution?

    a. What *repairs* should we make to address gaps in results?

    b. What *optimizations* should we make to exceed targets or reduce costs?

3. What *lessons* did we learn from this investment?

The BEM does not simply send a document to stakeholders. It's important to discuss results and ensure that questions that the business sponsor may have are answered. So, the BEM facilitates an *after-action review*. This session examines results and suggested future actions, if any. It provides transparency and ensures that the BEM understands the business's reactions to the solution.

After conducting the after-action review, the BEM revises the Results Report, shares the final version, and then ensures that actions identified in it are put into place. This is not too dissimilar from the work the BEM does up front with the Results

Contract when he or she ensures that the solution chartered is successfully launched into execution.

When Problems Arise…A Solution Falls Short of the Target Business Result

Investments are uncertain, and not all will pay off. So, no one expects that every item in the Learning Investment Portfolio will achieve its target results. At the same time, the business will expect its partner to proactively help it determine next steps. How should a BEM respond?

The good news is that by following the guidance in how to charter a solution, the BEM will have closed off a major possible source of contention. By following the principle of "L&D facilitates and the business decides," the BEM has not forced a solution on the business. By considering risk mitigation, the BEM will have made it clear what the challenges are.

At the same time, when a solution falls short, the money *has* been spent and it is easy for finger-pointing to begin. So, the BEM will need to be especially careful to maintain the "one team" collaboration between the business and L&D.

In short, the way that a BEM acts when a solution falls short is just the same way as she or he reacts when any problem arises. The BEM conducts discovery, identifies options, and facilitates selection of next steps. Then, the BEM goes back to identify what caused the gap to occur in the first place. Was it overambitious expectations for results? Was it an assumption about what would happen during job transfer that did not come true? While a business leader can understand that problems occur,

Chapter 12: Closing the Loop

the BEM will very much want to ensure that the same problems do not recur on later solutions!

It may be that some remedial effort is required. If so, it is unlikely to be in the budget. The BEM will also need to manage the challenge of mobilizing more budget. For guidance on how, see "There Is Insufficient Budget Available to Support a New Need" in Chapter 10.

Section 5: Implementing and Sustaining the A2B Methodology

The decision to implement A2B lies with the learning leader. If you are a learning leader and have chosen to implement A2B, how do you get started? Then, once A2B is in place, how do you sustain it over time?

Implementing A2B is not a simple "set and forget" change but rather an entry into a new way of engaging with the business. If you proceed, be prepared for a sustained effort. It can take nine months to get to a basic level of operations and perhaps another two years for a company to "feel it in its bones" as it becomes proficient in managing learning as an investment in demonstrated business results.

Chapter 13: Implementing A2B
Introduction

If you are a learning leader and would like to increase the demonstrated results your company achieves from learning investments by implementing the A2B Methodology, how can you proceed?

The basics of implementing A2B are just like those of any other organizational initiative. In this chapter, we highlight some specifics that can help you through the process. We focus on these key actions you should take when getting started:

- Establishing a compelling vision

- Configuring the implementation to suit your context

- Conducting change management with business leaders

- Conducting change management with HR

- Identifying team size and allocating staff to business groups

- Selecting staff

- Defining the toolkit and supporting roles

- Creating demonstrable wins

Establishing a Compelling Vision

As with any change, you should begin by defining a compelling vision. This vision must engage your business leadership as well as your L&D team. If business leaders view the effort simply as a shuffling of roles within an internal L&D effort, it will be difficult for them to get excited about the shift and, therefore, difficult for you to mobilize the support you will require to implement effectively.

To garner support, the learning leader should define just a larger vision. In our experience, this vision typically contains three elements:

1. *Business Imperative*—Our company is pursuing a business imperative that requires us to align our investments in learning to our business needs more effectively and ensure that we achieve the results we target.

2. *Problem Statement*—Historically, our company has struggled to provide business leaders the learning support to the level that they have desired and expected.

3. *Vision Statement*—We are implementing a new approach to driving alignment that will enable us to address our business imperative, provide the desired support, and increase the demonstrated impact our company generates from our investments in learning.

Chapter 13: Implementing A2B

In the following section, we describe each element.

Element 1: Establishing the Business Imperative

It is common sense that it is easier to garner support of business leaders for a change when that change clearly advances their goals. It's better to say, "You want to do X, so we want to do Y to help you succeed" rather than simply "We want to do Y because we think it will be better for you." You can accelerate implementation of A2B if you align it to a business imperative, particularly one driven by the CEO. Examples we have seen include the following:

- One company shifted its business strategy from "wide-but-thin" coverage of a target market to "narrow-but-deep" coverage. This shift required it to bring more insight and know-how to the customer segments it targeted; in return, the company expected to earn higher margins. As part of implementing the business strategy, the company altered its talent strategy, moving away from "buying" talent on the market toward developing talent itself. Being able to develop talent successfully required it to implement much stronger processes for identifying the investments to make in talent and then ensuring those investments succeeded. In short, it called for implementing A2B.

- Another company shifted its business development strategy from offering its broad portfolio of services through a decentralized set of independent business-unit-level sales forces to providing customers with a unified face via a single integrated sales force. To implement this strategy, the company needed to develop the abilities of the newly-unified sales force. It turn, this required the company to integrate a wide set of L&D initiatives that were once managed separately. In parallel, the company made a series of other changes that "moved the needle" from radical decentralization toward some centralization. Again, implementing A2B was central to enabling L&D to support the business strategy.

- A third company shifted its business strategy from being a "provider of equipment" to a wide set of markets toward being a "business partner" to a focused set of industry verticals. This company, like the first one, needed to mobilize deeper vertical know-how, bring broader solutions, and mobilize more effective consultative skills. It required product development, marketing, sales, and service to all demonstrate more savvy about the target verticals and move from a "components" to a "solutions" mind-set. Implementing A2B was again tied to the broader business strategy.

Element 2: Establishing the Problem Statement

If there is no problem, there is no need to change. It may seem scary to call attention to L&D's own shortcomings…but our experience is that in most companies, business leaders already know about them in any case. It can be refreshing for business leaders when L&D not only acknowledges problems but also puts forward a methodical and practical approach for overcoming them.

What kind of problems might business leaders see with L&D? In companies without the BEM role, we see problems like these arise:

Chapter 13: Implementing A2B

- Business leaders are unclear about the company's level of investment in learning.

- Business leaders are unclear on whether and how training programs are aligned to their needs.

- Business leaders are unclear on how investments are prioritized and suspect significant amounts are invested in low-value solutions.

- Business leaders are unclear on what results they get from their investments in learning.

- Business leaders are unclear on when and how to engage L&D.

- Business leaders view L&D as an order-taker not a strategic partner.

To establish the problem statement, it can help to get direct input from key business leaders themselves. One way is for the learning leader to hold a series of conversations to explore how satisfied they are with L&D. If the learning leader is new, it is natural for her or him to hold these conversations directly. If not, it can be useful to call in an external consultant to whom business leaders can speak freely without feeling like they are criticizing the leader to his or her face. In these conversations, the learning leader can ask, "What do you expect from L&D?" and "To what extent does L&D currently meet your expectations?" We have found these questions to elicit a wealth of insight from business leaders. At the same time, they establish the context for the learning leader to ask the business leaders

The CEO's Talent Manifesto

what they view as the critical question for this exercise: "Please rate the extent to which L&D serves your business group as a proactive business partner on a scale from 1 (low) to 7 (high)."

The chart shown in Figure 40 captures the results from one such set of interviews we did recently.

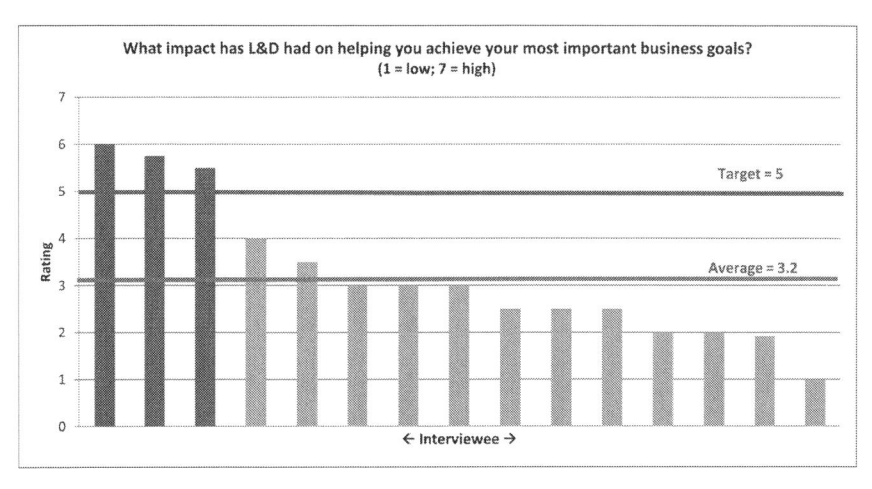

Figure 40: Example Results from Business Leader Interviews

Such a chart can serve as a pithy call to action by quantifying the gap between how L&D *should* help the business and how it *does*.

Element 3: Establishing the Vision

After business leaders see how improving L&D alignment will support their strategic business needs and are clear that there is a gap in how L&D achieves alignment today, most will be ready to hear about a vision for the future.

Many companies desire an L&D organization that:

- Proactively engages with the business

Chapter 13: Implementing A2B

- Educates business on how to best leverage L&D

- Adapts to the business as its needs change

- Provides effective solutions, evaluates results, and adjusts as needed

- Maintains efficient operations and, therefore, reasonable costs

If this describes a vision that matches your context, much of the heavy lifting of spelling out the vision has already been done. This is just the vision that was laid out by Adelsberg and Trolley in *Running Training like a Business*.[39]

> **TOOLS YOU CAN USE**
>
> We provide an example communication which specifies a vision itself and also the mechanics of how L&D will engage with the business by leveraging the BEM role.

As you move forward with implementing, it can help to capture this vision in a document that can communicate it consistently, both within and outside L&D.

Configuring the Implementation for Your Company

We have laid out a comprehensive approach for how L&D can help business groups improve their business results via their investments in learning. To configure an implementation, you:

1. Identify how comprehensively to implement the role of BEM

2. Identify additional tactics to implement in parallel to ensure that L&D can deliver on the commitments that BEMs will make to the business

Identifying How Comprehensively to Implement the Role

In the course of this book, we have made many specific recommendations. We have described a far-reaching definition of the BEM's role, including allocating BEMs full-time to driving business alignment and avoiding diluting their efforts with other responsibilities. We have recommended asking BEMs to:

- Ensure that L&D understands the business needs of their business groups and align investments to them by applying the Ability-to-Execute framework;

- Enable their business groups to organize, prioritize, and manage their portfolio of investments in learning;

- Ensure that individual learning investments are set up to succeed by chartering them via the Results Contract; and

- Evaluate results against targets for success that the business leaders have themselves established and are relevant to them.

We have also described a centralized budgeting and planning process in which the learning leader uses the outputs that BEMs produce to facilitate centralized decisions about which investments the company will pursue.

Chapter 13: Implementing A2B

You do not need to stick to each suggestion we have made in this book. Depending on the specifics of your company, you may choose to make adjustments to suit your context. For example:

- You may employ a federated or decentralized L&D model. So, having centralized budget approval may be a nonstarter for you.

- You may have already organized L&D so that some staff play a role similar to BEM but they manage staff and "own" the projects they charter. You may wish to alter how they spend time to increase focus on alignment but not completely rework their responsibilities.

You can be a strong leader by flexing in response to the prevailing winds like a willow instead of trying to simply stand straight like an oak. For example, in *The Business of Learning*, David Vance describes how when he was asked to launch Cat U, the CEO of Caterpillar suggested that he consider implementing full centralization of learning. However, Vance recognized that full centralization would not be supported by the business. The wiser course was to use a blend of centralized and decentralized approaches yet employ a centralized and shared approach to governance and budgeting.[40]

It's far better to get the heart of the BEM role into place than to insist on a change that will not be supported by your business leaders or which causes unnecessary flux in your L&D organization. Even so, we do recommend that you insist on three "non-negotiables." These form the heart of the alignment system:

1. *BEMs spend the vast majority of their time on alignment.* For example, you may ask them to oversee projects, but do not ask them to directly serve as project manager.

2. *All business groups use the Value-Added Matrix to track their investment portfolio on a quarterly basis, and these are published across the company.* Even if your company does not use centralized budget approval for learning, you can still manage investments inside of each group using the A2B approach. This ensures that business leaders recognize their accountability for making wise investments in learning. Furthermore, even if budgets do not require central approval, you can still have business groups share and probably even discuss investment plans. Doing so helps business leaders make better choices, as it makes it clear just how differently some groups leverage learning and gives you the chance to highlight best practices.

3. *All investments are chartered using the Results Contract, and after-action reviews are held against the commitments in it.* This ensures up front that targets for success are established; that business groups understand what they must do to achieve the results they seek; that a feedback loop is instituted so all are aware that their commitments have meaning; and that business groups and L&D can jointly improve over time by repeating best practices and eliminating failure points.

Identifying Additional Tactics to Ensure L&D Can Deliver

According to Ed Trolley in *Running Training Like a Business*, the single most important reason why more organizations have

Chapter 13: Implementing A2B

not realized the vision is that few have effectively implemented the business engagement manager role.[41]

At the same time, while the BEM role improves business clarity and alignment, it does not *create* core strengths in executing L&D solutions. It simply enables L&D to *apply its existing strengths* to the most critical business problems while establishing clear targets for success. As long as you are making a change, consider whether additional tactics will be required to achieve the levels of impact you seek. For example, does your L&D organization currently:

- Provide top-notch solutions? If not, you may need to mobilize better expertise.

- Provide efficient costs? If not, you may need to restructure.

- Ensure performance back on the job? If not, you may need to move business leaders and L&D staff to include in their end-to-end training designs the method through which training participants will apply what they learn back on the job.

- Evaluate solutions? If not, you may need to develop an evaluation capability.

If L&D has execution weaknesses, implementing the role may bring them to the fore. Now, seen from the perspective of continual improvement, this is good news. You want existing weaknesses to be systematically exposed so you can address them. However, if there are known substantial weaknesses in execution, address them as part of the implementation. If you are unclear, consider having an external evaluation performed.

Appendix B provides a short summary of how a learning leader can ensure a robust delivery capability.

Conducting Change Management with Business Leaders

Implementing A2B and defining the BEM role means more than simply changing who represents L&D to the business. BEMs interact with business leaders in a new and different way, not as "providers of training programs," but instead as "managers of investments in learning solutions." As such, they are concerned primarily with business value, efficient costs, concrete targets for success, and demonstrated results. BEMs bring a systematic and structured approach and a toolkit, which they use to rigorously manage the annual investment plan, charter individual investments, chaperone execution, close the loop, and "walk the beat" to keep up to speed.

Most business leaders enthusiastically embrace the notion of employing a systematic approach to achieving demonstrated results from learning. But for some, the specifics can appear to have mixed benefits. They may have to give up on some convenient and comfortable habits. For example, they may need to shift:

- From ordering L&D to "do some training" to being asked to identify specific business goals and target results for each investment in learning;

- From making independent ad hoc decisions about launching training to having their investments in L&D made visible to other senior business leaders; and/or

Chapter 13: Implementing A2B

- From considering accountability for results to be strictly L&D's responsibility to taking joint accountability for them.

As learning leader, you will need to conduct change management with business leaders. This means educating them about the vision and helping them understand concretely what it means for their group. If they may lose some direct control, it means acknowledging what is lost and what is gained as a result and exploring how to make the transition more comfortable without backing down from the change.

As you develop the vision, start the change management with a small circle of key stakeholders. Collaborate with these stakeholders to get their input and, accordingly, their buy-in. Exactly whom to include will of course differ according to your circumstances. However, we urge you not to shoot too low. Consider three categories of stakeholders:

- *The CEO*—Typically, your stakeholders should include the CEO. If you are not able to mobilize the CEO, it means that you probably have not identified a sufficiently compelling business issue to which to link the change.

- *The chain of command between you and the CEO*—If your bosses are not aboard, they will not jump in to help you when issues arise.

- *A handful of respected business leaders*—It helps if you have some success stories in hand to help build confidence that the change will "work." This can come from cases where L&D has already interacted with sponsors in a way like BEMs do or from cases where business leaders have experienced such engagement in past lives.

Once you have the support of this group, then you can move ahead with a more comprehensive communication and change management effort for all affected stakeholders.

Conducting Change Management with HR

Over the past twenty years, HR has increased its focus on the business. Led by David Ulrich and others, the call for "strategic human resources" has led HR groups to systematize and often outsource their transactional work and place more focus on identifying and addressing business needs.[42][43] It has encouraged HR groups to implement an "integrated talent management" approach that brings together the specialty functions of recruiting, compensation, succession planning, performance management, and learning. And it has led many groups to implement the role of "HR generalist" or "HR business partner" to serve in what seems to be much the same role that we advocate for the L&D BEM, albeit with broader scope. For example, *Strategic Business Partner; Aligning People Strategies with Business Goals* by Robinson and Robinson provides guidance for HR generalists just as we provide guidance for BEMs here. (As a note, this book has helpful guidance on several aspects that apply to the BEM, including managing stakeholders.)[44]

As you seek to implement the BEM role, determine how to integrate with HR. Our experience has been that simply asking the HR Business Partner to take on responsibility for L&D does not produce the best results. The challenge is that L&D solutions tend to operate at a different level, which is generally

Chapter 13: Implementing A2B

much more aligned to specific performance issues than many other HR specialties. Compensation, succession planning, and so on tend to put in place policies and systems that do not vary very rapidly. In contrast, L&D does tend to flex rapidly in response to specific business needs (as can recruiting). At the same time, the solutions perspective is important to retain. While L&D may typically operate at a more granular level than many other HR specialties, it can uncover gaps that are best addressed by them.

We recommend retaining both the BEM role and the HR generalist role and laying out some basic ground rules for how the two can interact. We have found this combination to be effective in supporting both integrated talent management and effective use of learning investments specifically. At the same time, we have also found it helpful to provide the individuals involved the freedom to work out how they will partner. The specifics can and should depend on the individuals in the roles. If an HR generalist has an L&D background or a strong and detailed performance focus, he or she may take on most of the management of the relationship. If a BEM brings particularly extensive business background, she or he may play more of a front role. The key is to get HR and L&D comfortable with complementary roles and coordinated communication and support.

Because this decision is critical to moving forward, we suggest including the HR leadership in the group of key stakeholders who help evolve the vision.

Identifying Team Size and Allocating BEMs to Business Groups

Our experience has been that L&D organizations usually do *not* require net new headcount to implement the BEM role. In fact, it can lead to a decrease in overall L&D effort. It is true that when you implement the role, you will increase the total person-hours that L&D spends helping the business manage learning investments. However, *someone* was spending time engaging with the business previously. And our experience is that the increase in focus and elimination of wasteful programs that the BEM role generates frees up more than an equivalent amount of person-hours in eliminating low-value execution work and forestalling execution problems.

Each BEM will manage one or more business groups. To figure out how many you require, start by deciding how you will identify business groups to be served. In theory, this sounds like a complex decision. Should you allocate BEMs to business units? To geographies? To functions like sales? In practice, however, this decision is easier to make than you might suspect. Simply follow what the business itself does. One wants BEMs to interface with senior business leaders, so one organizes the BEMs around how the senior executives themselves are organized.

Once you have a docket of business groups, you can then identify how many business groups each BEM can serve. This is a judgment call; it depends on the depth of service you will provide. It may be that a major function containing five thousand personnel will consume a BEM full-time. It may also be that a BEM serves a suite of corporate functions, such as legal, finance, and marketing. To reach a level, estimate how many stakeholders the BEM should maintain relationships with in

Chapter 13: Implementing A2B

each business group. Then remember that a BEM can maintain relationships with twelve to fifteen people. Overall, a company of twenty thousand people might employ four to five BEMs. Because the number of people in a job role tends to grow as companies do, the ratio of BEMs to employees is not constant. So, a company of one hundred thousand might employ double that.

Selecting BEMs

A successful BEM gets excited by the chance to improve business results through learning and is willing to proactively engage with a broad set of people to make that happen. Chapter 5 describes the tasks that BEMs perform. It's a broad list, so to be successful, BEMs require a broad set of skills and capabilities cutting across business acumen, specific and detailed understanding of the business groups he or she supports, skill in conducting needs assessment, the ability to get results through influence, and consultative skills.

You are unlikely to find all the skills required neatly prepackaged in one person you can recruit into the role. Instead, you will likely need to select candidates who have some prerequisite skills and then develop the others. The typical choice is between:

- *Background in the business*—Here, you select someone who has worked in the business group(s) to be supported. You seek someone who brings knowledge of how the business works, credibility, and a passion for improving the business. And you develop L&D skills.

- *Background in L&D*: Here, you select someone who has worked in L&D, preferably on projects for the group(s) to be supported. You seek someone who brings knowledge of how to solve business problems with learning solutions (more than deep technical skill, e.g., instructional design), who has developed credibility with L&D's clients and, again, has a passion for improving the business. And you develop his or her understanding of how the business works.

As a generalization, it's safest to select someone with background in the business. The highest risk you face when selecting a BEM is that the BEM will not be seen as a credible partner by the business. If the BEM is drawn from the business, you reduce the likelihood of this happening. In fact, one of the companies we spoke to while preparing this book reported that after trying both paths, they found that the only people who succeeded were those who came from the business. While we believe there is no "one path" to selecting BEMs, it's generally safer and faster to recruit from the business and develop L&D skills than to attempt the reverse.

When selecting people from the business, it is critical that they are already seen by business leaders as knowledgeable about the business, capable of getting things done, and easy to work with. If these criteria are not met, they should not be selected or L&D will be seen as a home for those who could not make it in the business.

Some candidates may feel that they will become sidetracked if they go into the role. You can turn this potential liability into a strength by using the L&D BEM role as a rotational position

Chapter 13: Implementing A2B

to develop a person for future business leadership or HR responsibilities.

Defining the Toolkit and Supporting Roles

For BEMs to be effective, they require an "operating system" within which they work. This operating system should spell out the major processes they employ, the tools they should use, and the roles with which they interact.

This book has described an operating system consisting of these major components.

Major Process	Major Tools
Managing a portfolio of investments	• The Ability-to-Execute Map • The Learning Investment Portfolio
Managing your relationship with a business group	• L&D Vision and Engagement Model • Account Management Plan
Managing the lifecycle of an individual investment	• Discovery Conversation • Results Contract • Results Report • Design architectures • Costing standards • Evaluation standards
Performance management of the BEM	• BEM job description • BEM scorecard

The CEO's Talent Manifesto

When implementing the BEM role, you will likely want to customize the tools we have provided to fit the specifics of your organization. It can be useful to involve the BEMs in performing this customization.

In addition to establishing the key processes and tools, define key support roles. We mention two key roles:

- *Senior instructional designer(s)*—The BEMs should be able to use standard design architectures to charter many projects, but some require more detailed attention. The senior instructional designers support the BEMs by defining the design architectures in the first place and then supporting them for complex cases.

- *Evaluation specialist*—The evaluation specialist plays a role parallel to the senior instructional designers. Often, organizations do not require a full-time in-house resource. Rather, it both saves money and provides better depth-of-experience to bring in an external consultant, such as KnowledgeAdvisors, to establish the standards initially and then to support particularly complex cases.

As part of this effort, it can be useful to establish some basic guidelines for how BEMs interact with HR generalists. As mentioned earlier, it is useful to leave flexibility in these guidelines so specific individuals can work out how to share responsibilities based on their individual capabilities and interests.

Chapter 13: Implementing A2B

Generating Short-Term Wins

It takes time to implement the BEM role and have it ramp up to full effectiveness. To maintain momentum, it's important to generate short-term wins along the way.[45] Over time, L&D will develop an improved track record for positive results. It helps to actively work up front to generate a set of concrete short-term wins that show how L&D is supporting the business. Look to your BEMs to consider what opportunities each has to create these wins and how you can lend extra support to help them materialize.

What counts as a "win"? Simple: demonstrated results. Pay particular attention to early opportunities to create these wins and then share them back with the business. Seek to generate a "catalog of wins" that cover the major proof points you wish to establish. These proof points should address what is important to business leaders and should be driven by the changes you make. Certainly one of those changes is the introduction of the BEM role itself. However, you may have also introduced other innovations at the same time to improve L&D.

Here is an example of a catalog of wins one learning leader might create.

- *Increased effectiveness* (e.g., The new version of Performance Management training has increased employee satisfaction with reviews by 33 percent. The HR leader felt that the major cause of the improvement was the BEM's insistence on inserting on-the-job practice into the new solution.)

- *Increased clarity on effectiveness* (e.g., For the first time, quality assurance tracked the number of errors made by project teams before and after training. They built confidence as the results showed a 40 percent reduction in errors. Better yet, they were able to fine-tune the solution as the results identified that three types of errors persisted, which are important to reduce going forward.)

- *More rapid rollout* (e.g., Operations was able to address 1500 regional field office personnel in one day using technology-based delivery as opposed to taking the four weeks that would have been required using the prior approach of instructor-led sessions.)

- *Higher leverage for experts* (e.g., The sales team received training directly from product development experts by capturing their insights in an online simulation versus filtering those insights through trainers. The sales leader was willing to try the simulation approach after reviewing sample sales simulations from other industries provided by the BEM.)

- *Lower cost and less time away from work* (e.g., The sales team was able to reduce the cost of training the sales force on new products by 75 percent while also cutting the time away from work by over 50 percent by using virtual delivery. The sales leader made the choice to move to virtual delivery after reviewing the business case for various delivery methods, which was provided by the BEM.)

Chapter 13: Implementing A2B

Once you have gathered a catalog of wins, you can then ask your BEMs to share them throughout the business. One simple way is to coach them to introduce case examples in their day-to-day conversations as they become relevant.

Conclusion

Implementing A2B is not a "one year and done" initiative. While A2B certainly has the potential to generate impressive early wins, it takes time to become a way of life. Business leaders must become accustomed to talking with BEMs who act as business-focused managers of learning investments. Business leaders must also become accustomed to sharing their investments with each other and discussing their strategies for how they leverage learning.

Even if you execute the implementation well, the new processes and roles will take time to become fully effective. Some business leaders will resist. Some old investments will survive even if they have no demonstrable alignment or results. Some BEMs will fail to generate trust with their business groups.

To maintain momentum, share the "quick wins" you realize. There will certainly be cases where you eliminate low-value spending and can provide new results based on evaluations against relevant business targets. Since you will need to give the business at least one full cycle through the annual planning process, you can expect the implementation to become mature only after eighteen to twenty-four months.

The hill is worth the climb. Implementing the BEM role will increase demonstrated results from learning investments. Even in the first run, the annual planning process will provide

The CEO's Talent Manifesto

"quick wins" you can use to sustain momentum. While sustaining the transformation takes effort, it's also worth it. In the next chapter, we describe how to do it.

Chapter 14: Sustaining A2B
Introduction
The last chapter discussed how a learning leader could implement A2B. We consider "implementation" complete when the BEMs are beginning to move into routine operations. This means that the learning leader has:

- Brought business stakeholders on board;

- Put in place a team of BEMs, each serving an assigned set of business groups; and

- Defined and shared the engagement model.

It also means that the BEMs have been through an initial round of work for each business group, including:

- Creating a docket of the existing investments in learning;

- Defining their Learning Investment Portfolio and Value-Added Matrix; and

- Chartering initial investments using the Results Contract.

It can take nine months for a company to reach this stage. This is a good start, but it does not mean that the company has learned how to manage learning investments "in its bones." Implementing the role is not a "set and forget" change but rather an entry into a new way of engaging with the business. It can take perhaps another two years for BEMs and their business groups to become fully productive at managing learning investments.

Even then, ongoing support and management are needed. As time goes on, the roster of players changes, business strategies evolve, and the potential impact of learning shifts business group by business group. With A2B, as with so many changes, it is in the sustain phase where the "heavy lifting" is often done.

In this chapter, we describe how a learning leader can sustain A2B. We focus specifically on the BEM role, as BEMs are the engine that drives A2B. Even though BEMs have a complex role, enabling them be productive is not so very different from enabling others to be productive. Much of what we say here could be considered management basics. To support learning leaders, we:

- Describe a working style based on joint accountability, which we have found effective;

- Provide a scorecard for evaluating a BEM's effectiveness; and

- Describe how learning leaders can prevent problems before they occur by ensuring BEMs are well-prepared for key interactions.

Chapter 14: Sustaining A2B

Managing Accountability: A Perspective

BEMs fill a complex, high-impact role. They require coaching and support to succeed. The way we suggest the L&D provide this is by having them be *accountable* on a routine basis, weekly or biweekly.

When we say "have them be accountable," we mean something a bit different than what an executive typically means when he says, "You better make sure someone's accountable!" or "I'm holding you accountable!" What *that* means is that they're talking about who's going to pay the price of failure. Such statements are meant to project a hard-nosed, no-nonsense tone that lets people know a *real executive* is in the room. They indicate a willingness to take action when work is not up to standard. However, for enabling BEMs to succeed (and we would argue for managing people in general), this hard-nosed sense of "holding someone accountable" is insufficient to generate great results. It simply focuses on what happens with rewards and punishments *after* the clock runs out. It offers no guidance on how to build a successful path from point A to point B *during the work* when there is a real opportunity to make a difference.

Since few people bring the full background required to succeed as a BEM, it is inevitable the BEMs will need to learn on the job. Few BEMs will find that their key stakeholders uniformly understand and appreciate what they are trying to accomplish, so it is inevitable that they will run into bumps in the road. What companies really require to help BEMs succeed is a way to coach them to success as they proceed. This means helping them:

- Reconcile competing objectives,

The CEO's Talent Manifesto

- Determine how they will take advantage of opportunities,

- Respond to unforeseen threats, and…

- Simply get the day-to-day work done.

What we mean by "accountability" is an approach for providing ongoing visibility into performance and support to help BEMs succeed. Under this approach, BEMs provide an accounting, on a regular basis, of their work. The following figure defines the "accountability principle" we employ.

The Accountability Principle

Effectiveness in a job is proportional to the ability of people doing that job to explain:

- What they are seeking to achieve,

- Why that's important to the organization,

- How well they are doing,

- What's causing their current level of accomplishment, and

- What they are going to do differently to fully achieve their purpose.

The principle holds regardless of how simple or complex a job is..

Chapter 14: Sustaining A2B

Under this principle, when we say, "The learning leader should implement accountability," what we mean is that the learning leader asks BEMs to provide a regular accounting about their goals, plans, actions, results, and growth.

This changes the notion of performance management for BEMs. Instead of a debate at the end of the year about whether results were achieved, this approach employs an ongoing set of precise and continuing conversations about accomplishments and opportunities as well as shortfalls and what needs to be done to overcome them. We suggest a set of weekly, monthly, and quarterly conversations.

> **TOOLS YOU CAN USE**
>
> The accountability principle is due to Tom. We provide a PowerPoint explanation of its application.

As the learning leader asks the BEM to account, he or she probes to understand:

- *Results*—Are the activities for which I am responsible achieving planned results or not? If they are, what is driving that success and what needs to be done to sustain performance? Are priorities appropriate and resources adequate?

- *Opportunities*—Are there opportunities emerging, and how can we take advantage of them? If they are not, what are the root causes and what am I going to do to remedy them?

- *Threats*—Are situations emerging that threaten results and how can we defend against them?

- *Growth*—Finally, what am I learning and what capabilities am I developing? The practice of accountability is the integrating method that connects all performance management processes.

While the BEM is doing this accounting, the learning leader uses her or his experience to:

- Ask questions to see if something has been overlooked

- Provide information that will help solve a problem

- Share a perspective that will shape more accurate thinking about a situation

- Give encouragement where courage is needed

- Stop a direction or decision that will impede success

- Obtain needed resources

- Secure the support of others

Accountability, employed this way, integrates learning into the job. Learning leaders expect BEMs to be fully responsible for not only doing their job but also for evaluating their work and determining their own growth needs.

This approach to accountability puts the learning leader squarely in the role of coach and collaborator. Providing feedback

Chapter 14: Sustaining A2B

and coaching is something organizations have been trying to get their managers to do for a very long time. But all too often, managers fail to create enough coachable moments. The practice of accountability creates those much-needed moments.

Structuring the Accountability Dialogue

This approach to accountability relies on a continuing series of meetings. In each, the BEM and learning leader run through what amounts to the typical annual performance management process: objectives and progress, assessment and root causes, opportunities and threats, learning and growth, and planned actions.

We suggest implementing a set of standing meetings to provide a dependable structure:

- *Weekly or biweekly operational check-in*—Review progress against the key actions underway. Ensure the BEM is prepared for upcoming events. Address current issues.

- *Monthly review*—In addition to the "check-in" agenda, review status against the scorecard. Any major changes? What is progress on the priority action plan? Would it be appropriate to alter it?

- *Quarterly review*—Time to step back and recalibrate. Rerate the scorecard. Adjust the priority action plan.

Of course, these will not be the *only* meetings between the BEM and the learning leader. As they work together, there will be many cases where additional time is required for "drill-down" tasks. For example, they may decide to do a dry run before a particularly important meeting with a key stakeholder. Or they may sit together to create an evaluation plan for a new business need that is beyond what the BEM has previously experienced. These meetings simply ensure that the BEM and learning leader remain in constant touch with clarity about performance and how to continually improve it.

The Effects of Implementing Accountability
The Effects of Accountability on the BEM

Accountability in this view calls for the BEM to provide a *first-person accounting*, not a disinterested bystander's report. It obliges people to *tell their own stories*. And in the telling, they are expected to know clearly what they are trying to accomplish and why that's important in the larger scheme of things. In short, just as BEMs are responsible for aligning the company's investments with its business needs, so this form of accounting asks them to align how they invest their own time to the results they seek to achieve.

Such an accounting asks BEMs to start with the results their actions have produced so far but then go deeper. They give their analysis of what has caused those results and what they plan to adjust based on what they have learned; what forces are at play and what they have done to manage them; where there are shortfalls or overruns and what they've done to overcome their causes; and what support they need. They are expected to demonstrate that they are monitoring and evaluating what is going on all along the way: exercising judgment, seeking counsel, soliciting help and making adjustments to overcome unforeseen obstacles and to compensate for unintended consequences.

Accountability is also an intensely emotional thing. Every time people need to tell the story of what they've done, they want the story to be a good one. So, they expand their awareness to take in everything affecting their goals and become keenly alert to threats and opportunities, with a hunger for all sorts of situational information. They feel concerned about other people: do they know their responsibilities, and are they all doing their parts; how are they feeling about what they're doing, and how are they holding up when the pressure is on? They feel worried about resources: are there enough and are they being used well? They live with a mindful of checklist questions: have all the right communications been made; are all the parts of the job getting done; are the customers satisfied; will we meet our objectives?

The Effects of Accountability on the Learning Leader

Managers tend not to generate enough coachable moments. One reason is simply time management. Even if doing so is helpful in the long run because it generates better performance, prevents problems, and keeps staff engaged, in the short run, it simply *takes time*. However, perhaps a more important reason is that to generate these moments, managers must put themselves on the line. When a learning leader holds BEMs accountable in the way we have described, coaching and leading become not just occasional tasks. Rather, the structure of accountability incorporates coaching and leading into each meeting they hold.

This may not be easy for learning leaders, but it certainly enables them to increase their effectiveness and drive their own learning. For them to fill their role in accountability discussions, they must provide meaningful support, challenge, and counseling for their BEMs. This gives learning leaders rich opportunities for real-time action learning during their everyday work.

By asking their BEMs to provide a regular accounting, learning leaders insert themselves into the day-to-day work of driving performance where their knowledge and experience can actually influence business results while they develop the people who report to them. In turn, they are then challenged to be leaders able to provide a meaningful dialogue about the direction of the business and the alignment of its direction to the BEMs' work.

A Scorecard for BEM Performance

Feedback helps people perform. With this in mind, it's useful for BEMs if they and their learning leaders maintain a clear, shared perspective where the BEMs' performance is strong and where opportunities lie. Figure 41 provides a scorecard BEMs and learning leaders can use to clarify BEMs' performance.

Define and Manage a Portfolio of Learning Investments
• The BEM understands business goals, strategies, key processes, and key operational objectives
• The BEM understands business needs (significant gaps in the above)
• Investments are clearly aligned to specific business outcomes
• Investments balance strategic-versus-operational needs
• Investments balance short-versus-long term needs
Manage Relationships
• The BEM has identified a productive set of key stakeholders
• The key stakeholders view the BEM as a trusted advisor
• The BEM is invited to staff meetings once a month or more often
• The BEM meets with key stakeholders quarterly or more often
Manage Individual Investments
• Investments have concrete targets for success and evaluation plans
• Results achieved meet or exceed targets
Manage Priority Action Plan
• The BEM has identified a high impact set of priority actions
• The BEM executes priority actions per the plan

Figure 41: Rating Criteria for the BEM Scorecard

Chapter 14: Sustaining A2B

The scorecard summarizes a BEM's performance with a single business group. Instead of trying to provide an exhaustive checklist of responsibilities, it focuses on the priorities, answering the question: "When a BEM performs effectively, what are the most important things that are true?" As a BEM and learning leader work together, we suggest that they discuss the scorecard periodically:

> **TOOLS YOU CAN USE**
>
> We provide an example scorecard format.

- During the monthly review, they review status of the priority action plan.

- During the quarterly review, they review the entire plan.

The scorecard should be self-explanatory with the exception of the "priority action plan." This plan is simply a short list of priorities the BEM should strive to achieve in a given business group. These plans vary widely between business groups. In one, it may simply be to build the relationship. In another, it may be to ensure successful roll-out of a major strategic program. In yet another, it might be to shift the group away from using unnecessarily expensive solutions or toward more systematically supporting evaluation.

The goal of the scorecard is not to rank BEMs against each other but rather to help each BEM learn how to better serve the business groups. Accordingly, there is no one fixed level of what constitutes "good performance" on these metrics. Some BEMs simply work with more difficult business groups than others. So, the BEM who implements an initial pilot of setting concrete targets for results and then evaluating performance against them in one business group may in fact have turned in a stronger performance than a BEM who already routinely sets and evaluates targets in another business group.

Keeping in Touch—The Three Actuals

As learning leaders sustain the BEM role, they should seek direct input on how well BEMs are engaging with the business, collaborating with HR, and working with L&D teams. There is no substitute for direct experience. Use what quality leaders call the Three Actual Rule: "Go to the actual place, talk to the actual people, and observe the actual process."

We suggest:

- For the *learning council*, it's best to protect their time and not ask for more meetings. However, if the learning leader is looking to add or change learning technology, introduce new significant functionality, enter into an outsourcing agreement, or any such high-level change, it is best to present the change to the council along with the rationale for it: (a) so that they can be an informed representative to the business community and (b) to get their feedback and advice.

- For *senior business leaders*, conduct a once- or twice-a-year check-in to ask about their satisfaction with L&D support along with an annual satisfaction survey with a drill-down meeting if there is any dissatisfaction.

- For *HR*, assuming L&D reports to the company's HR leader, the learning leader should use HR staff meetings

Chapter 14: Sustaining A2B

to build ongoing confidence in L&D's capabilities and should have touch-base meetings with individual HR leaders regarding the state of collaboration and mutual support.

- For *L&D teams,* conduct skip-level interviews with team members to understand their perspective on their work in L&D, including the BEMs' effectiveness.

Preventing Problems Before They Arise

One of the most valuable ways a learning leader can help a BEM is to ensure that the BEM is well-prepared. As they say, an ounce of prevention is better than a pound of cure. But what, specifically, can the learning leader do?

Ensuring a BEM Is Prepared for Quarterly Reviews

The highest-profile meetings that a BEM will run with a business group are the quarterly reviews. To ensure they are ready, it is helpful for BEMs to share their evolving plans for a review with the learning leader in a staged way leading up to the meeting. The learning leader can then consider the upcoming review as it shapes up. We suggest this staging:

- *Changes in business needs* (reviewed three weeks beforehand)—What changes have occurred in the business since the last review? What homework has the BEM done to learn about them? Is additional homework required?

- *Status against investment plan* (reviewed two weeks beforehand)—How have the business and L&D proceeded against the investment plan? Are results due? What were they? Is development due? What is progress? Are there issues?

- *Adjustments to the investment plan* (also reviewed two weeks beforehand)—Given the changes to business needs and status against plan, are there areas where the business should consider making adjustments? What are they? What are options to consider? Are there recommended options? Will additional investment be required?

- *Meeting planning* (reviewed one week beforehand)— How does the BEM plan to run the meeting? What are the key issues? Is it a simple status check-in, or is there specific work to be accomplished? What will count as success for the meeting itself? Who should be at the table?

As the learning leader works through each of the angles, it's helpful to probe for blind spots by taking the perspective of those with whom the BEM interacts. What would the leader of the business group think? How would the sponsor for this particular investment react? What would the L&D development team say to that idea?

Over time, these conversations help the BEM become a more effective and proactive partner to the business As the learning leader adopts first one and then another perspective with the BEM on a series of specific issues over time, the BEM learns to anticipate other people's views better and then plan ahead to address them.

Chapter 14: Sustaining A2B

Ensuring a BEM Is Prepared to Present Solution Options

A second area of exposure for BEMs is during a solution-planning session. This happens when BEMs are chartering an individual investment after they have identified the need and are bringing back solution options and a recommendation. The stance BEMs take when sharing solution options with a business sponsor is: "We will clarify the problem and provide a range of solution options. You will make the call." To enable the business sponsor to make a good decision, BEMs prepare a crisp summary of the need and criteria for the sponsor to consider when making a decision. BEMs also provide a set of options, each optimal under some set of business priorities, and a recommendation.

Some of the errors BEMs make during solution-planning sessions include:

- "Gilding the lily" by recommending a more expensive or comprehensive solution than is really required.

- "Taking the order" by simply reflecting back a solution the business sponsor requested when such a solution may not appropriately tackle the need.

- "Moving too early" by proffering concrete solutions when the need has not been appropriately understood.

The learning leader can help ensure the BEM is prepared by previewing what the BEM has brought and challenging it where appropriate. It can be particularly useful for the learning leader to put the BEM "on the spot" with tough questions that the business sponsor might raise. What will the BEM do, for example, if the business sponsor refuses to support the recommended job transfer activities? What will the BEM do if the sponsor will not provide the timeframe the BEM has requested? What will the BEM do if the sponsor continues to insist on providing face-to-face training even though the initial analysis shows that what is really most important to resolve the business issue is to provide a job aid?

Ensuring a BEM Is Prepared to Review Evaluation Results

When evaluation results from an investment come in, a BEM presents them back to the business sponsor during the after-action review. This is a one-time event for one-time solutions and a repeated event, with trend line results, for learning solutions that stay in place over time.

When actual results exceed targets, that is typically the end of the story. We chalk up another success, acknowledge those responsible for it, identify best practices to reuse, and keep moving. However, when results fall short, we must answer the question: "What, if anything, do we do to improve?"

The problem-solving component of this scenario is conceptually the same as when presenting solution options in the first place. The BEM seeks to offer options and a recommendation. To do so, the BEM must have a handle on why results fell under target…or at least be able to recommend steps to uncover why.

At the same time, the politics are different. When the investment was originally approved, it was approved based on a Results Contract that laid out budget, responsibilities, and specific targets. All agreed upon these and were probably excited by this "making of a new promise." However, now we are

Chapter 14: Sustaining A2B

looking backward at a promise that went unfulfilled. Given this situation, there are two requirements for handling the conversation that go beyond the original solution discussion.

First, it is important to maintain team cohesion. It is all too easy for finger-pointing to start when results fall short of target. The learning leader should ensure that the BEM does not become defensive and instead conducts an open, supportive discussion with the team to ensure that team members from the business, from L&D, and from vendors all understand the situation and share a perspective on root causes and possible repairs. When complete consensus is not possible, it is up to the BEMs to construct their best understanding and be clear about what they do and do not understand. BEMs do not take sides but rather seek clarity.

Second, just as it is important to determine how to resolve the issue in the immediate case, it is equally important to determine how to prevent it from happening again on other investments. Business leaders understand that not everything works to plan. In most cases, when a service provider does not hit a goal, if they see that the service provider reacts with energy, takes responsibility for carving out a path forward, and ensures that similar problems will not recur, they feel that the service provider is being a good partner.

So, as BEMs share their plans for the after-action review, the learning leaders should understand how they are viewing the results and what "second-level learning" they have generated from the project.

When Problems Do Arise

When the inevitable problems do arise, the primary responsibility that the learning leader takes is to coach the BEM to success. The learning leader does not want to undermine the credibility of the BEM by jumping in to directly manage every issue. However, if a significant conflict arises in the relationship between the BEM and a business leader the learning leader supports and isn't getting resolved, then the learning leader may want to meet with the business leader to hear his or her concerns firsthand and to then decide what next steps should be.

There is a special case where the learning leader may get involved earlier. If L&D will be introducing changes (technology, policies, etc.) that a particular business leader might oppose, it's best for the learning leader to proactively take on that issue with the business leader since the BEM has no control over that change.

Using BEMs to Identify and Sustain Other Innovations

So far, this chapter has focused on how the learning leader can sustain the innovation of implementing the BEM role. You can consider the BEM role to be an innovation that keeps on giving. Putting it in place can help learning leaders advance the other innovations they seek to implement.

BEMs are the learning leaders' business-focused front line. They can help the learning leaders *identify useful innovations*. The learning leaders can ask BEMs to identify what challenges and opportunities their business groups face in generating demonstrated business results through learning investments. By consolidating the results, learning leaders can then identify

Chapter 14: Sustaining A2B

where further innovation is required. New delivery methods? Better evaluations? More rapid rollouts? BEMs can help the learning leaders pinpoint where to focus improvements.

BEMs can also help learning leaders *implement innovations in progress.* Once an L&D organization has begun to implement innovations, it is the BEMs who will naturally lead the effort of employing those innovative concepts to real projects, learning along the way how to work with senior leaders, project sponsors, SMEs, and L&D staff to engage their best abilities in creating the desired outcomes. The hard part of innovation is usually less in the concept and more in the implementation. The BEMs carry out the work of client engagement, SME preparation, program communication, and participant preparation. They ensure that the learning design stays true to goal. And they work through where the innovation concepts need to be adjusted to realize results.

Appendix A: A Step-by-Step Example of the Ability-to-Execute Alignment Framework

Introduction

The Ability-to-Execute Framework provides a structure to help BEMs identify a business group's needs and thereby help it define and manage a productive portfolio of learning investments. Does this seem a bit abstract? To clarify, let's walk through an example.

We'll focus on a hypothetical company, Smith & Associates, an accountancy. Smith & Associates, like many accounting firms, has three primary service offerings, each of which is provided by a distinct business group (called a "practice" in professional services parlance):

- The *audit practice* conducts audits for public companies and issues opinions on their financial statements.

- The *advisory practice* provides consulting work.

- The *tax practice* helps companies plan and minimize their tax bills.

Each practice has a BEM dedicated to it. In our example, we'll focus on Sam, the BEM who serves the advisory practice.

The Ability-to-Execute Alignment Framework

As a reminder, Figure 42 shows the Ability-to-Execute Alignment Framework identifies the step-by-step links through which an investment in learning can advance a company's business outcomes.

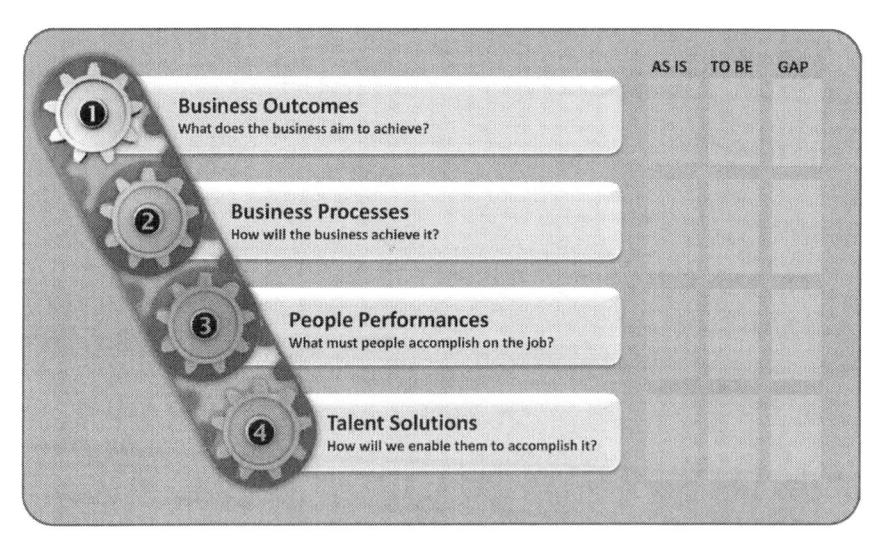

Figure 42: The Ability-to-Execute Alignment Framework

This framework shows that the linkage between business performance and people performance is through business processes. As a result, the way L&D *improves business outcomes* is through improving *business processes*, which it does by improving *people performances*, which it does by providing aligned, effective, and efficient *talent solutions*.

Overall Company Goals and Strategy

Like many industries, the accounting industry is crowded. So, to generate margin and growth, a firm must find some way to

Appendix A: A Step-by-Step Example of the Ability-to-Execute Alignment Framework

differentiate itself. Smith & Associates has chosen to be the premier accountancy in the energy and manufacturing industry verticals while supporting its clients with "best-in-class" advice in financial risk management in addition to basic accounting services.

To measure its success in implementing its overall strategy, the firm might focus on three key metrics above all others: a) market share in its target verticals, b) percentage of revenue from advisory versus accounting services, and c) operating margin.

Every BEM across the firm must know about its overall company strategy, Sam included. This is a prerequisite before beginning the Ability-to-Execute Alignment Framework.

Layer 1: Business Group Outcomes

Business groups within a company will have their own goals and strategies. In a well-run company, the goals will of course be solidly aligned to the company strategy. However, just because they are aligned does not mean they are the same. Group-level goals and strategies can vary dramatically across business groups. Obviously, BEMs must be clear on the goals and strategies for their group.

For example, Sam should be aware that the advisory practice within Smith & Associates has set as its primary goal that within the company's target verticals of energy and manufacturing, they will be accepted as the preeminent thought leader in financial risk management. Sam should also be aware of not just the goal itself but the size of the gap to be crossed. The good news is that Smith & Associates is starting from a foundation of having achieved strong results using innovative approaches from its engagements to date in this area. The bad news is that it has completed relatively few engagements.

To achieve its goal, the advisory practice has selected two strategies. First, it will invest disproportionately in R&D on financial risk management. Second, it will generate strong references from its clients for financial risk management. To do so, it will intentionally "overinvest" in the effort it dedicates to the financial risk management engagements it conducts this year, thereby providing unmistakably great service.

Sam notes that this second strategy actually goes against the company's overall success metric of high operating margin. However, the exemption has received executive support because the magnitude of the dollars at stake is relatively small, the scope of the exemption is tightly focused, and the importance of getting great client references to the firm's overall strategy is high.

So far, Sam has identified one set of needs at the level of the advisory practice's goals and strategy and seen how they are aligned to the foundational level of the company's overall goals and strategy. For brevity, we will skip over other potential needs. But even for the goal and two strategies we have identified so far, Sam is not done. Identification, alignment, and importance are all clear. But what about results?

Sam realizes that he needs to dig further and so invests some time to uncover how the advisory practice plans to evaluate its success. He learns that it has identified two metrics and targets:

Appendix A: A Step-by-Step Example of the Ability-to-Execute Alignment Framework

- *Penetration rate of 15%+* —The practice wishes to increase the percentage of its clients it serves with financial risk management to 15 percent or more during the year.

- *Client satisfaction scores of 4.7+* —The practice wishes to maintain its high client satisfaction scores. It sets a target of 4.7 out of 5 on the surveys it asks clients to complete after engagements.

Pulling what he has learned above, Sam is able to provide the Ability-to-Execute Map shown in Figure 43. The figure simply lists the desired business outcomes that he has analyzed.

Level	Target	Measure	Performance "As Is"	"To Be" Target
Outcome	Perceived thought leader in Risk Management	• Penetration	• <TBD>	• 15%
Outcome	Improved Risk Management R&D	• <TBD>	• <TBD>	• <TBD>
Outcome	Improved Risk Management references	• Client Satisfaction	• <TBD>	• 4.7

Figure 43: Desired Business Outcomes

Even just going this far highlights some open issues. It sounded reasonable when the practice lead said that he wanted to target penetration of 15 percent. But how far does he have to go? What is his current state? More important, to what extent is penetration really a good measure of his business goal?

Similarly, examining his table, Sam realizes that the business leader's desire to increase investment in R&D is more of an action than a goal. Does the practice really know what outcome it wants to accomplish through this investment? What kind of target should it set?

These types of questions, when judiciously asked, show that Sam is working hard to understand what the business is trying to accomplish. Since Sam brings a bit of an external perspective, raising such questions can even help the business leader think through his strategy. And then downstream, clarifying such questions will help Sam ensure that investments in learning are well aligned. (For example, imagine the practice leader requests Sam to run innovation training. On first blush, that seems like it's a well-aligned request since it targets such a critical business strategy. However, looking more deeply at it, Sam and the practice leader have no way to judge whether such an investment in training will produce the desired result. So far, they have not defined what the desired result actually is. Who can tell whether training is required or, if so, what kind of training?)

The BEMs who serve the other practices (audit and tax) will need to understand the particulars of those practices. For example, the BEM who serves the audit practice might identify that audit is a mature practice that routinely generates satisfied clients yet achieves only moderate margins. The practice faces turmoil in international regulations in accounting, which require it to make ongoing revisions in its work. These revisions must be made without fail across the practice. Given this context, the audit practice has set goals to increase margin, retain customer satisfaction, and avoid compliance errors. To achieve these goals, it has selected business strategies including: a) ensuring routine operational excellence, b) structuring engagements to further leverage more junior (and therefore lower cost) staff, and c) becoming a "fast follower" in reacting to how larger firms respond to international regulations. As these examples illustrate, even though both BEMs serve only a

Appendix A: A Step-by-Step Example of the Ability-to-Execute Alignment Framework

midsized company, they face quite different business environments and so will end up supporting quite different portfolios of learning investments.

Layer 2: Business Processes

Besides understanding goals and strategy, Sam must also identify which business processes are most important to the advisory practice. *In so doing, depth is more important than breadth. It's a mistake for a BEM to try to be comprehensive, as such an effort can rapidly become a bottomless pit. Rather, BEMs should seek to be clear about what's important.* In most companies, only the highest-priority business needs receive investment in learning solutions. It's far better to be crystal clear about the most important processes in a group than to strive for comprehensive breadth in understanding of each process in every nook of a group.

Let's take an example. Of the business outcomes identified in Figure 43, let's focus on getting improved references from risk management clients. The practice believes that if it simply pleases clients better (as measured by client satisfaction), it will then naturally get better references. From further exploratory discussions, Sam learns that the current ratings average is 3.8, a far cry from the target of 4.7. The advisory practice believes improving three processes will close the business outcomes gap:

1. Assigning staff to engagements,

2. Research and development, and

3. Conducting quality reviews to ensure customer delight.

The CEO's Talent Manifesto

What Sam is beginning to do now is take one business outcome and drill down into it. To capture his work, he begins to construct an Ability-to-Execute Drill-down Analysis as shown in Figure 44.

Level	Target	Measure	Performance "As Is"	Performance "To Be" Target
Outcome	Improved Risk Management references	• Client Satisfaction	• 3.8	• 4.7
2 Process	Assigning Staff	• <TBD>	• <TBD>	• <TBD>
2 Process	R&D	• <TBD>	• <TBD>	• <TBD>
2 Process	Quality Reviews	• <TBD>	• <TBD>	• <TBD>

Figure 44: The Start of a Drill-Down Analysis

Sam explores how each business process is evaluated. For example, the success of the last process, conducting quality reviews, is to be measured by:

- *Completion rate of 100 percent*—Percentage of engagements reviewed (a process excellence measure). The practice feels this happens perhaps 50 percent of the time today.

- *Quality investment averaging 7.5 percent of labor cost*— Hours invested in providing engagement "extras" to ensure delight. Decisions about these investments are made during quality reviews. The practice raised this number dramatically this year from its prior target of 3 percent and an actual result of around 1 percent.

Sam enters this into the evolving analysis (Figure 45).

Appendix A: A Step-by-Step Example of the Ability-to-Execute Alignment Framework

Level	Target	Measure	Performance "As Is"	"To Be" Target
Outcome	Improved Risk Management references	• Client Satisfaction	• 3.8	• 4.7
2 Process	Assigning Staff	• <TBD>	• <TBD>	• <TBD>
2 Process	R&D	• <TBD>	• <TBD>	• <TBD>
2 Process	Quality Reviews	• Completion Rate • Quality Investment	• 50% (Est.) • 1%	• 100% • 7.5%

Figure 45: Metrics Added for Quality Reviews

Sam now turns his attention to staff assignment. When Sam goes back to explore the staff assignment process, he learns that the practice head sees it as critical simply because it is so important to his practice's economics. The mix of staff has been leaning toward too many senior resources and not enough junior resources, leading to a high cost per labor hour. He wants to move the current weighted average cost per hour of $120 down to its target level of $100.

To capture this, Sam moves the "assigning staff" process out of his drill down for improved risk management references and instead enters a new top-level business goal: reduce costs (Figure 46).

This kind of shift is not unusual. It's hard work to untangle the lines of alignment, and business leaders often intermingle their goals in initial conversations. Furthermore, this is a *different kind of business outcome than before*. The outcomes Sam had pursued to date had to do with driving the strategy. Sometimes, a business group simply wants to get a bit better or even just maintain performance at a process it already operates. For example, the audit practice might want associates to write reports more clearly or the tax practice may want managers to coach junior staff better. Such changes are not tightly tied to

313

The CEO's Talent Manifesto

the group's strategy. In this book, we call them "operational changes" designed to better "run the business."

Updated Goals

Level	Target	Measure	Performance "As Is"	Performance "To Be" Target
Outcome	Perceived thought leader in Risk Management	• Penetration	• <TBD>	• 15%
Outcome	Improved Risk Management R&D	• <TBD>	• <TBD>	• <TBD>
Outcome	Improved Risk Management references	• Client Satisfaction	• 3.8	• 4.7
Outcome	Lower costs	• $/Staff Hour	• $120	• $100

Updated Drilldown on Risk Management References

Level	Target	Measure	Performance "As Is"	Performance "To Be" Target
1 Outcome	Improved Risk Management references	• Client Satisfaction	• 3.8	• 4.7
2 Process	R&D	• <TBD>	• <TBD>	• <TBD>
2 Process	Quality Reviews	• Completion Rate • Quality Investment	• 50% (Est.) • 1%	• 100% • 7.5%

Figure 46: Moving a Goal from the Drill Down to the Top Level

As we discuss later on, training to achieve such goals can add business value. However, in many companies, L&D spending on running the business begins to consume too much of the L&D budget, blocking out investment on advancing the strategy. Chapter 3 describes how BEMs can help business groups avoid this common problem.

As Sam explores further, he finds that the practice itself is unclear about the remaining gap he has for the outcome of improved client satisfaction: what is the impact of R&D? What does the practice want to achieve? BEMs should handle such known gaps by considering them to be on a watch list. One reason is strictly defensive, to prevent the company from investing money in low-value training. It's not unusual for a business leader to leap to a training solution in such areas (as discussed above, the practice lead might request "innovation training"

Appendix A: A Step-by-Step Example of the Ability-to-Execute Alignment Framework

without yet having defined what success would mean). At the same time, the more important reason is to stay on top of a potential way for L&D to add value. At some point, the business will identify its approach to R&D; that approach might well require learning, and unless the BEM proactively checks in on progress, the company might overlook the need.

For example, it might be that in another three months, the advisory practice decides to entirely revamp its approach to R&D, breaking down what was a low-priority monolithic process into separate components of identifying needs, generating new approaches, promoting them internally, and marketing them externally. The practice may choose to reengineer how it generates new approaches, moving away from a centralized R&D system and toward having engagement teams routinely try out new ideas as part of their work. This requires new skills for practice thought leaders, engagement managers, and line staff. Without Sam checking in periodically on R&D and proactively helping the practice think through the implications of its decisions, the advisory practice might not identify this skills gap and so miss a key enabling investment in learning it requires to achieve its goals.

At this point, Sam has completed his mapping for improved client satisfaction from the business outcome itself down to the layer of the business processes.

Layer 3—Required People Performances

In looking back at Sam's efforts so far, it jumps out that his conversations have had little to do with learning. Instead, Sam has acted first and foremost as a business consultant, trying to understand the advisory practice's strategy and goals so that he can then help it focus learning investments to achieve them. As we transition from the "business processes" layer to the "required people performances" layer, Sam moves from a pure business discussion into a talent discussion. For a business (and for a BEM), developing employees' skills, attitudes, and knowledge is not simply useful in its own right. Rather, it is useful because it enables a business to execute its processes with the levels of cost, quality, turnaround time, and so on that it seeks.

To pursue his investigation of required performances, Sam focuses on *required changes*. The key question he asks is "To achieve success in the key processes, what must people do differently?"

To see how this works, let's stick with the quality-review business process. Sam may have exhausted what the leader of the advisory practice is able to say. Now he must go out and do some of his own needs assessment. What is required to improve the performance of quality reviews? Upon tapping into his network and understanding how the process works, Sam learns some lessons. Once an engagement team identifies some action to take to improve quality, given enough advance warning before a client meeting, they tend to implement it successfully. The issue is that they can fail to identify high-impact actions. The pivotal role here is the partner in charge for the engagement.

What then are the required changes in people performance? The practice would like its partners to improve their performance by:

- *Conducting reviews early enough so that the team can act on their recommendations*—Currently, quality reviews often

Appendix A: A Step-by-Step Example of the Ability-to-Execute Alignment Framework

happen as late as the day before a client meeting. So, most actions are wordsmithing. The practice wants reviews to be conducted at least five days before a client meeting. Interestingly, this factor of timeliness turns out to be the major factor…but it was not even mentioned as a key measure of success when Sam first discussed the quality-review process with the practice lead.

- *Identifying more and better options for action*—Partners are generally good at critiquing work and spotting issues. So, no one is really blindsided by the instances of negative feedback that clients give. However, partners vary widely in their ability to brainstorm options to remediate the issues they spot. The practice wants all partners to perform more like the best do in this task.

- *Prioritizing options better*—Partners tend to fall in love with every idea they offer. Few step back and help a team prioritize the options for action. Combined with the lateness of many reviews, teams struggle to act on the options. The practice wants partners to help the team define pragmatic plans for which options they will actually implement so that the most important ones get the most effort.

Sam realizes that a really detailed needs analysis might identify more or other issues. But he has done sufficient investigation to feel confident he has gotten the key items and that addressing them will achieve the desired process outcomes. So, he enters what he learns into his map (Figure 47).

The CEO's Talent Manifesto

Level	Target	Measure	Performance "As Is"	Performance "To Be" Target
1 Outcome	Improved Risk Management references	• Client Satisfaction	• 3.8	• 4.7
2 Process	R&D	• <TBD>	• <TBD>	• <TBD>
2 Process	Quality Reviews	• Timeliness (Before Mtg.) • Completion Rate • Quality Investment	• 1-2 days • 50% (Est.) • 1%	• 5 days • 100% • 7.5%
3 Performances	• Schedule meetings early • Identify more options • Prioritize systematically			

Figure 47: Adding Performances for One Business Process

Note that Sam does not have measures or performance levels for the required people performances. This is not unusual; such details typically only arise during the development of a solution. What is important is that the business is confident that the gaps in these performances are substantial enough that resolving them will achieve the improvements to the business process that they seek.

Sam has now gotten to a relatively detailed level of clarity for the quality-review process. To do so, he has had to speak to a number of members of the advisory practice, some several times. It's useful to reflect on how he got there. It was not by asking for the order: "What training do your people need?" Nor was it even by asking about desired performances. Even though Sam got to desired performances, he only did so for a small corner of the work done in the practice. Even if Sam had the time to spend to try to get to a comprehensive view of desired performance (which would take him a *large* amount of his time), the practice would be unlikely to give him their bandwidth. It's only because the performance questions he has asked are so clearly aligned to what the practice wants to accomplish that Sam is able to carry out this exploration.

Appendix A: A Step-by-Step Example of the Ability-to-Execute Alignment Framework

Layer 4—Solutions

We finally reach the point of discussing learning solutions. How will the advisory practice achieve the changes it wants to make to performance? This is a layer where BEMs who come from L&D tend to be comfortable. It is where standard models of performance improvement come into play. To determine how to improve performance, Sam must understand the root causes of poor performance and then identify solutions that remediate them.

For example, based on Sam's explorations so far, he may already be able to provide an initial analysis as shown in Figure 48.

Even though L&D professionals may be comfortable working with such analyses, this work can be difficult for business leaders to get their arms around. Business leaders, like the rest of us, like things to be simple. Such a complex chart just to get quality reviews done better? In fact, looking at the chart, Sam might realize that the solutions cut across three different support functions. L&D is required to provide training. HR is required to alter compensation. And the Six Sigma team is required to update processes.

No wonder business leaders often look to cut to the chase. Every instructional designer has experienced being brought in to "create some training" only to realize that, for the problem at hand, training is at best only a partial solution. BEMs can provide substantial value for business leaders by simplifying this process for them and taking on some of the complexity of identifying root causes, identifying solutions, and mobilizing the various resources required.

The CEO's Talent Manifesto

Desired Performance: Conduct reviews 5+ days before client meeting	
Root Cause	**Potential Solutions**
Information	**Process change**
There currently is no standard for when reviews are conducted	Implement and communicate the 5+ day standard.
Information	**Process change**
Engagement managers do not know they should schedule the meeting	Communicate that the engagement manager is accountable. Include this in the Engagement Manager Manual.

Desired Performance: Conduct reviews 5+ days before client meeting	
Root Cause	**Potential Solutions**
Information	**Process change**
There currently is no standard for when reviews are conducted	Implement and communicate the 5+ day standard.
Information	**Process change**
Engagement managers do not know they should schedule the meeting	Communicate that the engagement manager is accountable. Include this in the Engagement Manager Manual.

Desired Performance: Identify more & better options to respond to quality issues	
Root Cause	**Potential Solutions**
Knowledge/Skills	**Resource**
Over time, the practice has responded effectively at some point or another to almost all of the types of quality issues that commonly arise. But partners are isolated. Most are unaware of what responses have been used before.	Publish a guide to common quality problems and typical actions to remediate them
	Training
	Train partners on how to use the guide

Desired Performance: Identify more & better options to respond to quality issues	
Root Cause	**Potential Solutions**
Incentives	**Compensation**
Partners' bonus payments are based heavily on margin but not customer satisfaction. They can be reluctant to invest in quality improvement actions.	Increase weightage of customer satisfaction
Knowledge/Skills	**Training**:
Partners tend to overestimate engagement managers' ability to prioritize improvement actions. They also struggle to do so effectively.	Train partners on the impact of failing to prioritize improvement actions and how to make the trade-offs required to do so

Figure 48: Example Performance Analysis

Appendix A: A Step-by-Step Example of the Ability-to-Execute Alignment Framework

In some ideal world, Sam might go and mobilize a compensation expert and the Six Sigma lead for the advisory practice, have them validate and improve his analysis, and then bring the results back for discussion with the head of the advisory practice. In the real world, however, BEMs have limited scope and organizational influence. Realistically, it is the rare BEM who has the access and skill to help facilitate solutions outside of HR. So, Sam should go as far as he can to support the advisory practice. How far is that? We have found that it's generally helpful for BEMs to adopt this tiered set of responsibilities:

- *Performance consulting*—The BEM will "own" performance consulting to provide the business with a clear sense of what performances are required, where the gaps are, and what the root causes of those gaps are.

- *Learning solutions*—To the extent that learning solutions are relevant, the BEM will directly manage the definition and chartering of those solutions.

- *Other HR solutions*—To the extent that other types of talent solutions are relevant, the BEM will directly work with HR to bring HR to the table and ensure that HR and L&D provide an integrated talent solution.

- *Solutions outside of HR*—To the extent that other types of solutions are relevant (e.g., a systems or process change), the BEM will help the business articulate the problem and will support the discovery process the relevant solution groups will themselves pursue. However, the BEM will not take responsibility for actually bringing these groups to the table nor will he or she manage them.

In our example, Sam and the advisory practice work through the required effort to jointly identify the solution, leading Sam to make the updates to his map shown in Figure 49.

Level	Target	Measure	Performance "As Is"	Performance "To Be" Target
1 Outcome	Improved Risk Management references	• Client Satisfaction	• 3.8	• 4.7
2 Process	R&D	• <TBD>	• <TBD>	• <TBD>
2 Process	Quality Reviews	• Timeliness (Before Mtg.) • Completion Rate • Quality Investment	• 1-2 days • 50% (Est.) • 1%	• 5 days • 100% • 7.5%
3 Performance	• Schedule meetings early • Identify more options • Prioritize systematically			
4 Solutions	• (Process) Engagement Mgr. schedules Quality Reviews • (Partner Compensation) Weight of client satisfaction for bonus calculation increased from 25% to 60% • (Partner Information) "Best practices" guide to how to remediate quality issues • (Partner Training) Remediating quality issues, prioritizing quality efforts			

Figure 49: The Solution to Achieve One Business Outcome

The last row captures the solution that the practice wishes to launch.

There are three important things to note about the solution.

First, the solution cuts across multiple areas (Six Sigma, compensation, and L&D). The BEM is acting to manage investments in learning. However, by being a good business partner, the BEM has actually uncovered requirements for an integrated talent solution—combined with an update to a business process.

Appendix A: A Step-by-Step Example of the Ability-to-Execute Alignment Framework

Second, there are no specific targets assigned to the solution itself. There is no "take up," "participant satisfaction," or "post-test" target. Why? Because if the business gets the business outcomes it seeks, it will view all the contributors to it as partners who delivered on their promises. As a corollary, the business will also be unlikely to care much about further efforts to evaluate the success of the L&D component specifically. Each area (Six Sigma, compensation, and L&D) contributes to success and each is jointly responsible for it.

Third, just because there are no specific targets assigned to the solution itself does not mean that L&D should hold back from further evaluation. The L&D organization can and should define a more comprehensive evaluation plan to ensure that its solution works and is efficient. However, L&D need not drag the business into this conversation.

Only if the advisory practice fails to achieve the targets will it then be likely to want more evaluation to support diagnosis and troubleshooting. The key point here is that while the BEM should ensure evaluation happens, he or she should start by ensuring that evaluation is *relevant* to business leaders.

Conclusion

This appendix has walked us through one path showing how a well-aligned talent solution can achieve targeted business outcomes. It shows how a BEM can use the Ability-to-Execute Map (and its associated drilldowns) to collaboratively work with the business to systematically explore a need, make sure to gather the critical information that is required, organize it in a way that makes linkage clear, and therefore charter a sound investment in learning.

Appendix B: Ensuring Robust Core L&D Capabilities
An Important Assumption

This book focuses on how companies can increase the demonstrated results they receive from their investments in learning. We describe how L&D organizations can use the Aligned-to-Business (A2B) methodology to engage with their businesses to collaboratively achieve strategic alignment. Under A2B, the business and L&D together define and manage a focused portfolio of learning investments that improves the company's ability to execute and thereby enables it to achieve targeted business results.

Why focus on how L&D and the business engage? Because, as we say in the book, the most pressing issue faced by most L&D organizations is not whether they have the right guns to fire but rather whether they know just where to point them.

In focusing on business engagement, the book takes an important assumption for granted: *L&D has robust core capabilities.*

Does the assumption hold true for you? This appendix provides a simple self-assessment that an L&D organization can use to evaluate its capabilities.

The CEO's Talent Manifesto

Defining "Robust Capabilities"

An L&D organization has robust core capabilities when four things are true.

1. L&D provides a *comprehensive set of L&D processes*, including being able to:

    o   Conduct needs assessment and performance consulting to identify the performance issues that undermine business results and diagnosis, which may be addressed by learning solutions;

    o   Define learning solutions using appropriate blends of delivery methods that provide effective and efficient means to achieve target results;

    o   Develop learning solutions that can serve the geographies, audiences, languages, and cultures that the business requires;

    o   Deploy solutions to ensure adoption and application of new skills back on the job; and

    o   Evaluate results.

2. L&D demonstrates *high process capability*, meaning:

    o   Rapid turnaround times;

    o   Efficient costs;

Appendix B: Ensuring Robust Core L&D Capabilities

- ○ High customer satisfaction; and
- ○ Effective outcomes.

3. L&D provides clear governance and ongoing improvement, meaning:

- ○ Transparency on the current performance of capabilities;
- ○ Benchmarking on best-in-class capabilities; and
- ○ Continual improvement.

Evaluating Your Capabilities

If you would like to take a quick self-assessment to identify whether your L&D organization has robust core capabilities, please consult the toolkit.

> **TOOLS YOU CAN USE**
>
> We provide a self-assessment.

What if You Find that You Fall Short?

Generating demonstrated value requires both an effective way to create strategic alignment and robust core capabilities. What if you feel that your L&D organization has room to improve on both?

The short answer is: fix both. The results your business will achieve are the product of your L&D organization's engagement capabilities and its core capabilities. You need strength in both to produce results.

That said, you do not need to fix everything yourself. The industry is growing a set of service providers who offer increasingly robust service offerings. For example, one author works with NIIT, a managed training services provider who offers a broad suite of capabilities. The industry also offers a series of more specialized service providers who can support more focused requirements. For example, if you wish to improve your ability to conduct evaluation, KnowledgeAdvisors is a well-known industry leader. Alternatively, if you wish to improve your ability to provide collaborative learning solutions, Q2Learning has had a long history of thought leadership. You can tap industry sources to help you accelerate your efforts to transform your L&D organization into one that generates demonstrated results from investments in learning.

Bibliography

Adelsberg, David Van, and Edward A Trolley. *Running Training Like a Business: Delivering Unmistakable Value.* 1st ed. Berrett-Koehler Publishers, 1999.

Aspesi, Claudio, and Dev Vardhan. "Brilliant Strategy, But Can You Execute?" *McKinsey Quarterly* (February 1999).

Bersin, Josh. *The Training Measurement Book: Best Practices, Proven Methodologies, and Practical Approaches.* 1st ed. Pfeiffer, 2008.

Blanchard, Kenneth H., Dana Gaines Robinson, and James C. Robinson. *Zap the Gaps! Target Higher Performance and Achieve It!* 1st ed. William Morrow, 2002.

Bossidy, Larry, Ram Charan, and Charles Burck. *Execution: The Discipline of Getting Things Done.* 1st ed. Crown Business, 2002.

Brinkerhoff, Robert O. *Telling Training's Story: Evaluation Made Simple, Credible, and Effective.* Berrett-Koehler Publishers, 2006.

Cascio, Wayne F., and John W. Boudreau. *Investing in People: Financial Impact of Human Resource Initiatives.* 1st ed. FT Press, 2008.

Chevalier, Roger. "Updating the Behavior Engineering Model." *Performance Improvement* 42, no. 5 (2003): 8–14. doi:10.1002/pfi.4930420504.

Chip Cleary. "Element K Strategic Learning Roundtable: Assessment of Annual Budgeting Practices." Unpublished, October 2010.

Davenport, Thomas H. *Process Innovation: Reengineering Work Through Information Technology*. Harvard Business Review Press, 1992.

Fisher, Roger, William L. Ury, and Bruce Patton. *Getting to Yes: Negotiating Agreement Without Giving In*. Revised. Penguin Books, 2011.

Friedman, Thomas L. *The World Is Flat: A Brief History of the Twenty-first Century*. 1st ed. Farrar, Straus and Giroux, 2005.

Liz Gryger, Tom Saar, and Patti Schaar. "Building Organizational Capabilities." McKinsey & Company, 2010.

Josh Bersin. *The High-Impact Learning Organization: WhatWorks® in the Management, Governance and Operations of Modern Corporate Training*. Bersin & Associates, May 22, 2008.

Kaplan, Robert S., and David P. Norton. *Strategy Maps: Converting Intangible Assets into Tangible Outcomes*. 1st ed. Harvard Business Review Press, 2004.

Karen O'Leonard. *The Corporate Learning Factbook 2012* Bersin & Associates Research Report. Bersin & Associates, 2012.

Kotter, John P. *Leading Change*. 1st ed. Harvard Business Review Press, 1996.

Bibliography

Mager, Robert F. *Preparing Instructional Objectives: A Critical Tool in the Development of Effective Instruction.* 3rd ed. Center for Effective Performance, 1997.

Michaels, Ed, Helen Handfield-Jones, and Beth Axelrod. *The War for Talent.* First Edition, First Printing. Harvard Business Review Press, 2001.

Jack J. Phillips, and Patricia Pulliam Phillips. *Show Me the Money: How to Determine ROI in People, Projects, and Programs.* Berrett-Koehler Publishers, 2007.

Phillips, Jack, and Ron Stone. *How to Measure Training Results : A Practical Guide to Tracking the Six Key Indicators.* 1st ed. McGraw-Hill, 2002.

Pyzdek, Thomas, and Paul Keller. *The Six Sigma Handbook, Third Edition.* 3rd ed. McGraw-Hill Professional, 2009.

Robinson, Dana Gaines, and James C. Robinson. *Performance Consulting.* Berrett-Koehler Publishers, 1996.

———. *Strategic Business Partner: Aligning People Strategies with Business Goals.* Berrett-Koehler Publishers, 2005.

———. *Training for Impact: How to Link Training to Business Needs and Measure the Results.* 1st ed. Pfeiffer, 1989.

Rossett, Allison. *First Things Fast: A Handbook for Performance Analysis.* 2nd ed. Pfeiffer, 2009.

Scott Mumma, Alan Todd, and Ed Trolley. *Running Training Like a Business: 2011 Research Update.* Corporate University XChange, 2010.

Ulrich, David. *Delivering Results: A New Mandate for Human Resource Professionals*. Edited by David Ulrich. Harvard Business Review Press, 1998.

———. *Human Resource Champions*. 1st ed. Harvard Business Review Press, 1996.

Ulrich, David, and Wayne Brockbank. *The HR Value Proposition*. 1st ed. Harvard Business Review Press, 2005.

Vance, David L. *The Business of Learning*. first. Poudre River Press, 2010.

Walton, Mary. *The Deming Management Method*. 5th printing. Perigee Books, 1988.

Womack, James P., Daniel T. Jones, and Daniel Roos. *The Machine That Changed the World: The Story of Lean Production– Toyota's Secret Weapon in the Global Car Wars That Is Now Revolutionizing World Industry*. Reprint. Free Press, 2007.

Yarow, Jay, and Kamelia Angelova. "Apple Is In The Middle Of The Pack On Revenue, But Crushing On Operating Profit." *Business Insider*. Accessed December 6, 2012. http://www.businessinsider.com/chart-of-the-day-revenue-vs-operating-profit-share-of-top-pc-vendors-2010-3.

"Process Classification Framework." APQC, n.d. http://www.apqc.org/process-classification-framework.

"Process Definitions and Key Measures." APQC, n.d. http://www.apqc.org/knowledge-base/collections/process-definitions-and-key-measures-apqcs-pcf-version-52-collection.

"Value-Based L&D Management Platform." In *Boosting the Predictability of the L&D Return*. Learning & Development Roundtable, Corporate Leadership Council, Corporate Executive Board, 2004.

About the Authors
Chip Cleary

Dr. Chip Cleary leads the Advisory Services practice for NIIT, a managed training services provider. Chip has worked with over fifty L&D organizations to help them improve the business impact they achieve from their investments in learning. He works on a range of efforts, including benchmarking L&D performance, defining learning strategy, creating more effective solution architectures, and allocating responsibilities between internal and external resources.

Chip brings a broad perspective to the learning industry; he has gained experience in business strategy having worked with the Boston Consulting Group; in learning theory and design, having worked as a solutions architect for CognitiveArts after earning a PhD in the learning sciences; and in technology, having started his career as a software engineer creating automated design tools.

The CEO's Talent Manifesto

Chip speaks regularly at industry conferences and events. He holds a PhD from the Institute for the Learning Sciences at Northwestern University, an MBA from the University of Chicago, and a BS in electrical engineering from Yale University.

About the Authors

Tom Hilgart

Tom Hilgart is a Partner at State Parkway Partners, LLC, a consultancy focused on strategic learning, talent, and performance management. He has thirty-five years of business leadership experience managing business operations and leading the learning function. From 2000 through 2007, he served as vice president of the Knowledge & Learning Group at CNA. CNA was recognized in 2004 by Corporate Executive Board research as a benchmark company for its approach to aligning learning investments to business strategy. In 2005, CNA was acknowledged by Bersin & Associates High Impact Learning Organization research as a best practice company both for its alignment of learning investments to business strategy and for the effectiveness of its balanced centralized/decentralized governance structure.

Tom earned a BA in philosophy from The University of St. Mary of the Lake in Mundelein, Illinois, and completed extensive graduate studies in philosophy, education, and social sciences at Loyola University and Northeastern Illinois University in Chicago, Illinois.

Notes

[1] "Value-Based L&D Management Platform."

[2] Josh Bersin, *The High-Impact Learning Organization: WhatWorks® in the Management, Governance and Operations of Modern Corporate Training*.

[3] Aspesi and Vardhan, "Brilliant Strategy, But Can You Execute?"; Bossidy, Charan, and Burck, *Execution*.

[4] Yarow and Angelova, "CHART OF THE DAY."

[5] Friedman, *The World Is Flat*.

[6] Michaels, Handfield-Jones, and Axelrod, *The War for Talent*.

[7] Cascio and Boudreau, *Investing in People*; Kaplan and Norton, *Strategy Maps*.

[8] Adelsberg and Trolley, *Running Training Like a Business*.

[9] Scott Mumma, Alan Todd, and Ed Trolley, *Running Training Like a Business: 2011 Research Update*.

[10] Ibid.

[11] Chip Cleary, "Element K Strategic Learning Roundtable: Assessment of Annual Budgeting Practices."

[12] Scott Mumma, Alan Todd, and Ed Trolley, *Running Training Like a Business: 2011 Research Update*.

[13] Karen O'Leonard, *The Corporate Learning Factbook 2012*.

[14] Josh Bersin, *The High-Impact Learning Organization: WhatWorks® in the Management, Governance and Operations of Modern Corporate Training*.

[15] Bersin, *The Training Measurement Book*; Phillips and Stone, *How to Measure Training Results*; PhD and Phillips, *Show Me the Money*.
[16] Liz Gryger, Tom Saar, and Patti Schaar, "Building Organizational Capabilities."
[17] BEMs can help business leaders with this thinking by coming prepared with concrete hypotheses. Our work here builds on the substantial and well-organized "process and measure checklist" generated by APQC. We show how BEMs can employ the APQC Process Classification Framework and its corresponding definitions and key measures documents.
[18] Chevalier, "Updating the Behavior Engineering Model."
[19] Blanchard, Robinson, and Robinson, *Zap the Gaps! Target Higher Performance and Achieve It!*.
[20] Robinson and Robinson, *Training for Impact*.
[21] Kaplan and Norton, *Strategy Maps*; Davenport, *Process Innovation*.
[22] Kaplan and Norton, *Strategy Maps*.
[23] Walton, *The Deming Management Method*; Womack, Jones, and Roos, *The Machine That Changed the World*; Pyzdek and Keller, *The Six Sigma Handbook, Third Edition*.
[24] "Process Classification Framework."
[25] "Process Definitions and Key Measures."
[26] Bersin & Associates, a research organization found that organizations with strong "performance consulting capabilities" (their phrase for a series of tasks including those we recommend be performed by BEMs) were seven times more likely to have an excellent measurement program. Josh Bersin, *The High-Impact Learning Organization: WhatWorks® in the Management, Governance and Operations of Modern Corporate Training*.
[27] Adelsberg and Trolley, *Running Training Like a Business*.

Notes

[28] Brinkerhoff, *Telling Training's Story*; Phillips and Stone, *How to Measure Training Results*.

[29] We use the term *business group* to identify an organizational unit supported by a business engagement manager. A business group could be a business unit like "commercial banking," a region like "EMEA," or a function like "sales." When implementing the BEM role, one of the decisions an L&D organization must make is how best to subdivide the company into business groups.

[30] Blanchard, Robinson, and Robinson, *Zap the Gaps! Target Higher Performance and Achieve It!*; Robinson and Robinson, *Performance Consulting*.

[31] Ulrich, *Delivering Results*.

[32] Robinson and Robinson, *Strategic Business Partner*.

[33] Note, the Strategic Account Plan serves an additional function. It helps BEMs keep track of change management activities they may plan with a group. For example, if a group has been resistant to use anything but instructor-led training, the BEM may have a plan to help them consider more efficient delivery methods. Or if a group has been resistant to setting concrete targets for results, the BEM may have a plan to address that.

[34] Bersin, *The Training Measurement Book*.

[35] Mager, *Preparing Instructional Objectives*.

[36] Rossett, *First Things Fast*.

[37] Chevalier, "Updating the Behavior Engineering Model."

[38] Fisher, Ury, and Patton, *Getting to Yes*.

[39] Adelsberg and Trolley, *Running Training Like a Business*.

[40] Vance, *The Business of Learning*.

[41] Personal communication.

[42] Ulrich, *Delivering Results*.

[43] Ulrich and Brockbank, *The HR Value Proposition*; Ulrich, *Human Resource Champions*.

The CEO's Talent Manifesto

[44] Robinson and Robinson, *Strategic Business Partner.*
[45] Kotter, *Leading Change.*

Made in the USA
Charleston, SC
11 October 2013